WHISKEY, SIX-GUNS & RED-LIGHT LADIES

~ ~ ~ ~ ~ ~ ~

George Hand's Saloon Diary, Tucson, 1875-1878

Transcribed and Edited by

Neil B. Carmony

~ ~ ~ ~ ~ ~ ~

Cover Art by M. Fred Barraza

Cover Design by Ann Lowe

Maps by Sid Alwin

High-Lonesome Books
Silver City, New Mexico 88062

DEDICATION

To the members and staff of the Arizona Historical Society, who have preserved
George Hand's diaries since his death, and to the editors of the *Arizona Daily
Star* who published excerpts from the diaries each morning for many years.

CONTENTS

George O. Hand, saloon keeper and diarist, ca. 1875. Detail from a photo by Henry Buehman. Arizona Historical Society, Tucson, #1483.

INTRODUCTION

"George Hand's diaries are sacred documents." C. L. Sonnichsen

Many frontier diaries have been published over the years. But you have never read one quite like George Hand's saloon diary. Most of the pioneers who took the time to keep a diary were serious and orderly folk, not much given to humor and certainly not frank about their love lives. George Hand, however, had a much different approach to life. A saloon keeper in the dusty village of Tucson, Arizona, during the 1870s, Hand was a fun-loving man. His friends and customers were miners, teamsters, troopers, gamblers, cowboys, and "soiled doves"--the rowdy, bawdy men and women who gave the Wild West its reputation. In his diary, George Hand captured the flavor of the ribald, fun side of frontier life, described the often violent West, and also revealed the loneliness and tedium of a life far from home and family. Not self-serving reminiscences, not an assortment of windy tales padded with fanciful exaggerations, his ingenuous writings are both rich reading and important historical documents. George Hand chronicled the lives and loves of the pioneers with a candor and style that is unique in the literature of the Old West.

The Diarist

George O. Hand was born in rural New York State in the village of Yorkville, Whitestown Township, Oneida County, on March 7, 1830. He did not have extensive formal schooling, but he learned to read and write and was quite well educated by the working-class standards of the day. The other members of the Hand family were George's mother, Sible (1810-1854), his father, Ira W. (1799-1867), his sisters Mira (1827-1886) and Emma (1838-1876), and his younger brothers Milton (1834-1891), Lewis (1835-1877), and Ira (1846-1875). George's father worked in a small factory and he trained his eldest son to be a draftsman. But George Hand was not destined to be a draftsman or factory worker.

In 1848, news of the discovery of gold in California spread across the country and around the world. Young George Hand caught "gold fever" and early in 1849 he sailed for California, leaving his parents and siblings behind. He kept in touch with his family by letter for the rest of his life, but never laid eyes on any of his relatives again. Hand knocked around the California gold fields for a decade, mostly in the vicinity of the mining camps of Little York, Grass Valley, and Dutch Flat. Like most forty-niners, he found more adventure than riches, the elusive big strike always just over the next hill.

In 1861, news of the outbreak of the Civil War reached the West Coast. Still single and unencumbered with wealth, George Hand, a patriotic Union

1

man, signed up as soon as the call went out for volunteers to fight the secessionists. He wrote: "By strict attention to business I had obtained possession of a very valuable piece of land for mineral purposes. No one could put a valuation on it. There was 'a million' in it, as Joe Gardner told me. He said, 'George, do you intend to leave what you have been years accumulating? Next year I will put water on that mountain and then no one can count your gold.' But as I had never before served my country, I thought it my duty to do so now, and, suiting the action to the words, I sold out for a trifle and left for the seat of war (or as near as I could get to it)."

George Hand was inducted into the Union Army at San Francisco on August 19, 1861. His army records list him as being 5 feet 6½ inches tall-- short by today's standards, but probably not much below average in the 1860s. He was assigned to Company "G," First Infantry Regiment, California Volunteers, a unit of what became known as the California Column. Hand was totally inexperienced in military matters, but presumably because of his age (thirty-one), and the fact that he was literate, he was made a sergeant.

The mission of the 2,300-man California Column was to march east and check the westward advance of Confederate forces that had invaded New Mexico and Arizona from Texas. In September 1861, George Hand and his comrades sailed from San Francisco to Los Angeles, then set out on foot for Camp Wright. The hastily-established camp was 100 miles south of Los Angeles, near Warner's Ranch. Here the volunteers settled down to the business of learning how to be soldiers. In March 1862, after training for five months, the Californians headed east into the desert. The column marched from water hole to water hole, a few units at a time, stopping at forts and towns to recuperate before continuing on. The soldiers trekked to Fort Yuma, then on to Tucson (a village with about 500 residents at that time), and finally reached the Rio Grande in southern New Mexico in the fall.

The Californians were too late to get in on any hard fighting. In late March 1862, a contingent of Colorado Volunteers decisively defeated the Texans at Glorieta Pass in northern New Mexico. The surviving Rebels fled south and eventually left the territory. The Confederates never attempted another westward thrust. In April 1862, an advance guard of the California Column encountered a small, retreating Confederate force near Picacho Peak, about forty miles west of Tucson. A brief fight ensued, and three Union men were killed and three wounded. Two Texans were wounded and three captured. The Rebels continued their retreat to the east, left Tucson (which they had held for two months), and the Californians did not make contact with them again.

The Southwest remained a backwater of the Civil War and George Hand and his companions spent the balance of their three-year enlistments performing routine garrison duty in New Mexico, Arizona, and West Texas. There were a few skirmishes with Apaches, but most of the casualties among members of the column were the result of disease, bad food, and drunken accidents and brawls. Hand never saw a Rebel soldier or Apache warrior, and never fired his weapon except in practice. One thing he did do was keep a diary during the war years. He stopped keeping it, however, shortly after mustering out of the Union Army at Fort Craig, New Mexico, in August 1864.

When their terms were up, a few of the Californians reenlisted in the army, as the war was winding down but not yet over. Many returned to California. Some headed for the eastern states. But a number of them, including George Hand, stayed on in New Mexico and Arizona. For a quarter of a century many of the region's most prominent citizens were men who had first come to the Southwest as members of the California Column.

After turning in his sergeant's stripes, George Hand began a beef contracting business in southern New Mexico, with the military as his primary customer. He had little success in this venture, and after a frustrating year as an entrepreneur, Hand moved to Fort Bowie in southeastern Arizona and went to work for the post sutler. He stayed at Fort Bowie for about two years. In December 1866, Hand was appointed the first postmaster for Apache Pass, the little civilian community adjacent to the fort. For a time, he also engaged in the mail contracting business, in partnership with an old friend from Company "G," Tom Wallace. This enterprise also went sour, and the partners left Bowie and moved to Tucson in 1867. The town had grown a great deal since Hand first saw it in 1862.

Upon arriving in Tucson, Tom Wallace opened the "Pioneer Butcher Shop" in partnership with George F. Foster, who had come to Arizona from California in 1864 as a private in the Union Army. Illness soon overtook the hard-drinking Wallace, however, and he died on September 14, 1867, of "liver complaint." He willed all of his worldly goods, including his interest in the butcher shop, to George Hand. George Foster and George Hand became close friends and remained so for life.

In the summer of 1869, Foster and Hand sold their butchering business and opened "Foster's Saloon." Their partnership ended for a time when, in 1873, George Foster left the saloon and again opened a butcher shop. George Hand continued to run the saloon, and in 1874 moved his operation from Main Street to the northwest corner of Mesilla and Meyer streets. His new location was directly across Mesilla Street from Foster's meat market. Tucson's *Arizona Citizen* newspaper took note of the move on May 23: "George Hand has removed 'Foster's Saloon' from Main Street to the corner of Meyer's and Mesilla Sts., the old restaurant corner. George is a good man and says he means to make the boys behave themselves in their bibitory experiments." George Foster gave up butchering for good in 1876 and again became partners with George Hand in the saloon. The site is now occupied by a Holiday Inn hotel.

There is evidence that George Hand resumed keeping a diary in 1872. However, the only diaries that are known to exist from the years that he was a saloon keeper cover the period January 1875 to December 1878. These are the writings that are presented in this book. Hand regretted abandoning his diary for so long after leaving the military. In the back of one of his Civil War diaries he wrote: "I have not attended properly to my diary since I left the army. I am very sorry that I did not continue it and kept record of the hundreds of good and true men who have been murdered by the red devils [Apaches], but I neglected it."

FOSTER'S SALOON

MAIN STREET
(Opp. Lord & Williams)
Tucson

DRINKS
> Plain
>> Fancy
>>> or
>>>> Ornamental

And made to order.

SMOKING--Best of Cigars, or you can go on the cheap native plan, and roll 'em yourself while the music plays.

COME IN--Plenty of room, seats, etc. "You know how it is yourself."

Ad published in the Arizona Citizen *(Tucson) in 1872. George Foster got out of the saloon business in 1873, and George Hand moved the saloon from Main Street to the corner of Mesilla and Meyer streets in 1874. Foster rejoined his friend as a partner in the saloon in 1876.*

The Territory: Arizona in the 1870s

The part of Arizona that lies north of the Gila River became U.S. territory in 1848 as a result of the Mexican War. The lands south of the Gila were added in 1854 when the Gadsden Purchase was ratified by the U.S. Congress. The town of Tucson, the most northerly non-Indian settlement in Spanish Sonora, was founded in 1775 as a *presidio* or fort. The Spanish garrison was replaced by a Mexican one in 1821. Thirty-three years later, Tucson technically became an American town, but its residents were protected by Mexican troops until the spring of 1856. It was located about sixty miles north of the new international boundary, and in 1856 it had about 200 residents, all but a handful of them Hispanics. At first, what is now Arizona was part of New Mexico Territory. Congress passed legislation dividing the huge territory in 1863.

Prior to 1912, Arizona was a territory rather than a state, and its highest government officials, including the governor and the supreme court justices, were appointed by the president. These men were usually from outside the region and unfamiliar with the territory's special characteristics. A few were merely political hacks receiving patronage appointments. Some of Arizona's early governors could not be found in the territory except during the few weeks the legislature was in session every other year. An exception was Anson P. K. Safford, who served as governor from 1869 to 1877. Safford lived in Arizona while in office, invested in the territory, married a Tucson woman (Margarita Grijalva), and worked hard on behalf of his constituents. The town of Safford was named for him.

By 1875, Arizona had been divided into six counties: Maricopa, Mohave, Pima, Pinal, Yavapai, and Yuma. All the counties were large in size, but Yavapai was truly enormous, encompassing half the territory. The largest town in Arizona was Tucson, the territorial capital (from 1867 to 1877), with about 4,000 residents. Prescott was next in size with some 3,000 inhabitants; Yuma had a population of 1,500; Phoenix, a new farming community on the Salt River, only had about 500 residents; Florence, a farming town on the Gila River, was beginning to grow and was home to about 500 people. The entire territory had approximately 25,000 non-Indian inhabitants. Good estimates are hard to come by, but it appears that some 50,000 Native Americans lived in Arizona. They were not regarded as U.S. citizens, however, and did not participate in the territory's political affairs.

Mining was the lure that brought most immigrants to Arizona in the 1870s. By 1873, the Indians in the territory, including the Apaches, had been settled on reservations and for the first time the back country was relatively safe for outsiders. This period of calm would not last, but while it did prospectors swarmed over the countryside. Although the territory would become famous for its copper mines, before the railroads arrived in the 1880s copper mining

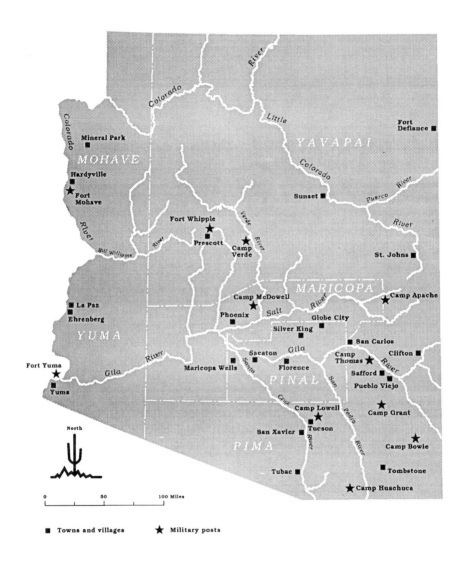

ARIZONA SETTLEMENTS CIRCA 1878

was not very profitable. Gold and silver were the minerals sought, and nearly everyone in Arizona, farmers, doctors, lawyers, merchants, soldiers, as well as bona fide miners, prospected and bought and sold claims and shares in mining properties. They all hoped to strike it rich, but not many did. Mining methods were crude and working in the mines was extremely dangerous, ill-paid ($2 to $3 a day), and involved inhuman toil. Therefore, few miners came to Arizona in the 1870s merely to find work--almost all of them prospected on the side, hoping to find the mother lode.

Several new ore deposits were discovered in southern Arizona in the early 1870s, and a few old Spanish mines were reopened, most of them near the Mexican border. Some gold and silver were extracted from the Yellow Jacket, Ostrich, Old Mine, and Oro Blanco mines west of present-day Nogales. To the east, the Salero Mine, the Aztec group of mines, and the Mowry, Trench, and Patagonia mines were actively worked. But, while these operations looked promising at first, none of them ever really amounted to much.

In 1874, placer gold was discovered on the northern slopes of the Santa Rita Mountains a few miles south of Tucson, and the community of Greaterville developed near the placers. North of Tucson, the Silver King Mine was opened in the spring of 1875, causing much excitement. Large chunks of nearly pure silver were found and displayed throughout the territory. The Silver King was located a few miles north of the Gila River, not far from the present-day copper mining town of Superior. This was a sizable discovery and a few fortunes were made there. But the big strike south of the Gila would not be made until the fall of 1877 when silver was discovered about seventy miles southeast of Tucson. The town that developed near these mines was named Tombstone.

Next to mining, supplying army posts was the most lucrative activity in the territory. During and after the Civil War, clashes between settlers and Apache Indians intensified and many people were killed. In order to pacify the hostiles, a number of army forts and camps were established in Arizona. Besides providing security, the posts themselves were a financial boon and supplying them kept many farmers, stockmen, and merchants in business. Then as now, government paychecks were important to the local economy--many of George Hand's customers were off-duty soldiers.

Prior to the arrival of the railroads in the 1880s, travel in Arizona was slow and uncomfortable. Tucson was on a government-subsidized, cross-country mail route, which from 1874 to 1878 was known as the Southern Pacific Mail Line. Mail stagecoaches came through town three times a week from both east and west. The stage line carried passengers as well as mail, but fares were high. A ticket to go from Tucson to Yuma cost $55 in 1875, a lot of money in those days. The stage contractor boasted that the 800-mile trip from the Rio Grande Valley in southern New Mexico to San Diego, via Tucson and Yuma, took only eight days. The horse-drawn coaches could only make about five miles per hour over the unimproved roads, so to meet their schedule they had to

A stagecoach takes an excursion party on an outing near Tucson. Although these folks were having fun, spending several days and nights riding across the country in a jolting coach was no fun at all. Arizona Historical Society, Tucson, #61654.

It took twenty mules to pull these freight wagons. Traveling at a slow walk, trains of freight wagons were hard pressed to cover fifteen miles in a day. Arizona Historical Society, Tucson, #2978.

travel day and night, stopping only for meals and to change teams and drivers. Frequently, passengers were given shovels and asked to help repair washouts, for there were no road-repair crews on call. This they were glad to do, for to linger in Apache country was unwise.

Sleeping was impossible in the coaches as they lurched and bounced over the rutted roads, and a few days of riding in one was a brutal ordeal. As a result, Tucsonans who wished to visit the eastern states usually headed west, not east, to minimize the time spent in horse-drawn vehicles. Many would board a river steamer at Yuma, chug down the Colorado to the Gulf of California, transfer to an ocean-going sloop, and sail to San Francisco. They would then ride the transcontinental railway (completed in 1869) to their destinations in the East. Others would continue on from Yuma to San Diego or Los Angeles by stage and then sail to San Francisco and the Central Pacific-Union Pacific railhead.

Freight also was sent by the roundabout but faster route. Goods from the East bound for Arizona were usually shipped by the transcontinental railway to San Francisco, then were loaded on ships that sailed all the way around the tip of Baja California and up the gulf to the mouth of the Colorado River. At that point the freight was transferred to flat-bottomed river steamers and taken 150 miles upriver to Yuma. The goods ordered by Tucson merchants then were packed into huge freight wagons drawn by teams of as many as twenty mules (oxen were not used as often in the desert) and slowly, slowly, brought to town. Three weeks to cover the 280 miles from Yuma to Tucson was considered fast time for freight wagons. From time to time, some freight bound for Tucson was taken by ship to the Sonoran port of Guaymas and then brought to town by wagon, a distance of 320 miles. However, there were recurrent political problems in hauling freight overland through Mexico, and the Guaymas route was never popular. With the completion of each section of the Southern Pacific Railroad--San Francisco to Los Angeles (1876), Los Angeles to Yuma (1877), Yuma to Tucson (1880), Tucson to the Rio Grande (1881)--the transportation of goods and passengers became cheaper and more efficient.

The Town: Tucson in the 1870s

In George Hand's day Tucson resembled a Mexican pueblo in many ways. A journalist named Hiram Hodge visited Tucson in the mid-1870s, and he described the town in his book, *Arizona as It Is*, published in 1877:

> Tucson is the county town of Pima County, and since 1867 has been the capital of the Territory.... It has a population of about 4,000, one third being whites and two thirds Mexicans.... The town of Tucson is built up almost wholly of adobe (sun-burned brick), and to one

unaccustomed to that kind of material, it presents a quaint and curious appearance.

Tucson has two hotels, a county court-house and jail, fifteen general stores, a branch United States depository [a kind of bank], two breweries, six attorneys, five physicians, one news depot, ten saloons, two milliners, two flouring mills, three barbers, four boot and shoe stores, four feed and livery stables, a public schoolhouse and about three hundred pupils, a Catholic school under the charge of the Sisters of St. Joseph with about two hundred pupils, one photographic gallery, two jewelers, several small establishments, and one newspaper, the [*Arizona*] *Citizen* [a weekly founded in 1870], edited and published by John Wasson, Esq.

The business of Tucson is quite large.... A good proportion of this business and trade is with Sonora, the merchants exchanging dress and fancy goods, boots and shoes, groceries, notions, etc., for flour, oranges, lemons, tobacco, cigars, and silver coin.... General good feeling exists between the white and Mexican population, and a large number of white men have married Mexican women, who make kind, pleasant, and affectionate wives.

The location of Tucson did much to determine the way of life there. The town sits at the northeastern edge of what is now termed the Sonoran Desert. The elevation is about 2,400 feet above sea level. It is a hot and dry place-- Tucson receives an average of about eleven inches of precipitation per year; maximum temperatures greater than 100 degrees are common in the summer and they occasionally top 110 degrees; winters are mild and snows and hard freezes are uncommon. In the 1800s, Tucson's existence was made possible by the then perennial Santa Cruz River which flowed past the western edge of town. Springs issued forth about two miles upstream from the village and provided enough water to power two small gristmills and irrigate a few hundred acres of wheat, corn, melons, and other crops. These springs have now ceased flowing owing to groundwater pumping and the lowering of the water table.

The desert town is surrounded by high mountains, some of which exceed 9,000 feet in elevation. The tops of these mountains are clothed with ponderosa pines and other conifers, providing a limited amount of timber. In the mid-1870s a small steam-powered sawmill was in operation in the Santa Rita Mountains about thirty miles south of town. The mill supplied Tucson and nearby ranches and mines with lumber, but wood was scarce and expensive and unfired adobe remained the building material used the most.

There were very few trees or shrubs in the adobe town and to visitors from the eastern states the community had a drab, dusty, unkempt appearance. Sanitation left much to be desired. The system for trash removal was rudimentary, and many folks simply threw their garbage out the back door. The more fastidious residents often complained about disgusting odors emanating from heaps of fetid refuse. Animal waste in the streets and stables was also a source of unpleasant effluvia. Flies were a constant annoyance. Sewers were far in the future and outhouses were standard equipment. It is no surprise that diseases related to poor sanitary conditions, such as typhoid fever, were common. When available, prisoners from the county jail were organized into chain gangs and compelled to sweep the unpaved streets.

Some homes and businesses had their own wells--water could be found by digging down about thirty feet. Unfortunately, the wells and outhouse pits were often perilously close together. A few of the well-to-do residents installed windmills to raise the water out of the depths. However, most Tucsonans bought household water from a vendor who dispensed it from a tank on horse-drawn wagon. The water, from a spring south of town, cost a penny a gallon. With water being scarce in the homes, many people took their weekly bath and washed their clothes in a small spring-fed irrigation ditch or *acequia* that flowed past the western edge of town. A hot bath could be had at a barber shop for a few cents.

Tucson incorporated as a village in 1871 and held its first municipal election that year. The town now had a mayor, "common council," marshal, and a full compliment of other civic officers. The council and mayor promptly set about passing ordinances designed to bring a little order to the rough-and-tumble pueblo. One provided for keeping the stray dog population under control; another directed property owners to remove putrid carcasses of dead animals from their premises; emptying chamber pots in the streets was proscribed; displaying a weapon in a threatening manner was made an offense; riding a horse or driving a buggy faster than a trot was prohibited. Being also a county seat and territorial capital, it seemed at times that every adult White male in town except George Hand was some sort of government functionary. Hand's partner, George Foster, was elected Tucson's assessor and tax collector in 1873, a post he held for many years. Tucson adopted a new charter in 1877 and proclaimed itself a "city."

The only church in Tucson in the mid-1870s was Roman Catholic. It was dedicated to Saint Augustine (*San Agustin*), and the congregation was led by Bishop John Baptist Salpointe. He was assisted by several priests and an order of nuns, the Sisters of St. Joseph, whose convent was adjacent to the church. Traveling Protestant preachers would come to town from time to time and were allowed to hold forth in the Pima County courthouse. George Hand was raised a Protestant but was not religiously devout. However, he loved music and singing and enjoyed oratory, and occasionally attended preaching sessions for entertainment. On special occasions such as Christmas Eve he attended the Catholic services. Protestant churches began to organize in Tucson in the late 1870s.

11

Looking east across Tucson ca. 1880. At the upper left is the San Agustín church, built of adobe, with the church plaza in front and the Sisters of St. Joseph convent at the right. Note the flat earthen roofs in the foreground. Carleton Watkins photo, Arizona Historical Society, Tucson, #13927.

There was a plaza in front of the San Agustín church, used mostly for religious ceremonies, and another one in front of the courthouse where secular assemblies were held. A large open area known as Military Plaza was located on the eastern edge of town. This was the site of Camp Lowell until the army post was moved farther out of town in 1873. At the western edge of town, near the bull ring and the fields on the Santa Cruz River floodplain, German-born brewer Alexander Levin had planted several acres of cottonwoods and other trees adjacent to his brewery and saloon. Known as Levin's Park, his outdoor beer garden had a pavilion where dances, concerts, and holiday celebrations were held. The grove provided a shady, semipublic retreat enjoyed by all. Nighttime activities at the park were lit with bonfires. Levin eventually developed a bowling alley, shooting gallery, and opera house on his property. Not far from Hand's saloon there was a large courtyard where traditional Mexican entertainments were given. Small circuses from Sonora performed there, and puppet shows and theatrical plays were popular.

Looking west on Pennington Street in the 1870s. Alexander Levin's Park Brewery is at the end of the street. Special Collections, University of Arizona Library, Tucson.

Many of Tucson's Hispanic residents were indigenous, but quite a few were immigrants from Mexico, especially Sonora. The Hispanic population was divided into two distinct groups--a small, well-to-do elite, and a much larger number of poor, mostly illiterate farm workers, adobe makers, woodcutters, shopkeepers, maids, cooks, and general laborers. The wealthy and influential Hispanic businessmen and property owners participated fully with the American and European newcomers in the running of the town. The poor majority remained mostly outside the political and economic mainstream. However, they were the people who gave the community much of its distinctive Latin character. They were the most ardent fans of the bullfights and cockfights held on Sundays. They were the best customers for the little Mexican circuses and theatrical troops that came to town from time to time. The *tamales* and other traditional Mexican foods were made and sold by them. The poor people were the mainstays of the local celebrations and feasts--they were the people who kept the old customs alive.

The non-Hispanic population included native-born Americans like George Hand, but also many immigrants from Europe--Irish, Germans, English, French, Swiss, Poles, Portuguese, and other nationalities. Several prominent Tucsonans were Jewish. A small number of African-Americans lived in the town--two of Tucson's barbers were Blacks. A few Chinese had arrived by the

1870s, and, true to the customs of the day, they operated laundries, restaurants, and truck farms. Most of the non-Hispanic Tucsonans came to Arizona after first giving California a try. Almost all of the women in town were Hispanics, and, as Hiram Hodge observed, Tucson men of all nationalities married Hispanic wives.

The three main elements of Tucson's culture in the 1870s are represented in this photograph: Mexican burros loaded with mesquite firewood are at the left; in the center, a Papago (Tohono O'odham) woman carries a load of hay on her head; a Euro-American sits astride his horse at the right. Arizona Historical Society, Tucson, #26458.

A number of former Union soldiers lived in Tucson, like George Hand and George Foster, but the town was also home to Confederate veterans and sympathizers. The Union men were mostly Republicans, the Southerners were Democrats. Tucsonans took politics very seriously in Hand's day, but the two groups seem to have gotten along remarkably well. This lack of bitterness was made possible by the fact that, although Tucson was occupied briefly by a Rebel force in 1862, no battle was fought there. The Southwest did not experience the terrible destruction during the Civil War that left deep scars.

Besides the thrice-weekly mail stage, Tucson was connected to the outside world by telegraph. Built and maintained by the military, the telegraph system also carried civilian messages. The line was brought to Tucson in 1873 en route to new Camp Lowell, located seven miles northeast of town. The camp was first established on the edge of Tucson during the Civil War. It was moved farther out in 1873 to a site on Rillito Creek where the grazing for the troopers' horses was better and Tucson's saloons were not so handy. Nonetheless, when off-duty, soldiers from Camp Lowell still made a beeline for Tucson to patronize establishments such as the one run by George Hand.

The Saloon

George Hand's saloon on the corner of Meyer and Mesilla streets was in a building he rented from businessman and politician James H. Toole. (James Toole was elected mayor of Tucson in 1873, 1874, 1878, and 1879. Toole Avenue was named for him.) The structure was a one-story adobe affair with a flat, earthen, often-leaky roof. The furnishings of the saloon were very simple, consisting of a plain counter top that served as a bar, and a few tables and chairs. There were no pool tables or elaborate gaming devices, and no fancy woodwork. The walls were whitewashed and decorated with some Currier and Ives prints, and the barroom was lit at night with kerosene lamps. (Tucsonans had to wait until 1882 for gas lights and the 1890s for electric ones.) Hand bought water for the saloon from a vendor. It was stored in *ollas*, large earthen jars holding about five gallons each. The ollas were made and sold by Papago (Tohono O'odham) Indian women who lived at San Xavier, a village about ten miles south of Tucson. There were three or four smaller rooms at the back of the saloon, and Hand, a life-long bachelor, slept in one of them. The others were rented out to roomers. In the spring of 1876, a partition was installed in the main room of the saloon, separating the front barroom from a card room in the rear.

Behind the saloon there was a courtyard or patio which Hand called the "corral." It housed the privy, and during the hot months Hand would often take his bed outside and sleep there. Before the advent of air conditioning, sleeping out of doors where it was cooler was a common summertime practice in southern Arizona. Outside the saloon the dirt streets produced billowing clouds of dust most of the time, and were a sea of mud after rains.

The drinks served by George Hand were as plain as the saloon itself. Whiskey was the mainstay of the business. Hand did not buy bottled brand-name whiskey, however. Instead, he filled a few bottles and jugs from a wholesaler's barrel every day or two. His customers were primarily interested in quantity rather than quality, and this rotgut met their needs just fine. Beer from Levin's brewery was also available to slake a desert thirst, and by all accounts he made a pretty decent product. Surprisingly, as early as 1877 Foster and Hand began selling bottled Milwaukee beer brought from Wisconsin by way of California. Before a steam-powered ice plant went into operation in Tucson in 1879, customers drank warm beer or none at all. Many Tucsonans cauterized their innards with *mescal*, a fiery liquor made in Mexico. It was brought to town from Sonora by the barrel. Cheap and potent, the frontier version of this cousin of tequila was usually harsh on the palate and always cruel to the liver.

Looking south on Meyer Street in the late 1870s. The man on the right is standing in front of Foster and Hand's saloon. The two-story building farther down the street on the right is the Palace Hotel. Buehman photo, Arizona Historical Society, Tucson, #41115.

Sin was legal in Arizona in the 1870s. It was legal to sell liquor to anyone regardless of age, twenty-four hours a day, seven days a week. Opiates and other powerful drugs could be purchased from a druggist without restriction. Gambling was legal and a constant feature of frontier life. No special onus was attached to gambling in those days, and professional gamblers, if honest, were accepted as ordinary members of society. Since there were no real casinos in Tucson, the itinerant professional gamblers would set up shop in the saloons. The owners of the establishments might take a small cut of their winnings, but the gamblers themselves were independent operators. The saloon keepers liked them because they drew customers who would spend money on drinks. Sometimes the saloon owners were also gamblers and would deal faro or monte on the side. Now rarely played, faro and monte were the most prevalent card games in the Southwest in the 1870s. They were "banking" games in which the players bet against the dealer or bank. Poker was also popular, and roulette wheels were sometimes employed to separate miners and cowpokes from their pay. George Hand liked to bet on horse races and election results, but was not addicted to games of chance.

Looking south on Meyer Street from the top of the Palace Hotel. Photo taken ca. 1880 by Carleton Watkins. Arizona Historical Society, Tucson, #14841.

Prostitution was legal in Tucson in the 1870s and practiced openly. But by tacit agreement with the city fathers, the ladies-of-the-evening stayed out of the "better" parts of town where the well-to-do had their homes. The prostitutes worked the saloons, including George Hand's, and there were brothels where they were the primary attraction. Most of the bordellos were in the town's red-light district, which was known as Maiden Lane, but there were bawdy houses elsewhere. Of course, venereal diseases were constant threats to the health of the customers and inmates of the sporting houses.

Life was hard on the frontier. The golden dreams that brought the pioneers to the Southwest were rarely realized. Many found only dashed hopes, loneliness, and despair. It is no wonder that George Hand and his customers sought comfort in oceans of booze, and bought love from the girls on Maiden Lane.

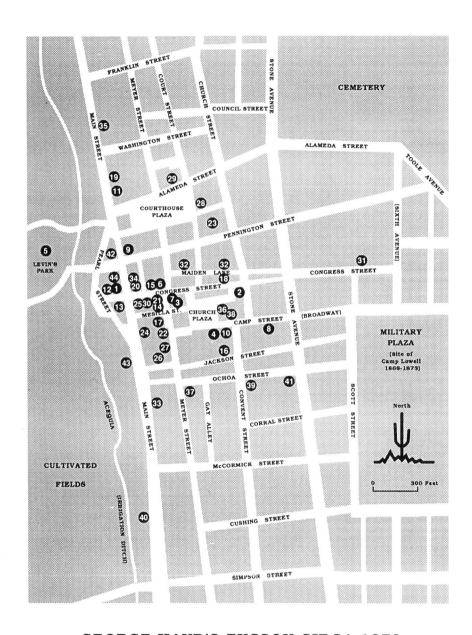

GEORGE HAND'S TUCSON CIRCA 1878

KEY TO THE MAP OF TUCSON

1. Arizona Citizen newspaper office
2. Arizona Star newspaper office
3. Big Carmel's place
4. Bishop Salpointe's home
5. Bull ring
6. Charles Meyer's drugstore
7. Charles O. Brown's Congress Hall saloon
8. Charles O. Brown's home
9. Cosmopolitan Hotel
10. Dr. John Handy's office
11. Edward N. Fish's home
12. Etchell's blacksmith shop
13. Foster and Hand's saloon (1869-1874)
14. Foster and Hand's saloon (1874-1881)
15. Gem Saloon
16. George Foster's home
17. George Foster's meat market (1873-1876)
18. Henry Buehman's photo studio
19. Hiram Steven's home
20. Jacob Mansfeld's news depot
21. Jacobs brothers' store
22. Joseph Neugass' Tucson Restaurant
23. Leatherwood's corral (stable)
24. Leopoldo Carrillo's home
25. Lord and Williams' store
26. Mexican circus corral
27. Palace Hotel
28. Pima County courthouse and jail
29. Pima County hospital
30. Post office and stage station
31. Public school
32. Red light cribs
33. Residence of Governor Frémont (1881)
34. Sam Drachman's store
35. Sam Hughes' home
36. San Agustín church
37. Simpson's Hole-in-the-Wall saloon
38. Sisters of St. Joseph convent and school
39. Smith's corral (stable)
40. Steam-powered flour mill
41. Territorial capitol (1867-1877)
42. Tully and Ochoa's store
43. William Oury's home
44. Zeckendorf's store

George Hand's Partner

George Franklin Foster was born in Boston in 1832. Like George Hand, he sailed for California in '49 when he was still in his teens. Nothing is known about his life in California except that he enlisted in the Union Army there in 1864. George Foster's unit was immediately sent to Arizona and he spent an uneventful three-year stint at various posts in the southern part of the territory. He mustered out of the army in 1866, and settled in Tucson, where he lived for the rest of his life.

How Foster and Hand became partners in the saloon business has already been discussed. During their partnership, George Foster always seemed to be out front, the person mentioned most in newspaper notices about the saloon, while George Hand stayed in the background. The establishment always bore Foster's name, and he seemed to be the more efficient businessman. During the years that George Hand ran the saloon by himself (1873-1876), the business did not prosper.

George Foster married Juana Moreno in 1876. However, they had lived together as man and wife for years before they were formally united, and they already had several children. This was a common practice in old Tucson, and no eyebrows were raised. The Foster children were Maggie, George, Clara, Annie, and Mary. Young George's middle name was Hand, given in honor of his father's friend. As was so common in those days, several other children died in infancy.

From 1873 to 1877, and again for several years in the 1880s, George Foster served as Tucson's assessor and tax collector. He was still the city tax collector when he committed suicide in 1890 at the age of fifty-eight. There was speculation that irregularities regarding tax monies might have precipitated his desperate action. But the books were found to be in order and no money was missing. George Foster had simply come to the end of his rope and was tired of living.

George Hand's Last Years

George Hand continued to make his living as a saloon keeper until the fall of 1881, when he and George Foster closed down their saloon. Their friendship continued undiminished, however. The *Arizona Weekly Star* (founded at Tucson in 1877) commented on the event on November 17, 1881: "Foster & Hand have been partners for twenty years, and although now out of business, they propose to remain as partners for twenty years longer."

The Southern Pacific Railway was completed across southern Arizona in 1881, and a few months later a branch line (owned by another company) was built south along the San Pedro River. In March 1882, George Hand traveled on the new railway system to Contention City. Contention was a raw, unruly ore-milling town located on the San Pedro about sixty miles southeast of Tucson and ten miles west of Tombstone. William Bradley, an old friend and veteran of the California Column, had opened a saloon there and Hand went down for an extended visit. The Tombstone silver boom was at its peak, the Earp-Clanton feud was still in progress, and there was much excitement in the air. As far as is known, this was Hand's only trip away from Tucson after he came there to live in 1867.

George Hand returned to Tucson in July 1882 and Pima County Sheriff Robert H. Paul hired him as night watchman and janitor for the new Pima County courthouse. Hand opened the doors in the morning, closed up at night, kept the gas lights in order, swept up, emptied the spittoons, and saw that workmen made major repairs as needed. The county jail was in the same building, and Hand used prisoners to do much of the work when they were available. He had a small office at the back of the building, with a desk and a cot where he slept at night. Hand spent most of the day in his little office, reading newspapers and magazines, and writing letters, both for himself and for illiterate Tucsonans (for a small fee). His diary was always on his desk, and Hand carefully recorded the comings and goings around the courthouse and the details of the shootings and stabbings in Tucson's saloons and bawdy houses. He usually spent weekends and holidays at George Foster's house where a bedroom was reserved for his use. Hand was considered a member of the Foster family, and he often mentioned the Foster children in his diary.

Tucson was still a pretty rowdy place in the 1880s, and George Hand visited the saloons often, but, now in his fifties, he did not spend much time in them. Nor did he patronize the "soiled doves" as in earlier years. Old George did not give up drinking, however. He kept a large demijohn of whiskey in his room and did most of his tippling there. Hand's whiskey jug proved a strong attraction for thirsty friends short on cash. On payday, he promptly replenished the whiskey supply.

In December 1881, Negley Post No. 35 of the Grand Army of the Republic was founded at Tucson. The G.A.R. was an organization of Civil War veterans who fought for the Union, and posts were eventually established all over the country (except in the South). The fraternity became a powerful national lobby for veterans' benefits. George Hand was active in Negley Post No. 35 (named for James Negley, a Civil War general) and participated in meetings, rallies, and parades. Amusingly, he served for several years as the post chaplain.

Another organization in which George Hand was active was the Society of Arizona Pioneers (now the Arizona Historical Society). The organization was founded at Tucson in 1884 and George Hand and George Foster were charter members. Prior to 1897, membership in the Society was limited to men who had settled in Arizona before 1870. In those days the Society was more of a social club than the scholarly historical institution of today.

Tucson notables pose for a photograph on the steps of the Pima County courthouse in 1887. This was the county's second courthouse, a substantial brick building completed in 1882. The short man with the long beard in the center of the top row is George Hand. The man leaning on Hand's shoulder is Charles Shibell, a former Pima County sheriff. Arizona Historical Society, Tucson, #21950.

In Hand's day, a person in his fifties was considered to be getting on in years, and if an older man had ever served in the military he was usually "promoted" out of respect. George Hand, the former sergeant, became known to Tucsonans as Captain Hand. A kindly, good-natured man, he was a beloved fixture about the courthouse. And no other Tucsonan was as highly regarded as a storyteller. Whenever a newspaper reporter wanted a humorous anecdote or a pithy quotation, he consulted the genial old Captain. For example, this little note appeared in the February 16, 1884, issue of the *Arizona Daily Star*: "Capt. George Hand, the venerable janitor at the court house, says things ought to be enlivened by a killing, if nothing more than a chuckle-headed reporter is killed." The Tucson newspapers published a number of other humorous articles during the 1880s giving George Hand's views on the town and its inhabitants, and on life in general.

Although he had complained of feeling poorly for months, in February 1887 George Hand began to feel especially ill. The symptoms he described in his diary indicate heart disease--chest pains, shortness of breath, and discomfort in one shoulder. His doctor prescribed an array of pills, but none was effective. As his illness increased in severity, many old friends called on him, bringing their favorite home remedies. Saloon keeper Charles O. Brown brought him a sack of *yerba buena*, a trusted herb used to treat many illnesses in Mexico, but a tea made from the plant did not help. By April 15, Hand was too sick to do any work and he left the courthouse and moved in with the Fosters. He made his last diary entry on April 25. On May 3, 1887, Tucson was rocked by the most severe earthquake to strike the region in recent times. The next day, George O. Hand, the old Captain, died at the age of fifty-seven. He was buried in the G.A.R. plot in the Tucson cemetery. George Hand's obituary in the *Arizona Daily Star* ended with this observation: "He was one of the few who could say, 'I have many friends and no enemies.'"

A Note about the Diaries

George Hand's diaries are housed in the archives of the Arizona Historical Society in Tucson. They consist of ten small leather-bound books. Eight of them have been in the Society's possession since Hand's death. Two books, those that contain the record of his years with the California Column, were originally part of the Hand collection, but somehow were removed from the archives at an early date. They were recovered by the Society from a private party in 1946. The existing diaries are not continuous--there are two major gaps, dividing them into three distinct periods: the "Civil War diaries," August 1861 to October 1864; the "saloon diaries," January 1875 to December 1878 (reproduced herein); and the "courthouse diaries," March 1882 to December 1883, and January 1885 to April 1887 (there is no book for 1884). The Hand collection also includes three of his scrapbooks containing newspaper and magazine clippings. Nothing remains of the voluminous correspondence between Hand and his friends and family members to which he devoted so much time throughout his life.

There is no doubt that George Hand first began keeping a diary upon entering the army in 1861, stopped writing in it when he left the army in 1864, and did not keep one for several years thereafter. It is also clear, however, that he resumed keeping his diary before 1875 and that some of his diaries have been lost. Arizona Historical Society records show that diaries for the years 1861-1864, 1873-1878, and 1882-1887 were received from Hand's estate after his death. Evidently the Civil War diaries and those for 1873, 1874, and 1884 were removed from the collection in the early days of the Society. Only the Civil War diaries have been retrieved. Today, the diaries are kept in a special locked compartment with other rare and valuable documents.

1861

Aug 19 George O Hand was mustered
into the service of the United
States as a Soldier at the
Presidio. Near San Francisco
went into quarter first
at Oakland.

Sept 16 Monday left Oakland
crossed the bay to San Francisco
left the same night on the
Steamer Senator from San
Pedro. with Cos B, I & H. 1st Inft

" 18 Wednesday arrived at San Pedro
Camped late at night.

20 Left en route for Los Angeles

21 Arrived at Camp Latham 9
miles from Los Angeles.

Oct 16 Left Camp Latham for Warner
with "G" & H. 1st Inft as two Cos Cav
Ranch. Camped at Stearns
Ranch 22 miles. Oct 17 Camped
at Rowlands Ranch 18 camped
three miles from the Chino Ranch

George Hand began keeping a diary upon enlisting in the California Volunteers in 1861, and wrote in it on and off until his death in 1887.

There is some indication that George Hand returned to his diary as early as 1872 and that he attended to it continuously through 1887. In the back of his diary for 1885 Hand compiled an annotated list of people who had died in southern Arizona (see Chapter 5). The first entry is dated January 1, 1872. There are numerous entries for each year through 1885. It appears that he extracted the accounts of these deaths from his diaries. The wording in the list for the years 1875 to 1878 is very similar to the discussions of these deaths in the diaries for those years. It is possible that Hand's diaries for the years 1872 and 1879-1881 were inadvertently discarded or otherwise lost before the Society of Arizona Pioneers obtained his precious legacy.

In 1907, twenty years after George Hand's death, the *Arizona Daily Star* (Tucson's morning newspaper) began publishing excerpts from his diaries as human-interest features. From 1927 to 1972, with a few lapses, the *Star* published entries from the diaries as a daily feature on its editorial page. The selections from Hand's diaries that were used were always for the same day of the year as the issue of the *Star* in which they were reproduced. For example, on January 1, twentieth century Tucsonans could read how their forebears celebrated New Year's Day in the 1800s. For more than four decades, thousands of Arizonans began their day reading George Hand's laconic comments on frontier life. Of course, the editors bowdlerized the diaries, and accounts of Hand's dealings with prostitutes were never published. Nonetheless, the *Star* received angry letters from some readers complaining about the descriptions of saloon life and drunkenness which were printed. Prohibition was still in force in 1927 and the attitudes that spawned the Volstead Act remained strong. But to the newspaper's credit, George Hand's diaries survived the critics and delighted two generations of Arizonans.

The saloon diaries have never before been published in book form. Readers have not until now been able to enjoy Hand's chronicle of daily life on the frontier as an uncensored, coherent story. The value of publishing the diaries has long been recognized, however. In the late 1940s, Arizona Historical Society officials sent a sample of them to a university press. The editor liked Hand's narrative, but was timid about publishing an unexpurgated version: "We have all got quite a bang from [Hand's] salty comments on his life and times...our fear is that some of the very best parts of the diary would have to be excised if it were to be published...there is a risk of libel at almost every jump." Readers can rest assured that "the very best parts" are included in this new transcription of George Hand's diaries.

George O. Hand. Photo taken in Adolpho Rodrigo's studio in Tucson in 1874. Arizona Historical Society, Tucson, #1831.

Chapter 1

KEEPING TIGHT DAY AND NIGHT--1875

"Got tight again today. Pearson and I had a fight. Davis hit him in the head with a bar pitcher and he ran out in the street hollering 'murder.' Lawyer Clark is tight. Everyone is tight." George Hand, July 5, 1875

George Hand was just barely getting by in the saloon business as the year 1875 opened. There was a flurry of mining activity in southern Arizona, and new people were coming to Tucson every day, but not much money was being passed around. The forty-four-year-old pioneer was having trouble paying his rent and taxes, and sometimes there wasn't enough money in the till to buy whiskey for the saloon. Times were tough, but George Hand managed to keep his sense of humor and get some fun out of life.

One of the diversions enjoyed by Hand and many other Tucsonans was horse racing, and one of the best places to hold races was the Halfway House. In 1873, A. G. Scott built a roadhouse in the desert about halfway between Camp Lowell and Tucson. The army post, completed that same year, was about seven miles northeast of town. Scott was determined to get first crack at off-duty soldiers on their way to Hand's saloon and other places of amusement. He cleared off a horse-racing track near his tavern, and thus was able to attract business from Tucson as well as Camp Lowell.

~ ~ ~ ~ ~

January 1, 1875 (New Year's Day). Cold but pleasant morning. I made some eggnog. Everywhere the boys were all drunk before breakfast. I went to the races with Davis. We rode out with Sam Hughes. I got very tight [drunk]. Bought into a pool for $10. The race was a single dash of one mile. Results-- Tom Gardner's Grey Eagle, 1. Smith Turner's Gila Grey, 2. Jim Lee's Grey, 3. Soldier's horse, 4. Red Fox, 5. I won every bet. We rode home with Frank Griffen. Everyone was drunk all evening. I went home with Bedford and slept with the sister of Bernardo. Expenses today $10.00. Won on Grey Eagle $48.00.

Jan. 2. Sober today. Moore, Hall, Holmes, and Rivera clubbed Sawyer and escaped from jail last night. Two more races were made today between Grey Eagle and Gila Grey. Jim Brown of Utica got shot in the hand accidently by a soldier. The mail stage came in late--no letters for me. Walker is drunk. Dave Davis is drunk. Expenses $2.50. [The jail breakers had been convicted of murder and their escape caused considerable alarm in the area. They were believed headed for Mexico. See Chapter 5, June 5, July 9, and July 24, 1874. Jerome B. Sawyer was the night guard at the jailhouse.]

Jan. 3 (Sunday). Pleasant morning. There are several drunken men in town. J. B. Brown is on the warpath, Tom Gardner also. There is preaching today at the courthouse. The bullfight at Smith's corral was the best of the season--one Mexican was nearly killed. Went to the *titeres* [Mexican puppet show] in the evening--the house was full. The streets were full of drunken men all night. I closed at 11 o'clock. Expenses $1.50.

Jan. 4. Went to see the hall of the legislature. Helped Steve to hoist the flag on the building. Sent newspapers to William Bradley, Ira [Hand, George's youngest brother], and John E. Roberts [a brother-in-law, Mira Hand Roberts' husband], and wrote to Joe Phillips. The stage arrived--I got some newspapers from John B. Hart. The Honorable Peter R. Brady came in. I closed up at 8 o'clock to save stock. Expenses 75¢. [The eighth territorial legislature convened in Tucson on January 6. The law-making body met for a few weeks in the capital every other year. Peter Brady, a prominent Arizona pioneer and former Tucsonan, now lived at Florence and was a member of the legislature.]

This unpretentious adobe building on Ochoa Street served as Arizona's capitol from 1867 to 1877. Arizona Historical Society, Tucson, #47863.

Jan. 5. Very pleasant weather. The municipal election is today. The stage left for California. Jack Ferrin left town. Jonesy [Fred C. Jones] came in from Governor Safford's ranch. [Governor Anson P. K. Safford's sheep ranch was near Arivaca Creek, about 50 miles southwest of Tucson.] Jim Hart and [John] Cady came home. Hart filled up with whiskey. The election closed without a fight. Estevan Ochoa mayor. Dave Davis marshal by 20 votes majority.

Jan. 6. Lots of drunken soldiers are in town. One named Jacob Burch was shot by someone at the French Brewery. The doctor pronounced the wound mortal. [The French Brewery, owned by Paul Abadie, soon went out of business leaving Alexander Levin Tucson's only beer producer.] I went to a restaurant and found fat Carmel there, half drunk. Took her to my room, stripped her to the bare pelt, and put her to bed. I then left her, and walked around town till two in the morning. Went home and found the girl gone. Went to sleep. Expenses $4.00.

An unidentified cantina woman--a friend of George Hand? *Special Collections, University of Arizona Library, Tucson.*

Jan. 7. Frenchy Rageon and Grey Jack came in town from Camp Grant. The soldier who was shot died this morning. The coroner's jury sat but did not finish. [In Hand's day, coroner's juries were empaneled to help the county coroner investigate violent or otherwise suspicious deaths for evidence of foul play.] Puck Ryan arrived in town. I kept sober all day. Tom Smith returned from Aravaipa [located 50 miles northeast of town]. Taylor sent me a pair of pups. There was a concert of the 5th Cavalry band this evening at the courthouse. Expenses $1.00.

Jan. 8. Fine day. I was summoned before the coroner's jury. Jacob Burch, Company "C," 5th Cavalry, was buried today. [According to the *Citizen*, Burch's assailant, a stranger, was arrested and charged with shooting the soldier in the back.] This is the anniversary of the Battle of New Orleans where Jackson gave the British beans many years ago. I was sober all day, got tight at night. Expenses $3.00.

Jan. 9. Tinker [one of Hand's dogs] got loose and Ginger and him had a little set-to. I commenced drinking to be able to perform the operation of cutting dogs' ears. Cut three. Then got tighter in the evening. Davis and I went to make some calls. Puck Ryan fell over a big *Olla*, broke it, spilled all the water and rolled in it. Grey Eagle is lame--think he will not run tomorrow. Expenses $8.00. [George Hand loved dogs and always had several around. He served the community as its unofficial canine veterinarian, looking after sick dogs and docking tails and trimming ears as per the customs of the day.]

Jan. 10 (Sunday). Pleasant morning. No horse race today. Bill Henry and Captain Devers came in to town. Long Henry Brown came in. Portuguese Joe gave a *bronco* ball [wild party] at his house [saloon--when Hand uses the term "house" he usually means "house of business"]. Brown, Frenchy, and Puck Ryan got sober because everyone with money had gone to bed. Tom McClellan is on the warpath. Born to E. N. Fish and wife, a son. Expenses $1.50.

Jan. 11. Nothing new, very dull. I got full of rum and went to bed. The mail stage came in--received a letter from my sister with a pocket handkerchief in it.

Jan. 12. Sober today. Several natives of Sonora are on a bender. Davis got his bond signed and enters upon the duty of marshal today. Ryan, Frenchy, Cuff, and Old Brown are quite sober. Cady and Jim Hart held a dance for the members of the Arizona legislature. Two more Browns came in from the mines today.

Jan. 13. Nothing of importance transpired today. John Justice left on his ear [fighting mad] for Cal. Cruz--$5.00. [Cruz was a prostitute--Hand recorded his dealings with the "soiled doves" of Tucson in this manner.]

Jan. 14. Fine weather. Still very dull. The supreme court is still in session. I had a row with Prentiss about a seat in the courtroom, but I held the bench. Finished the day by getting drunk. Lost one dollar at keno. Davis made one arrest and received a $2 fine. He got drunk also.

Jan. 15. Fine weather but looks like rain. Sober today. No whiskey in the house this morning--the boys look blue. Cuff leaves today for Camp Grant. Puck Ryan went to work for Tom McClellan. Frenchy left with Dutch Fred.

John Cady reopened my old place on Main Street. Davis is not very drunk. Very dull times. Expenses $3.75.

Jan. 16. Very pleasant morning. The air is full of dust from sweeping the streets. The mail stage arrived--no news. Cady opened his place with a dance. Doña Flavia had a "kept man's" dance. Doña Bernarda also held a dance. [*Doña* is a title of respect bestowed on older Hispanic women, especially widows. These particular *doñas*, however, were keepers of houses of ill-repute]. Davis got pretty full. I saw notice of the death of I. N. Dawley, Dec. 31, Denver, Colorado, of heart disease. Judge Tweed [a supreme court justice] came in my place and bought a cigar. Expenses $2.50.

Jan. 17 (Sunday). Delightful weather, too warm for a coat. Seems so much like summer that I was almost tempted to get tight. Milligan brought me another dog from the post [Camp Lowell]. 12 noon--appetite got the best of judgement and I did get tight. Went to a dance at Cady's, danced a few times, ate some lunch, and went home. Closed up at 11 o'clock. I escorted Marshal Davis home to his little bed, saw him turn in with his little woman, went home and retired. Born to the wife of W. J. Osborn, a daughter. Expenses $6.00. Carmel--$3.00. [Hand always distinguished between a man's "woman" and his wife, formal marriage being the criterion.]

Jan. 18. John Sweeney came to town. I took too much juice today. Went home with Davis. Went to bed full. Unknown girl--$2.00.

Jan. 19. Got up at 8 o'clock. Took one drink and was tight. Kept drinking till 11 a.m., then went to bed full of rot and slept till three p.m. Ate no dinner. Frenchy Rageon came to town. Brown was very tight all day. Davis is playing pool in C. O. Brown's saloon. I closed up at 11 o'clock. Went to bed sober. [Although nothing special by San Francisco standards, Charles O. Brown's Congress Hall Saloon was the fanciest one in Tucson, with an ornate bar, pool tables, and better-than-average booze. His saloon was on the corner of Meyer and Congress streets, close to Hand's place, and George Hand often reported what went on there.]

Jan. 20. Cloudy, but warm. Seven Mexicans were put in jail last night. Charley Rice came to town. John Sweeney came up with a pocket full of money and checks. Davis, nearly as drunk as Sweeney, took the money from him and put it in John Archibald's safe. The whiskey gave out in the house. I sold a ball ticket and won it back shaking dice. Bought a bottle of rot from Shorty Holt and went with Hunt and McClellan to the old army camp. We left Hunt there, tight and asleep. Came home at 1 o'clock.

Jan. 21. Rice commenced bleeding at the nose at daylight. The boys all quit drinking to take a new start. There is to be a grand ball this evening at the hall of the legislature, tickets $5.00. Ladies are invited free by the committee. I took Charley Rice to the hospital. [The Pima County Hospital was supervised by Dr. John C. Handy and was little more than a pest house where the sick were quarantined and given basic nursing care. Tucson's first private hospital, St. Mary's, was founded by the Sisters of St. Joseph of Carondelet in 1880.]

The interior of Charles O. Brown's Congress Hall Saloon, Tucson's finest in Hand's day. The man at the right is C. O. Brown. Arizona Historical Society, Tucson, #60832.

Jan. 22. Fine weather again. The ladies' ball was a success. One cake sold for $100--Robert Leatherwood bought it. 100 ladies and 200 gents were present. It is supposed to have netted $1,200. [The ball was thrown to raise money for a new public schoolhouse.] Big Jesús--$2.00. [In Hand's day, Hispanic women, as well as men, were often named *Jesús.*]

Jan. 23. I am sobering up. Very dull today. Davis cannot quit drinking-- he took three drinks inside of 20 minutes. Brown is quite sober today. Tom McClellan and Jim Hart are very much intoxicated. McClellan found a girl this morning and proposed marriage to her. He is to settle the arrangements this evening. There is a dance at Cady's, one at Big Carmel's, and a kept man's dance at Flavia's. I drank a bottle of beer and went to bed at 12 o'clock.

Jan. 24 (Sunday). Got up at 8 o'clock. Had only one drink before breakfast. Ate quite hearty. Bedford took my watch to raffle off. 12 noon-- very pleasant. All the stores are closed this morning. Bullfights today. Davis has really quit drinking. Davis commenced again. I gave a dollar to see the bullfight. Went to the *títeres.* Closed up at 12 o'clock. Cruz--$2.00.

Jan. 25. Cloudy. Again I took only one drink before breakfast. Received a letter from J. D. Phillips with stamps to send papers. 12 noon--clouding up thick. It rained a little in the evening. [Deputy] Jack Long came in from New Mexico on the trail of an outlaw. I closed early, went to bed.

Jan. 26. It rained quite hard all day. Jonesy and Norm Eldridge came in from the sheep ranch. Dr. Peter Thomas (a Negro) was arrested on complaint of his adopted daughter. [Peter Thomas was a barber who practiced quack medicine on the side.]

Jan. 27. Still cloudy but no rain. Davis and Long are going to the Rillito post [Camp Lowell] to look for an escaped murderer. They returned, went to Nine Mile Water Hole [nine miles northwest of town], and returned. We had cold rain and some snow today. William C. Dunn married Dolores Sierras. Tinker got loose, went for Ginger, and had a hard fight. Tinker got the best as far as punishment, but Ginger had the best wind. Several of the boys got tight, myself among the number. I put the nigger barber [probably Charles Glasco] and Brown out the door. Went to bed vexed.

Jan. 28. Cloudy, muddy, disagreeable day. Very cold. The bummers are all out in full blast. The mail stage arrived--no letters for me. The legislature passed a bill creating the County of Pinal [with the town of Florence, 70 miles north of Tucson, as county seat]. Nothing new or interesting. Carmel--$2.00.

Jan. 29. Pleasant day. Hart, Conwell, etc., left for the Patagonia mines [60 miles southeast of town near the Mexican border]. We heard about the escaped murderer--he is reported to be at Sacaton [80 miles northwest of Tucson]. The nigger doctor is still in jail. Old Brown is still drunk. Everybody is drunk this evening. Went to Cady's, had a few dances, came home, shut up the house. Took a walk with Davis. Went to bed. Jesús--$5.00.

Jan. 30. Pleasant morning. 12 noon--no mail stage yet. Very dull. I am giving no credit today. The mail stage arrived late at night. Davis is again under the ardent. I closed up at 10:30. Went to bed sober.

Jan. 31 (Sunday). Very pleasant. Very dull. Took a hot bath, changed clothes, and went to the bullfight. Went to the *titeres* in the evening. I closed up at 10 o'clock and went with Davis and took in the whole town. We brought up at a masquerade ball at the upper end of town. There was nothing to drink, so I filled a bottle with water. Bought a few *cascarones* [eggshells filled with confetti] for the girls. Came home at 1 o'clock, took a drink, and went to bed. Jesús--$1.00.

~ ~ ~ ~ ~

February 1. Dull morning. Sick today. The dogs broke out of the kennel and ran all over the house. No whiskey in the house today--the boys and bums all look very blue. Davis is very hot, says he will never take another drink. I paid the [territorial saloon] license today [$30 per quarter]. The rent is also due, no money to pay it [$30 per month]. The common council meets this evening. Doña Juana was arrested for keeping a disorderly house. I sent papers home [Oneida County, New York] and to Billy Bradley and J. B. Hart. Closed up early. Went to bed sober.

Feb. 2. I have not bought any whiskey yet. The bummers all got sober and left. Good riddance to bad rubbish. Sent little Jimmy [a dog] to Dick Hudson in Silver City [New Mexico]. I was sober all day--drank **NO** whiskey. This evening I went to hear Judge Dunne deliver a lecture on education and the propriety of dividing the school fund. I fully agree with him. Went to bed at 9:30 o'clock. [Edmund F. Dunne was chief justice of the Arizona supreme court. A devout Catholic, he argued that the territorial school fund should be shared with parochial schools. Although Hand was not a Catholic, he agreed with the proposal. However, most non-Catholic Arizonans were hostile to the idea.]

Feb. 3. Very fine morning. No whiskey yet. Davis has the prisoners at work cleaning the streets. Patterson came in from Camp Grant, brought Burk and Lt. Woodson. I received an invitation to a ball to be given at the Cosmopolitan Hotel Feb. 12. Davis arrested two niggers and some Mexicans. I took a walk with Judge Osborn to his place one mile out. Closed at 9 o'clock. Davis slept in my room.

Feb. 4. Still sick. No rot in the house. Quite cold this morning. Mail arrived yesterday--no through mail. I called on McClellan's paint shop, Sam Hughes' assay office, and other places. 12 noon--wind, cold, and cloudy. Looks much like rain. The legislature passed the compulsory education bill. Jim Douglass is drunk. He is playing against faro and monte and is very abusive. Martin Sweeney came in town. I closed at 9:30 o'clock.

Feb. 5. Pleasant weather. The capital bill passed both houses. It [the territorial capital] is now on wheels, bound for Prescott. Purdy from Yuma is supposed to have sold his vote to the Prescott party. There is free wine by the basket at Brown's saloon, bought by the winning party. Faro and monte games are running heavy at Brown's. There are several drunken men in town. Jim Douglass is on a bust. [Prescott was selected to be Arizona's capital when the territory was established in 1863. Tucson politicians managed to bring the capital to their town in 1867. Unhappy with this result, legislators from Prescott worked to recapture the capital and finally succeeded in 1877. However, in 1889 the legislature voted to move the capital to Phoenix, which has been Arizona's seat of government ever since.]

Feb. 6. Fine morning. Several cartoons displaying Purdy and others were posted on my house by Joe Neugass--they caused great excitement. The mail coach arrived--no papers, received a letter from J. B. Hart. Ginger went to W. W. Williams' house. Smith's Fanny had pups. There was theatre and a dance at Cady's saloon tonight. Davis pricked Coyote Drumm with a knife and Justice Meyer ordered him to jail but he did not go. [German-born Charles Meyer was a justice of the peace and the town druggist. Meyer Street in

Tucson was named for him.] John Day is drunk and sleeping in a chair. I kept open till past 1 o'clock. Sick all night, slept very little.

Feb. 7 (Sunday). Very pleasant today. Everyone is going to church. Drumm says he nearly bled to death. I called on Charley Rice in the hospital-- he is improving quite fast. Bullfights again today. Went to see Smith's pups. Saw the bullfight. Davis got drunk and got a French lip put on him. There are plenty of drunken men in town. Rooney came to town and gave me a ham of venison. Jack Hill came back from San Carlos [headquarters of an Apache Indian reservation on the Gila River, 120 miles northeast of town]. Cady sold half his dance house. I went to bed at 10:30 o'clock. Expenses (foolish) $2.50.

Feb. 8. Finest kind of weather. Davis has a lip as big as a beefsteak. John Metzger and John Hastings arrived. Pat O'Meara and Tom Banning are drunk already. Davis was tried today for cutting Coyote's behind--he got clear. A dance of the kept men was held tonight at the Pioneer Brewery [the old name of Alexander Levin's Park Brewery]. Davis spent $11 for eggshells [*cascarones*] to break on the little heads of the beautiful *putas* [whores].

Feb. 9. Cloudy. Davis is on trial again today for drawing a pistol on a woman. The woman swore that Davis tried to shoot her and threw her down from a platform. I was called as a witness and the woman was impeached. A little windy today, but very warm. More cartoons are out this morning--Purdy and his love, Mabel, are the subjects. Davis' examination closed at 2 p.m. Sentence received--$40 fine or 40 days in jail. The capital goes to Phoenix if this bill is approved. Hand got tight. Closed at 11 o'clock.

Feb. 10. Very pleasant morning. Had only one drink before breakfast. At a meeting of the common council last night, it was resolved to invite Davis to resign as marshal. He received notice from the clerk this morning, also an acknowledgement from W. W. Williams of the withdrawal of his bond. Another bill passed both houses to keep the capital here. Lutz sold his dance house for $20. Trooper John and Yankee Joe came in town. Pat O'Meara is drunk again. I ate a pig's foot and went to bed.

Feb. 11. Davis quit drinking. Jack Long returned this morning with a prisoner, one of the Bender family. John Burt and Thomas Roddick came in town today. Jack took Davis, Joe Phy, and myself down the road to see the man that he has arrested for one of the Bender gang. Billy Harrison and some other boys came in today from the Colorado River. There was a big dance at Smith's- -I did not attend.

Feb. 12. Fine day. Got tight early. Last day of the legislature--the capital remains here. Someone stole my old pipe. Davis resigned the office of marshal [and began working and rooming at Hand's saloon]. 12 o'clock--Hand is drunker. Three o'clock--Hand is quite sober, but got drunk again. 9 in the evening--Hand is very tight. Went to bed early.

Feb. 13. Pleasant day. The boys are all getting drunk, Hand included. Went to bed at 2 p.m. and slept till dinner. Went back to bed after dinner and slept till night. Louise the squaw cut Big Carmel badly in the back and breast. I went to bed tight, slept very little.

Ad for Alexander Levin's Park Brewery published in the Arizona Citizen *(Tucson) in 1875.*

Feb. 14 (Sunday). Cloudy and cold. Drank no whiskey today--have to quit drinking to get well. Several of the boys are tight. There is a bullfight today. Tom McClellan is tight. Everybody went to the bullfight--were badly sold. At night some of the boys went to shivaree the Roadrunner who just got married. Dave Davis and Tom Roddick were the leaders of the band. [Refugia Rivera, a prostitute, was nicknamed "*La Churra*" or "The Roadrunner." She married a man named Robert Frazer.]

Alexander Levin, Tucson's master brewer and developer of Levin's Park. Levin, a German immigrant, began making beer in Tucson in 1866. Buehman photo, Arizona Historical Society, Tucson, #166.

Feb. 15. Rainy and muddy all day. The mail stage left taking some of the members of the legislature. Louise was fined $15 for cutting Carmel. French Joe paid the fine. Davis and Long received a letter from Sulphur Springs [70 miles east of town] stating that the prisoner, Bender, had escaped. Fred Eland is still on a spree. I closed early and went to bed.

Feb. 16. Feel pretty well--I have drank nothing since Sunday night. It rained all last night and it is very muddy this morning. Old Brown hired out to drive some hogs up the river. He got drunk and did not go. Davis then gave him the name of "Hog" Brown. The mail stage arrived this morning--no letters for me. I felt sick all day. Ate a pig's foot at Cady's and some Oregon apples.

Went with Clark to the Mexican restaurant and got supper. Closed and went to bed at 11:30 o'clock.

Feb. 17. The weather cleared off fine. Hargrave, Tompkins, Doc Moeller, and others [legislators] left today for home. I bought some apples for Foster's children. Sick again today. Mail arrived--no letters for me. The prices of all kinds of groceries were raised by a combination of the merchants. The first who undersells forfeits 1,000 dollars.

Feb. 18. Cloudy and windy. Dick Munson from Silver City came to town en route to Cal. There was another death in town. The election for marshal was advertised for February 22--five candidates are already in the field. It rained this afternoon. John Day and Norm Eldridge are drunk. Tom Banning is drunk.

Feb. 19. It rained nearly all last night, cleared off fine this morning. Very muddy. Bill Elliott has posters out announcing himself for marshal. There was a great argument in the house on religion between Morgan and Sawyer. It lasted one hour, and ended when they commenced in another argument, this time about President Grant--Sawyer said he was an idiot. Nigger Charley [Glasco] is on a spree. Tom Roddick and Bill Harrison came back from the mines. Ginger got loose, came down and had a fight with Tinker. Only one round and they were parted. Ginger was hurt worse. Closed up and went to bed at 11 o'clock.

Feb. 20. Very pleasant today. Went to see Ginger--he was pretty well shook up last night. Prisoners are sweeping the streets this morning. Both faro games in the house lost last night, everybody won. One game is still running at 3 p.m. today. The game finally closed with Blade the loser. He went against Bob and Brown and lost several hundred. There was a big dance in the alley tonight. Big Jesús and others got into a fight and were arrested and lodged in jail. Nigger Charley got drunk and took charge of the French barber shop and landed his boat in jail. The mail stage came in today--I got no letters. Closed early and went to bed. Paid $3.00 for medicine.

Feb. 21 (Sunday). Very cold and windy. Big Jesús and Refugia were each fined $7 by Justice Neugass and went to jail for want of funds. [Joseph Neugass was a justice of the peace and the proprietor of the Tucson Restaurant and a small hotel.] I had a nice bath. The boys all went to the horse race between [James] Speedy's bay pony and Smith's dun horse. Speedy's horse got beat by 3 lengths. There was a bullfight at 4 p.m. and a puppet show in the evening. Quite cold this evening.

Feb. 22. Cold morning, quite windy. Flags are flying all over town in honor of Washington's Birthday. Nigger Glasco had his trial this morning on complaint of the French barber [John Baker], was fined $12.50 for breaking one piece of glass. I bought some new pants. 12 noon--rain, snow, and hail. It was cold, rainy, and muddy all day. Roddick, Johnson, and others are tight.

The mail stage left for Cal. Goldberg's wagon train arrived. Lew Davis came in from Yuma.

Feb. 23. Cloudy but no rain. Election for marshal today. Two candidates, Bill Elliott and Pancho Esparza. Not much excitement. Jack Long and Sawyer returned from prospecting, did not find a mine. A telegram today says that Old Bender is again arrested, this time at Florence. Davis or Jack will start tomorrow for Old Bender. The mail stage came--no letters for me. 5 p.m.-- Pancho is elected marshal by 26 votes majority. I closed at 9.

Feb. 24. Cloudy, cold morning. 12 noon--the clouds cleared off. Roddick left for the mines. Dr. Lord and his wife left for the States. I wrote to John Roberts and Billy Bradley and sent them some papers. Morgan is drunk. Billy Munson left for Pueblo Viejo [a settlement on the Gila River about 120 miles northeast of Tucson]. Dixon came in town, got drunk, and talked for 3 hours steady. I was obliged to shut up the saloon to stop him.

Feb. 25. Quite cold this morning. A new lot of men are leaving for Boyle's mines [in the Santa Rita Mountains]. I washed out my dog kennels. 1 p.m.-- Boyle's wagon full of miners just left town. Fred Eland is drunk again. The mail stage arrived--no Atlantic papers. The coach was full of goods for Zeckendorf's store. I played freeze-out for a saddle. Won the saddle, $2.00, and one new deck of cards. Very poor saddle.

Zeckendorf's store on Main Street. Arizona Historical Society, Tucson, #56749.

Feb. 26. Pleasant morning but cold. Sawyer and Jack Long are going out again prospecting. I wrote a letter to C. J. Nickerson, Sutter Creek, Amador County, Cal., and one to Milton F. Hand [a brother], Joliet, Ill. Davis' dog, Trouble, died and was buried today. The stage left for Cal. There was a trial today before Justice Neugass of McKey's woman for beating another woman.

Jack Klingenschmidt came in from Sonora today. He was near being killed there last year by a Mexican in his employ.

Feb. 27. Fine morning. McKey's woman appeared this morning for sentencing--30 days or $30. She paid the fine and the case was appealed. Old Brown dug a new vault for the outhouse. I cleaned out the corral [courtyard] and was very sober at night. Baker commenced fixing rooms in the corral. Very dull day and night. Wrote to Joe Phillips. Davis and I retired very early.

Feb. 28 (Sunday). Seems like rain again. Did not get up this morning till past eight o'clock. Took a bath. Brown went to the mines driving a team. 12 noon--quite pleasant, sun out, but windy. George Fields' wagon train is in. Fred Eland is drunk. Yankee Joe came in. Very dull. No money in sight. Closed at 10 o'clock.

~ ~ ~ ~ ~

March 1. Cloudy, cold, and windy. 10 a.m.--rain. It cleared off and at 3 p.m. was very windy and dusty. Contreras' wagon train came in. I went to Smith's to get my dogs but could not get in the house. Got another bottle of medicine from Meyer. Tom McClellan is here tonight, blowing as usual. Sawyer and Morgan had another argument this evening. Closed at 10:30.

Charles H. Meyer was Tucson's druggist and a justice of the peace in the 1870s. There were no restrictions on the sale of drugs in his day. Buehman photo, Arizona Historical Society, Tucson, #242.

Mar. 2. Cold--water froze in the ollas. Got my pups from Smith, gave one to Davis, one to a Mexican, and one to Goodrich. Dan Kehoe went off owing me $4.25. Fred Eland left for San Pedro, drunk. [San Pedro was a settlement on the San Pedro River about 50 miles east of town.] Cady held a dance at the Halfway House. The mail stage came today--received a letter from my sister. Davis is drunk again. There was a big argument in the house this evening on the profit of raising cattle vs. that of sheep. Davis is dealing monte. Cold tonight. I closed at 11 o'clock and went to bed.

Mar. 3. Cold and windy, rain and snow. Wrote to Ira and Emma [a sister]. Sent papers to Nickerson and Bradley. Pleasant this afternoon, but cold. No beef to be had for dinner today. The stage left for Cal. H. S. Stevens left on it for Washington--several men in buggies went to see Hiram off. [Hiram Stevens was a Tucson merchant and the new delegate to the U.S. Congress from Arizona Territory.] William Zeckendorf left for New York. Very cold night. Closed at 11 o'clock.

Mar. 4. Cold and windy. George Esslinger is drunk again. The stage arrived at 2 p.m. Davis dug a hole and put a post in to tie Tinker. John Sweeney and Faher are in town.

Mar. 5. Went to Etchells' blacksmith shop and saw the new quartz mill [a steam-powered machine for crushing ore]. There is great excitement about town in regard to mines. Called at the soda [soft drink] factory. I drank some whiskey today. Tinker caught a woman and tore her dress. Juan Rodriguez was married last night. Esslinger is still on the spree. Davis is drunk. Hand is drunk.

Mar. 6. Fine day. The mail stage came in--no letters for me. The cook at Foster's house got her back up and left. Smith held a dance at the Halfway House.

Mar. 7 (Sunday). Looks very dull for business. The stores are all shut up. Today is my birthday--45 years of age. Took a hot bath. Lots of the boys are drunk today. Pat O'Meara got tight, fell down, and someone stepped on his nose. Overstreet hit a Mexican, and the Mexican hit Harrison with a rock and cut his head. There was a puppet show this evening. Took a walk after I closed up. Came home at 3 in the morning.

Mar. 8. Fine morning. Nothing new. Billy Harrison's head is swollen. French Joe was on a bust, raised a row with Billy Wall, and got shot in the right side of his belly. In the row [which took place in Hand's saloon], Mr. Sothers, while in the character of Lord Dundreary [a popular comedic personality of the day], was shot in the leg. Great excitement. The priest here confessed Joe. Wall was arrested and put in jail. Esslinger is still drunk. I received $10 cash from Tom Smith and his note for $70. Antoine took his pup today. No more excitement.

Mar. 9. Fine morning. French Joe Provencie is easier today. Fred Eland died this morning of lung fever. He swelled and turned black in a short time. I got tight today and made a fool of myself again. I sued John Hovey for $18.80 and attached his pay in Goldberg's hands. [Hovey was a teamster in the employ of Isaac Goldberg, who had a freighting business.] Went to bed at 1 o'clock. Expenses $1.25.

Mar. 10. Sick this morning. Eland was buried at 11 this morning. I was sick all day today. Had a fearful lot of bums around. Davis quit drinking at 10 o'clock and started again at 12. Jack Long and Sawyer returned from prospecting. Billy Wall was indicted and released on $2,000 bail. George Esslinger is still drunk. I closed at 11 o'clock and went to bed.

Mar. 11. Fine day again. Joe Provencie died this morning and was buried this evening. John Rageon (Frenchy) came in from Picacho [a stage station 40 miles northwest of town] with a bruised head and got drunk in less than half an hour. Hand got drunk also. I ate supper with John Day at Cady's. Called on Mrs. Cady this afternoon. Sent papers to Nickerson and Bradley. Closed at 11 o'clock. Got up in the night to get water and fell over some chairs and broke my washbowl.

Mar 12. Very pleasant morning. Frenchy and the darky barber are drunk. The trial of Billy Wall is to be held today before Justice Neugass. I was sober and sick all day. The trial of Wall is not over. Frenchy is drunk. George Esslinger is still on the spree. Closed at 11 o'clock.

Mar. 13. Sick and very cross. Bummers are plenty. Windy, dusty, and disagreeable. The decision by Justice Neugass was rendered at 2 p.m.--Wall was acquitted. Mail stage arrived--received a letter from Mason, San Luis Obispo, Cal. The house was measured again for a new floor. Dixon was drunk and bawling all over town all night. Closed at 1 o'clock.

Mar. 14 (Sunday). Fine day. The church is busy this morning. There were cockfights at noon. There was a bullfight and circus at 4 p.m.--I was foolish enough to be found there myself. Billy Wall, Johnny Burt, Lew Davis, and Hog [Dave] Davis got drunk on *mescal*. I came home at dark. Had dinner at the "Hotel de Neugass." We had singing during the evening. Davis sang some of his favorite songs, "She's Mine Wherever I Find Her," and several others equally good. Closed with 6 sleepers.

Mar. 15. Fine day. Roddick and Stroud came in town and both got drunk. Nothing new. McClellan got an assay of his mine--no good. He is red hot, says Brown is a bilk and a liar. I closed at 9 o'clock.

Mar. 16. Windy day. I was sober all day. Nothing new. The mail stage came.

Mar. 17. Fine morning. St. Patrick's Day. I treated all the boys. Everyone got drunk. No fights. I made some egg drinks and served them to the girls in the corral. Got tight myself and kept full all day. Went to bed early.

Mar. 18. It rained in the night. Cold, windy, and very dusty and disagreeable today. I slept nearly all day. Got a money order from Tom McMahon for $25. Old Brown changed his name back to get a pension as a soldier of the Mexican War. His right name is J. H. Brumfield.

Mar. 19. Cold and damp--it rained last night. Some villain threw a big rock in Joe Neugass' window and broke and scattered glass all over him while he was sleeping. I wrote letters to Mason, J. Phillips, and Bill Ferguson. Sent papers to P. R. Brady, Joe Phillips, and Puck Ryan. Got full of whiskey. Played two games of quoits with Dave Davis and others. [Quoits is a game in which metal rings are thrown at an upright pin.] Got drunker and drunker. Went to bed drunk. Maria--$2.00.

Mar. 20. Windy in the morning, fair after 12 noon. Sick all day. The barber moved his mother and family. Men are cleaning the streets today. The mail stage arrived--no letters for me. Davis is drunk. Frenchy and McMahon are sober. I saw the gold on display from the new placer mines [in the Santa Rita Mountains about 30 miles south of town]. Cady broke my axe. I was very sick at night--had to go to bed. Closed at 10:30.

Mar. 21 (Palm Sunday). Fine morning. Metzger is tight. The two Davis's are drunk. Hand is drunk. Frenchy is sober. I took a bath. Got drunker by night. I cleaned the lamps, got mad, and shut up the house. Took a long walk with Jim Abbott and Hog Davis. Came back and opened the front door. Rageon and myself ate some enchiladas. I sat in the corral until bedtime. Went to bed early.

Mar. 22. Pleasant day. Very dull. Received a letter from Billy Bradley speaking of LaRose, Potter, Savage, and Brown. I was sober all day. There are several new faces in town. No one killed today. Closed early.

Mar. 23. Fine day. Mail stage came--no letters for me. Very dull. Tom McClellan is on a bust. Davis is trying to keep sober. Cherokee--$2.00.

Mar. 24. Fine day. Got tight again today. Sent papers to Bradley, John Roberts, and C. J. Nickerson. Dr. Handy brought a black and tan pup from the Rillito post [Camp Lowell] and gave it to me. I christened her Sue. She did not whine a whine all night.

Mar. 25. Sullivan and Hunt commenced on the new floor for the house. We moved the bar and everything out. The boys got drunk in a very short time, myself not far behind. Frenchy is very drunk. The floor was nearly done by 6 o'clock and Sullivan set up three bottles. McClellan and myself were drinking and wrestling. We tore our clothes and nearly broke our necks. I bought some bacon from Dickey and kept drinking. Nothing to do at night but run around and love the girls. Foster is drunk. I took Jerry Kenny home. Went to bed early but in my senses.

Mar. 26. Good Friday. No meat in the house but bacon. Hand is sober. Davis is sober. Frenchy is sober. All the boys are sober.

Mar. 27-April 3. [No entries.]

~ ~ ~ ~ ~

April 4 (Sunday). Sick and sore and very lame.

Apr. 5. Commenced tearing the wall around the corral down to build a new room. Tom Banning fell in a fit. Hand got full of rot. Very windy and dusty. Very dull times.

Apr. 6. Cold morning. Windy and very dusty. Frenchy went to Levin's this morning. Mail stage came in--no letters for me. I was sober all day. Jack Long came in from the mines. 4 p.m.--cloudy. 5 p.m.--light rain, the wind calmed down. Very cold but no firewood.

Apr. 7. Mail stage arrived--received a letter from Mason, San Luis Obispo, and Ira. Got tight. Went to a dance at Doña Luisa's. Went to bed at 12 o'clock.

Apr. 8. Very cold--ice in the ollas. Sick today. Sober all day. Morgan is drunk. Pleasant day but very dull.

Apr. 9. Pleasant day. Cold. Jack Long took Spot [dog] to the mines. I received an invitation to attend a dance in Maiden Lane [the red-light district], but did not go. John Moore came to town yesterday. Some of the boys got tight at the dance today. Jones came in town from Governor Safford's ranch. I had a terrific time cleaning the privy. Metzger is drunk. Davis is drunk. Ginger came down again tonight.

Apr. 10. Pleasant weather. Worked hard cleaning up. The stage came in-- no letters for me. I got full after noon. Daly got tight at night and was near having a fight with Prentiss. He came to my house with H. B. Jones, stayed an hour. I went to a dance, got ashamed of myself, and went home. Big Refugia-- $2.00.

Apr. 11 (Sunday). Sober all day. The town is pretty lively with discharged soldiers. Professor LeRoy [an itinerant magician] performs tonight at the courthouse. Hastings is drunk. Banning is drunk. The two had a fight this morning--Banning won. There was a dance this evening--it ran till 2 in the morning. All the boys were tight.

Apr. 12. Pleasant morning. 9 o'clock--wind and dust. The soldiers are still on the drink. Nothing very interesting so far. I was sober all day. Lew Davis stole a collar from Red, a dog belonging to Davis & Kelson [tinsmiths]. Hastings was sober all day. A soldier gave him $10 this evening and he was drunk in 20 minutes. Hog Davis slept all the morning. I had a sleep after noon. Closed at 12:30 o'clock.

Apr. 13. Slept late. Windy this morning. Hastings is still drunk. Levin brought some of his new beer in this morning--very fine beer. I drank several bottles of it but kept sober all day. Plenty of soldiers are on the drink this evening. Professor LeRoy and the Mexican puppet show were hired by Cady to show in his corral. There is great excitement in town tonight, the streets are full of people. The boys were anxious to have a dance here after the performances but I did not want it. Closed at 1 o'clock.

Apr. 14. Fine day. Some soldiers are tight this morning. Tinker bit Belle, the black-and-tan, over the left eye and for four hours I thought her eye was lost. I gave Tinker a good whipping and was vexed all day until the little dog showed that her eye was good. The mail stage left today. Some ladies came around selling tickets for the ball to be held on the 100th anniversary of the Battle of Lexington [April 19]. Dave Davis is full. He received a dog from Silver City--no good. Very dull in the house this evening. Closed at 10 o'clock.

Apr. 15. Slept late. Had breaded tripe and fried mush with eggs and beans for breakfast. Very warm, no air stirring. Lawyer Howard returned to town. Shibell and Moffat returned. Very dull. Mail stage came from Cal.--no letters for me. Jim Blade bought some property from Ruelas on Mesilla Street.

Apr. 16. [No entry.]

Apr. 17. Jim Hart came in town. The mail stage came from Cal. I bought a flag from Zeckendorf--$5.00. Got drunk. All the boys got drunk. We had some excitement--Tom McClellan wanted to shoot Fletcher. I had to throw him down and take his pistol from him.

Apr. 18 (Sunday). Fine warm day. Took a bath. Got tight. Kept tight all day. Was very tight. Had a row with Jim Hart about money. I put up a flagstaff and the wind blew it down. I left it lay across the road till morning. Got pretty sober by nighttime. Went to bed sober, but was sick all night.

Apr. 19. Sick all day, felt very bad. Drank very little. Tom Roddick came in town and got tight very quick. McDermott got tight. Closed at 9:30.

Apr. 20. Very warm. Still sick. Slept considerable during the day. Jonesy came in from Governor Safford's ranch. Lew Davis and Charley Stuart leave for Prescott today. I commenced to tie Jo [a female dog] up.

Apr 21. Still warm. Sick in bed nearly all day with a cold and piles [hemorrhoids]. Jonesy and Tom Roddick are tight. There was a big argument between Morgan, Sawyer, and Hastings. They made so much noise that I was obliged to get up and stop it. Nothing new. Closed at 10 o'clock.

Apr. 22. Still sick. Mail stage arrived--got a letter from P. R. Brady and answered it immediately. Felt bad all day. Very dull in the house--did not make expenses. Jonesy, Mawford, and Roddick left for home. Very windy and dusty. I was obliged to retire early.

Apr. 23. Warm and pleasant. Felt some better today, then worked too hard and made myself sick again. I had to go to bed nearly all the rest of the day. Foster took 17 drinks and Fred Jones 12 in a very short time. Very dull day. Sent papers to John Riley, Bradley, and Nickerson. Davis had a presentiment this evening and would not sleep in his room. I paid the road tax. Went to bed at 9 o'clock. [Both the territory and village had road improvement taxes whereby all male residents between the ages of 21 and 50 were charged one day's labor or $2 per year.]

Apr. 24. Got up early. The first man I saw was Sam Wise. Worked considerable today. The *Citizen* came out with a full account of the party of the 19th. The stage arrived with a bride for W. C. Davis the tinsmith. Jacobs also came on it. No mail for me. Tied Jo up today.

Apr. 25 (Sunday). Very warm and very dull. Nothing new except a bullfight by candlelight. Two *bravo* Mexicans (drunk) were hurt badly by the bulls. Closed and went to bed early.

Apr. 26. Windy and some cooler than yesterday. Very dull. Got my sprinkling pot fixed. A load of whiskey came for Lord & Williams [the wholesalers from whom Hand usually got the whiskey for his saloon]. John Hovey arrived with Lazarus' wagon train. Closed at 9 o'clock.

Apr. 27. Warm. Windy after noon. The mail stage arrived. They laid the first adobe on Toole's new house [of business]. Davis the tinsmith was married this evening. Very dusty this afternoon. Closed early.

Apr. 28. Windy and very dusty. Sent for the Utica *Herald*. Also sent photos to Ira and Mit [Milton Hand]. The mail stage left today for Cal. I worked nearly all day binding last year's *Spirit of the Times*. [The *Spirit of the Times* was Hand's favorite periodical and he subscribed to it throughout his adult life. A sporting magazine published in New York, it featured articles on yachting, boxing, horse racing, wingshooting, etc. Hand bound and repaired books, both for himself and for others in town.]

Apr. 29. Very dusty. The barber moved and the Mexican lunch house moved into his old room. The stage arrived--no Atlantic mail because of a railroad blockade. [Mail from the eastern states came to Tucson via the transcontinental railroad and California. A late spring storm had blocked the tracks in Wyoming.] Jo [dog] got married. Cloudy today. There was a very light sprinkle of rain, not enough to lay the dust. Had *pinole* [parched corn] and milk for dinner. I was very sleepy all the evening. A new saloon opened today in the building formerly used by Sullivan as a carpenter shop. 8 p.m.-- very cloudy.

Apr. 30. Pleasant morning. The stage leaves today. Prince called on Jo again. Very warm. No wind today. The work stopped on Toole's house. Cause--no adobe. There are dead dogs all over town. [After posting notice so that pets could be kept in, the marshal and poundmaster had placed strychnine baits about town to get rid of stray dogs.] W. W. Williams gave a dance at his private house last night. The soldiers got paid today, but it is still very dull in town. I went to bed early. Davis kept the saloon open till three in the morning. Hastings got drunk and pissed all over the new floor.

~ ~ ~ ~ ~

May 1. Cloudy this morning. Company "H," 5th Cavalry, and the band, leaves [Camp Lowell] today for New Mexico. [Music was in short supply on the frontier, and the 5th Cavalry band was sorely missed by Tucsonans.] Hastings is drunk. H. B. Smith caught Billy Gardner in bed with his wife. He called several others in to see the sight and prove the truth. He advertised in the *Citizen* today, warning all persons against crediting her on his account. The mail coach arrived--no through mail. Dickey commenced work at Lord & Williams' store today. Some soldiers had a dance at Big Carmel's. They strayed in my house late and I got the late game. Closed at 2:30 o'clock.

May 2 (Sunday). Pleasant day. Drank gin all day, but did not get tight. There was a bullfight after dark. I was sick this evening with pleurisy. Frank Belar got rolled. Closed at 10 o'clock.

May 3. Fine day. Taken sick this morning with pleurisy-- obligded to take medicine. Very sick all day--nearly driven crazy with pain. [Pleurisy is an extremely painful inflamation of the membrane covering the lungs.] Sent papers to Bradley, Nickerson, and J. E. Roberts. There was a housewarming at Greek Alex's this evening. [Alexander Wilkins, "Greek Alex," had opened a new barber shop.] I closed at 10:30.

May 4. Fine morning but warm for the season. Feel some better. Ate some milktoast and eggs. Sick all day. The stage came--no letters for me. There was a dance at the house of Jim Douglass. The latter was very drunk in the evening. Today was the warmest day this year.

May 5. Fine day. Warm, no wind, no dust. Ate very little this morning. Paid the internal revenue tax [a federal tax on the making and sale of liquor and tobacco products--the tax on saloons was $25 per year]. Sick and taking medicine all day. Some men came in from Boyle's mines [in the Santa Rita Mountains]--work has stopped there. Cady opened a bit house [a saloon that sold a shot of rotgut whiskey for a "bit" (12½¢), two shots for a quarter]. The soda man opened a saloon.

May 6. Fine morning. I feel some better. Paid the county [saloon] license today to [Deputy Assessor Charles] Shibell. The stage came in today. Charles H. Wells of Wells Fargo Express is in town. [C. H. Wells was the son of Wells, Fargo & Co. founder Henry Wells.] New goods are coming in every day. Very dull in the house--receipts today $3.00. Closed at 9:30.

May 7. Very fine morning. Sent papers to P. R. Brady, J. D. Phillips, and C. J. Nickerson. Terrible dull. Bill Morgan, Jim Lee, and others returned from Sonora--they found the stolen stock and brought it home. [Thieves stole six of Morgan's mules and two of his horses and fled into Mexico. The Tucsonans caught up with them a few miles across the line and recovered the stolen animals.] Foster sold 3 turkeys for $12.

May 8. Windy and dusty. The day opened dull as usual. The mail stage arrived at 11 a.m.--no letters, but I received some papers from Bradley. I put a pane of glass in a window. Hastings went to work for Osborn. Cady had music and a small monte game at his house. He made all the boys sick with his belly-wash. A dance was held at the Yaqui's place. Davis is sick. I closed at 1 o'clock.

47

May 9 (Sunday). Fine day. The flower girls came around early. There are several dances in town. Some drunken soldiers are about. No bullfights today.

May 10. Fine day until noon, then wind and dust. Drunken fellows were pretty thick today. We played freeze-out for drinks--I won one and lost another. The stage left for Cal. Metzger is drunk. I went to a dance this evening.

May 11. Pleasant day. I bought a new hat--$2.50. The stage came. Lt. Ross, Pretty Steve, Leatherwood, and others went to the Oro Blanco mines today [located south of town near the Mexican border]. Charley Conwell came to town. Bill Morgan left for the Sonoita country [about 50 miles southeast of town]. I paid the dog tax this morning. The street is quite lively tonight with music, etc. Closed at 12 o'clock. [The first ordinance passed by the Tucson Common Council upon incorporation of the town in 1871 mandated the licensing of dogs ($2.00 per dog per year) and instructed the marshal to catch and destroy strays. Rabies was a real threat and the primary reason for keeping the stray dog population down.]

May 12. Quite warm. Joe Kelsey came to town. Very dull in the house. The stage left today. Conwell got full and wanted to take a girl in my bed. He got quite mad because I would not let him. Very warm this evening. Someone gave a woman croton oil [a powerful purgative]. Closed at 12 o'clock.

May 13. Windy. Worked all day cleaning and covering pictures with netting. Stage arrived--no letters for me. I filled myself with mescal. Blade is repairing his house. Nothing new. Closed at 11 o'clock. Cruz--$2.00.

May 14. Windy, hot, and dusty. Finished cleaning the pictures today. The stage left. I slept for 2 hours after dinner. Ate some enchiladas at night. Robinson had a party--did not invite me. I closed at 11 o'clock and went to bed.

May 15. We scrubbed the house out. Davis got sick--overtaxed his muscles. The streets are full of freight wagons and teams with goods for Lord & Williams, Wood, and Fish. Very windy, very dusty, very disagreeable day. Mercury at 12 noon--90 degrees. Hastings is in town, drunk. Matt Bledsoe took his monte game from my house to Jim Blade's place and went broke. Davis tried very hard to catch a girl, but they are all posted on him and call him "Bilky." Closed at 12 o'clock.

May 16 (Sunday). Pleasant cool morning. Nothing new, very dull. There was a dance at Baker's barber shop. Charley was drunk. Mrs. Fuller died this morning. Closed at 11 o'clock. Big Carmel--$2.00.

May 17. Cool morning. The funeral of Mrs. Fuller was at 7 o'clock. Louise Oury [daughter of Pima County Sheriff William Oury] was married this morning to Dr. Girard of Camp Lowell. Mercury 80 degrees at noon.

May 18. Cool morning. The stage came in. Davis finished his kite but could not raise it and was oblidged to pronounce it a failure--very little wind. Mercury 84 degrees at noon. Topsey killed two rats. Pleasant evening. Closed at 10:30.

May 19. Very dull. Davis and Fletcher are making another kite. Dickey lost two kittens in the well. Mercury at noon 88 degrees. They raised the kite tonight--it did not go well.

May 20. Pleasant, cool, and cloudy. Plenty of wind at noon--the boys raised the kite. It stayed up first rate until the cord broke. Big Carmel had a row with Louise, was arrested and fined seven dollars. Some Indians are catching stray dogs today. We had a little sprinkle of rain at ten o'clock. 12 noon--it rained quite hard for a few minutes. Closed at 11 o'clock.

Main Street in Tucson bustles with activity in the 1870s. Buehman photo, Arizona Historical Society, Tucson, #47258.

May 21. Cool, a little cloudy. Jo killed a big rat. I wrote to Dr. Lord. Very windy after noon. Lots of kites are up today. Davis put his up, but lost it and the cord. Foster sold a horse to Cockeyed Jones. Johnny Moore licked a fellow today. There was a big dance at the house of Doña Luisa this evening. Davis and Jones went to the dance. Topsey has a bad cold--I think she is getting distemper. Closed at 11 o'clock and went to bed sober.

May 22. Fine morning. Charley Russell made his appearance. Topsey is quite sick with a cough. Davis' partner (Jones) got put in jail last night for the indecent exposing of his person in public. The stage arrived at 12 noon--got a letter from J. D. Phillips. I went to bed at 11 o'clock. Davis kept the house open. I was aroused in the night by the noise of a dancing party of gents and whores trying to eat everything in the house. They succeeded and left.

May 23 (Sunday). Fine day. Topsey is better. Very dull. Green Rusk got tight, had a row with John Luck and got a cut in his head from a cane. Hand got a little too much juice. Ate dinner at the Hotel de Neugass. Took a walk with Jim Abbott in the evening. Went to a dance. Came home and closed up. Ate some tamales with coffee. Went to bed. Cruz--$4.00.

May 24. Feel well this morning. Very dull in the house. Topsey has nearly recovered.

May 25. The mail stage came today--I got a letter from Joe Phillips. Sent him some papers and a paper to Bradley and Roberts. Got tight today. Closed early.

May 26. Warm day. Mercury at noon--92 degrees. Got tight again today. The whiskey gave out in the house. Did not light up the saloon in the evening--closed and took a walk with Davis. Saw McWard's woman Lula--she had a girl baby yesterday. Dick [dog] left home today. Ate some enchiladas and went to bed.

May 27. Windy. The mail coach came in--no letters for me. No whiskey in the house today--Davis was sober all day. Closed at 10 o'clock.

May 28. Pleasant morning. Bob Morrow came in from the Verde. He told me of the death of Victor Boley--he died in Sherman, Texas. I wrote to Joe Phillips. 12 noon--mercury 95 degrees.

May 29. Joe Steele and Mr. William Boyle came in from the north. Jonesy came in from the governor's ranch. Hand is tight. Davis is tight. Strangers are tight. Puck Ryan is drunk. There was a circus performance this evening--Davis went, I got too drunk. Boyle hit a fellow in the eye for calling him a son-of-a-bitch. Later in the evening I knocked a man down. Closed at 11 o'clock and went to bed. Cruz--$2.00.

May 30 (Sunday). Sick all day. Very dull. Ryan was drunk all day. Theatre and circus this evening. Closed at 9 o'clock. [A small Mexican circus had come to town from Sonora. It featured jugglers, acrobats, clowns, trained dogs and ponies, theatrical players, but no large exotic animals.]

May 31. Fine day. Windy and dusty after dinner. Humpy Moore and Tom Roddick came in from the Yellow Jacket Mine [located near the Mexican border]. They brought in $50 in gold, the product of one ton of ore worked with an *arrastra* [a simple mule-powered mill for crushing ore]. Simpson and Bill Walker went to Prescott. Topsey is getting better. Closed at 11 o'clock.

~ ~ ~ ~ ~

June 1. Pleasant. The wind blew early. 9 o'clock--Roddick left for the mines. I had boiled mackerel for breakfast. Topsey is improving. Gave her cod liver oil last night. Gave her some more this evening. The saloon kept by Mr. Reise went broke today. He is quite sick from drink. 94 degrees at 12 noon. There is a dance at Levin's Park this evening for the benefit of the new schoolhouse. Closed at 10 o'clock.

June 2. Fine morning. Topsey is tip-top. Mr. Reise took an overdose of laudanum [a dangerous medical preparation containing opium] and is supposed to be dying. 10 o'clock--he seemed better and is supposed to be out of danger. 12 noon--died. Hastings helped me put in posts and poles for a shade at the back door. We both got tight.

June 3. I sued a man (a discharged soldier) for a bar bill of $30.75. Got the money and $3.10 interest. Had a pain in my stomach and got drunk on the strength of it. Received a letter from C. J. Nickerson. Big Carmel--$2.00.

June 4. Sick all day. Mercury 97 degrees at noon. Topsey is nearly well. Trouble [dog] is sick.

June 5. Still sick. Received letters from Joe Phillips and Largo Tom. Slept nearly all day. Mercury 98 degrees at 12 noon.

June 6 (Sunday). Warm morning. Commenced doctoring Davis' dog Trouble. There is a picnic today at San Xavier. [San Xavier was a Papago (Tohono O'odham) Indian village about ten miles south of town. Nearby was an impressive mission church built in the late 1700s when Arizona was part of New Spain.] Bob Morrow left today for San Carlos. Mercury at 12 noon--104 degrees. 1 p.m.--103 degrees. Rooney, Captain Devers, and Ed Marshall came to town. Theatre and circus tonight. Very warm evening. Very dull times. Closed at 10 o'clock.

June 7. Very warm. Mercury at nine o'clock--100 degrees. 12 noon--102 degrees. Davis made a big kite 7 feet high. He took up a subscription to buy twine and played the money off against the game of monte just introduced in this country. Mercury at 6 p.m.--100 degrees. Closed at 10 o'clock. Louise--$1.00.

June 8. Warm. Coyote Drumm came in town and got tight. Mercury at 11 a.m.--100 degrees. Steve and Conroy came in town. Davis went to bed at 8 o'clock.

June 9. Everyone got drunk, me also. I nearly got broke up wrestling and fooling around. Got a black eye, skinned nose, and my leg nearly broke. Went to bed early. Davis got drunk, went to bed, and left the money in the drawer and the doors open.

June 10. Am very sore, lame, and can scarcely walk. Davis was tight before breakfast. He won a few dollars playing seven-up and got drunk as a fool. Bought himself some shirts, etc., and then got beastly drunk. I kept sober all day. Closed early and had a good night's rest. Davis came to my room to serenade me by singing his favorite song.

San Xavier del Bac Mission, located ten miles south of Tucson, had fallen into disuse in Hand's day, but even then it was popular with sightseers. The church was built of fired brick in the late 1700s by the Franciscan order. Today the restored building is an active place of worship. Buehman-Hartwell photo, Arizona Historical Society, Tucson, #15926.

June 11. Fine morning. Davis is full again. Jim Fletcher took his dog Dick home. 8 a.m.--Davis is drunk in bed. 10 a.m.--Davis is up again. He cannot sleep without another drink. The dog Dick left again.

June 12. Very warm and dusty. The stage arrived--received a letter from Ira. I was sober all day. Old "Oneida" Brown came to town. Circus tonight.

June 13 (Sunday). Warm, not much wind. Several drunken fellows around today. Nothing new. Ate a fly this evening and was sick all night.

June 14. Cloudy and warm, lots of dust. Hastings got drunk and pissed all over himself and the house. Several Mexican vagrants were arrested. One was killed by a pistol-shot fired by Pedro Burruel, the police constable. I closed at 10 o'clock.

June 15. I was woke this morning by rain on the window. Davis, Rooney, Jones, Burns, and others were summoned by the coroner as a jury on the body of the Mexican killed by Pedro Burruel last night. Dr. Peter Thomas (colored) was arrested and tried for giving bad medicine to a woman, thereby causing her death. He was sentenced to a fine of $250 or three months in prison. John Burt and Steve came in. Burt got tight and caused me to get so. The mail stage arrived--no letters for me. Louise--$2.00.

June 16. Cleared off fine, no dust. Went to work cleaning up. Morgan left for the sawmill [in the Santa Rita Mountains south of town]. Rooney and Ryan also left for the mines. I had several calls from ladies. Stage left--I sent papers to Bradley, Roberts, and Nickerson. The whiskey gave out and I closed up at 10 o'clock.

June 17. It rained a little early this morning. No rot in the house--Davis is blue. I slept nearly all day. At night I had a strange dizziness come over me, caused by a too-sudden stoppage of spirits. I sent out and bought 50¢ worth of whiskey. After drinking some of it, I felt better. Went to bed early.

June 18. Up early. No whiskey left--Davis used it up. After breakfast, I went to Levin's Park and drank some beer. Went to Smith's and had some whiskey. Went to see some girls, had a social chat with them for an hour, and went home full of beer, etc. Did not light up the house tonight. I sat in front of the house till 11 o'clock and went to bed.

June 19. Very dull times. Everyone is grumbling. Mail stage arrived about noon--no letters. I was sick all day and in bed most of the time. Did not light up the house. Had supper at the China restaurant [probably Hop Kee's Celestial Restaurant]. Went to bed at 10 o'clock.

June 20 (Sunday). Fine day. Very warm in the early morning. Had a bath. Hastings came in town, bought a bottle of mescal, and got tight. Davis is in bed from the effect of Hastings' mescal. Theatre tonight.

June 21. Cloudy and quite warm. Cockeyed Jones left for Sonora--what for, no one knows, not even himself. Stage left--sent some papers to John Davis and Dick P. Someone dies every day, the church bell is tolling all the time. Watermelons are in town from Altar, Sonora, $1.50 each. Very dull. Awful dull.

June 22. Still cloudy. This morning Leopoldo Carrillo brought a big rat up, turned it loose in the street, and Jo killed it very quick. Another funeral today. I was sick all day and drank very little. Archie McIntosh [a scout for General George Crook] arrived in town this evening. A wagon load of potatoes came in from the Gila River, 12½¢ per lb.

June 23. Fine morning. Baldy Johnson, Rose, and some others came in, discharged from the 5th Cavalry at Camp Bowie. Baldy paid me $5. Rose slid off owing me $10. I went this evening to see Maloney's Merino sheep--2 rams and 3 ewes--and his four fine Berkshire pigs. He showed me a picture of the champion cow of the world. E. D. Wood whipped his wife, and her father whipped him. Wood was placed under bond to appear in court tomorrow. I got several drinks under my skin before night and was nearly tight at bedtime. Juana--$2.00.

June 24. San Juan's Day opened as usual with singing and music. Very warm. Did very little work today. At four in the afternoon the fun commenced--pulling the *gallo* [rooster] and horses running all over town. Very dusty and disagreeable, everyone was filled with dust. Wood made his father-in-law bring back his furniture. Jerry Kenny bought a bottle of mescal and we sat in the dark and drank it. Closed at 11 o'clock. [San Juan's Day, the feast day of Saint John the Baptist, was celebrated with gusto by Hispanics in the Southwest in the 1800s. By tradition, it was supposed to rain on this day, thus ending the spring dry period. Pulling the *gallo* was a sport in which a live rooster was buried up to its neck in the ground and horsemen tried to pull it out while riding past at top speed. San Juan's Day was very much a horseman's holiday, the men showing off their steeds and their riding skills with reckless abandon.]

June 25. Nothing new today. Two men came in from Sonora, ragged and broke--they got robbed. They curse Mexico and everyone in it. Not as warm as yesterday. Sold my saddle today, $10 silver.

June 26. Fine day. The mail coach came in--no letters for me. Roddick and Stroud came in from the Yellow Jacket Mine. They give good reports on the mine's prospects. Hastings is in town, drunk. I got all ready to cut Topsey's ears but had not the courage. Got half tight on Hastings' mescal. Theatre tonight.

June 27 (Sunday). Pleasant day but very dull. Took a warm bath and lay in bed all day.

June 28. Windy weather. Got tight somehow today. I played a game of billiards, the first in 7 years. Jo pupped three little ones. Went to bed early.

June 29. San Pedro's Day [the feast day of saints Peter and Paul]. Windy and dusty. I was sick and in bed nearly all day. There were terrific times after dark, horsemen riding all night and dust blowing everywhere. No chance to get a fresh breath for drunken Mexicans riding and kicking up dust. Closed up at 9 o'clock. I took off all my clothes and took a big fan to bed with me.

June 30. There is great excitement in town over some big pieces of gold brought in by Dave Britton. Everyone wants to go to the placer mines [in the Santa Rita Mountains south of town]. A little cloudy today. Got somewhat tight. Went to bed early.

~ ~ ~ ~ ~

July 1. Looks like rain this morning. The streets are very dirty and terrible dusty. Stage arrived--received a letter from Joe Steele. Wagons are loading up to go to the mines. Billy Wall and Tom Steele went to the placer mines. I paid the rent today. A wind sprang up, with clouds thick and dark. It was very dusty at night and I had to shut up the windows and doors. We expected rain for sure. After blowing one hour, it quit, cleared off, and no rain. I went to bed.

July 2. Fine day but very warm. Several people came in from the mines, others are going out. In the afternoon, clouds came up and it looked very much like rain. In the evening, it became even darker in the sky. A wind sprang up and the dust blew, making it very disagreeable for an hour, but, alas, no rain. No such good luck. Went to bed at 9:30 o'clock.

July 3. Still cloudy but no rain. Fred Hughes returned from the placer mines and says they are quite extensive, but there is a scarcity of water. Brocky, Dearg, and some other soldiers came to town from Camp Grant. Very warm and sultry today. 3 p.m.--still cloudy but no rain. 5 p.m.--rain commenced good. We had a fine shower which finally laid the dust. It was a cool and pleasant night.

July 4 (Sunday). The day opened with the national salute of 13 guns by John Burt. I raised my flag. It was a very dull day for the 4th of July. A procession formed at 4 p.m. and marched through town to Levin's Park as per orders. The Declaration of Independence was read by Dr. Goodwin. There were orations and the children had a fine time marching and singing in Levin's pavilion. There was a dance in the evening at the same place. Mayor Ochoa sent a constable to arrest me, for nothing, but he failed to accomplish his object. I left the dance at 12 o'clock and went to bed.

July 5. Fine morning. Got tight again today. Pearson and I had a fight. Davis hit him in the head with a bar pitcher and he ran out in the street hollering "murder." Lawyer Clark is tight. Everyone is tight. Closed at 11 o'clock and went to bed. The faro game ran all night at Brown's saloon.

July 6. Sick this morning. Stayed quite sober all day. I hired Alcario today to help around the saloon. The stage came in, brought another of the Wood brothers. It rained a little this afternoon. John Moore came in town.

July 7. John Clark was arrested by a policemen. Three Chinamen had a fight, and [Sheriff] Bill Oury arrested them. Justice Meyer sent them all to jail. The mail stage left. Jerry Kenny came back from Desert Station [a stage station about 100 miles northwest of town]. Rooney, Old Brown, Davis, and Hastings are here, all sober. No rain today.

July 8. Warm, cloudy, and very sultry. It rained in the afternoon and the roof sprang a leak. Cool and pleasant at night--it rained considerable. The stage came in, Dave Beardsley the driver.

July 9. Fine morning. Hastings helped me fix the leak in the roof. No rain today. I managed to get tight but stayed at home. The stage left today. I closed at 11:30 o'clock.

July 10. Pleasant day. The street is full of carts from Sonora loaded with flour. Stage arrived--no letters for me. It rained some this evening. Leopoldo Carrillo was dealing monte in the house all night. I closed up at 11 o'clock.

July 11 (Sunday). Very pleasant. It rained nearly all night. Theatre tonight, also a dance at Levin's.

July 12. Cloudy all day. The mail stage left today. Simpson and Matlock had a fight in Brown's saloon--nothing desperate. Tom Roddick came in today. There are a great many strangers in town. Hastings, Jones, Davis, and Drumm went on a picnic today. They took 3 bottles of mescal and one watermelon. Hastings got tight and was left on the river. I closed up at 11 o'clock.

July 13. Cloudy but warm. Davis gave Roddick his dog Trouble, and Tom McClellan took him home to keep for a few days. Dave Davis and Cockeyed Jones left for Prescott. Roddick left for the mines. Several people went to the mines today. Very dull in the house. No rain today. Jim Watts arrived, has been in Dutch Flat [California] since he left here.

July 14. Cool, pleasant, and cloudy. It rained quite hard today. People are still going to the mines. Yank Markham is in town, Bill Morgan also.

July 15. Pleasant cloudy morning. Several people came in from the mines. The stage arrived, and a report from Florence says that they picked up 400 pounds of nearly pure silver in a lead [ore deposit] owned by Brown, Dorsey, and others. [This silver strike was made north of the Gila River near the rich Silver King Mine.] It rained this afternoon and it continued until late at night. No letters for me by the mail. Had a roast mutton lunch this evening.

July 16. Still cloudy. It rained a little early in the morning. Dr. Handy, Neugass, and Lazard left for the mines. Yank went also. I had to kill the pup Jack this morning. Hastings and Jim Watts were both sick all last night from eating mutton. Very dull today. The Rio Grande mail did not get in--the Cal. mail stage left before it arrived. Richard Mawson came in from Cal. Señora Carmel and all the demi-monde [prostitutes] are on a bust today. The sky is very dark this evening. It commenced raining at 8 o'clock, stopped at one in the morning. Bob Crandall and Jim Blade returned from Hot Springs. Louise--$2.00.

July 17. Very wet and muddy. We had another shower this a.m. Cady came back from the mines. It rained all morning, cleared off at 1 p.m. Pleasant this afternoon. Dick Mawson got tight, did not start for home. The mail stage came in late. Fine cool evening. I sat outside till 11 o'clock, then went to bed.

July 18 (Sunday). Cleared off fine. Everyone is going to church. Dick Mawson and his pard left for the placer mines. 9 a.m.--sun out, very hot. Report says Dick Mawson went to the Rio Mimbres [New Mexico]. Very dull in my house. There was a dance tonight at Baker's barber shop. Fisher had a row there with some Mexicans and got put in jail. I went to bed at 11 o'clock. Cloudy, but no rain until two in the morning.

July 19. Cloudy, a little rain in the morning. Fisher got out of jail, was fined $5. The two French carpenters are on a bust today. I was sick all day. Got very tight. Governor Safford left for Cal. It rained again late at night.

July 20. Fair, no rain. The mail stage arrived. There are plenty of strangers in town, all getting ready to go to the mines. Very dull in the house.

July 21. Fair today, no rain, no wind, very warm. Strangers are continually arriving from every direction--they are all going to the mines, some to those north of the Gila, others to the placer mines. Nothing new today. Very dull. Closed at 10 o'clock.

July 22. Very warm. Received a dead letter for Davis--I put a stamp on it and sent it to him. Saw the 34 lbs. of silver in one piece from the Gila mines on display in Brown's saloon. Drumm's woman had a pup yesterday--a boy. Very dull yet. Kelly Hoag is in town. Windy and dusty after dark. Closed at 10:30 o'clock.

July 23. Had a light rain very early this morning. Very warm after sunrise. Not much breeze today. Still dull. Very dull. Foster killed a very fat beef today. The stage left for Cal.

July 24. Pleasant, warm morning. John T. Smith, Abe Dunning, and Tom Gardner came to town. 12 noon--very warm, but Dunning is only about 10 degrees above zero. Jim Quinlin and George Fields arrived today from Yuma with their freight wagons. Dutch Fred is drunk. Hastings and Troy are drunk. We had a terrific wind and sandstorm after dark--oblidged to close all the windows and doors. Closed up at 10 o'clock.

July 25 (Sunday). Fine day. Frank Francis came in town. Very dull today. Singing Mexicans were wandering all over town after dark. Hastings, Troy, and lots of the boys are drunk.

July 26. Dunning left this morning, took the Swiss boy with him. Sam Campbell and Hastings got tight. I got Trouble from McClellan and sent him to Tom Roddick. Topsey died at 5 p.m. today. Hastings and old man Crosby went to the soda factory and got in a row. The old man was on it big and got put in jail. I closed up at 10 o'clock.

July 27. Sam Campbell left for his ranch and Hastings left for the mines. Old man Crosby is still in jail. Very warm today. I met a man named Anson from Oriskany Falls, Oneida Co., N.Y. It is very lonely without Topsey. The mail stage came from Cal.--no papers but Zeckendorf got 5 sacks full of merchandise. I received a letter from Joe Phillips and one from Dad Overton in Wyoming. Another party just started for the placers. Cloudy and quite pleasant this evening. Closed at 10 o'clock.

July 28. Fine morning. Old man Crosby is still in jail. It appears he tried to take charge of several houses and run them himself. 2 p.m.--the Rio Grande mail stage just arrived. Wrote to Joe Phillips today. Big John Miller brought his family to town. Very Dull in the house--closed early. Ate a 15¢ piece of watermelon and went to bed.

July 29. Fine morning but still very dull. Bill Morgan came in from the sawmill. Stage arrived at 11 o'clock--I got a letter from Lame Morgan. The first extension on the Silver King Mine, owned by Johnson, Goodrich, and others, is about to be sold. There is great excitement about mines. The army paymaster returned to town. Troy is drunk. He sold his blankets to bail old man Crosby out of jail and got drunk on the money. Pedro Burruel got put in jail for whipping his wife. I closed at 10 o'clock.

July 30. Very warm, very dull. Sent papers to Steele in Florence. George Esslinger is on a spree again--he drinks wine now. The mail stage left today.

July 31. Fine day. Stage arrived--no papers but I received a letter from Dave Davis. Very warm day. Very dull. Settled a bar bill with Esslinger today. He owed me a balance of $76. The barber had a dance this evening in the corral. The French carpenter left town.

~ ~ ~ ~ ~

August 1 (Sunday). Fine day but dull. A great many strange people from Sonora are in town to buy goods. Theatre this evening. Nothing new today.

Aug. 2. Warm and sultry. Old man Crosby got out of jail and left for the mines with Bill Morgan. I wrote a letter in answer to Joe Phillips' telegraphic dispatch. Sent papers home and to Cal. Also sent a bundle of old letters to Dave Davis at Prescott. The Rio Grande mail stage arrived at 5 p.m., and the Cal. stage left immediately after. I finished reading Hiram Woodruff's book today [*The Trotting Horse of America: How to Train and Drive Him* (1868)].

Aug. 3. Very warm today. Stage came late--received a paper from C. J. Nickerson and a letter from John L. Shipler. Mercury today 107 degrees. No excitement in town. The streets were deserted early at night. Closed at 10 o'clock.

Aug. 4. The usual hot weather. John Clark returned from the mines and is on the drink again. Tom McClellan got half tight today. Hotter than yesterday. I gave Alcario the little black pup.

Aug. 5. Lost my little dog early in the evening.

Aug. 6. My little dog came back home this morning.

Aug. 7. Got tight today. A Mexican cart ran over my little dog and killed him--had the funeral after dark. Shut the doors and two fellows had a square fight, one round.

Aug. 8 (Sunday). Very warm day. Several drunken men were about. We had a light rain today. Closed at 11 o'clock.

Aug. 9. It rained early this morning. I went to court--was excused till 10 o'clock tomorrow. [Hand had been called for jury duty.] We had rain in the evening. Jerry Kenny is drunk.

Aug. 10. Went to court again. After a long argument between lawyers, they found that no case was ready. We were excused again until 10 a.m. tomorrow. It rained today. Ferg has been sick, is better today. Stage arrived. Big Carmel--$1.00.

Aug. 11. In court again this morning. We found at 12 noon that no case was ready yet, and were excused again till 10 a.m. tomorrow. 2 p.m.--clouding up and windy. Rain in the evening. Very dull in the house. The stage left for Cal.

Aug. 12. At court again but nothing for the jury.

Aug. 13. Court again--nothing for the jury. We were excused till 10 tomorrow. Bedford and his family arrived from Prescott. I got full today. Juana (new)--$1.00.

Aug. 14. Rainey and cloudy. Stage arrived--received a letter from J. B. Hart, Owyhee Camp, Idaho. I got very full again today. Dixon came in from Prescott, broke and sick.

Aug. 15 (Sunday). Pleasant day. Very warm. Bob Morrow and Sherman came in from Camp Grant with cattle for Fuller [owner of a meat market]. Both got drunk, of course, I along with them. Theatre tonight. John Day got drunk--Jerry and I found him in the church plaza and Jerry took him home. I closed at 1 o'clock. Juana--$1.00.

Aug. 16. Very warm this morning. The boys are trying to get drunk but have not money enough. We had a light sprinkle of rain today.

Aug. 17. Got tight again today. Received a letter from J. B. Hart. New girl--$2.00.

Aug. 18. Everybody got drunk.

Aug. 19. Everybody still drunk. Bedford got put in jail for drawing a knife on a man named Moore.

Aug. 20. Bill Morgan left for the mountains and took all the sawmill boys with him but John Day. I got drunk again today. Closed at 10:30 and went to bed.

Aug. 21. Very warm. Got tight again. The mail stage came in--no letters for me. There are plenty of strangers in town. A telegraph dispatch from Prescott says that Dave Davis was sent to jail in default of a $100 fine for assault with a pistol. It was very hot indoors and Jerry Kenny and I slept on the sidewalk.

Aug. 22 (Sunday). Fine day. Quite lively in the house today. Clark is very tight. Dr. O'Connor [an itinerant foot doctor] and Esslinger are also on it big. I kept quite sober. It rained enough to make the air cool. Closed early.

Aug. 23. Fine day. People commenced fixing the [courthouse] plaza for the feast. Nothing strange happened. [The feast day of Saint Augustine of Hippo, August 28 (the day of his death), marked the beginning of the biggest celebration of the year in Tucson. Saint Augustine (*San Agustín*) was the Patron Saint of Tucson and the local Catholic church was dedicated to him. The carnival-like festivities lasted for several days and drew visitors and hucksters from throughout Arizona and northern Sonora. It was a typical Hispanic-Catholic celebration, a wonderful mixture of religious observances and boisterous revelry. There was much eating, drinking, gambling, dancing, and ribald carousing, as well as solemn church services.]

Aug. 24. We had a little rain last night. It is cool and cloudy this morning. Musick came in from the mines. The mail stage arrived from Cal.-- received a paper from C. J. Nickerson. Clark, Nigger Charley, and the tailor are all drunk. Ferg is also drunk. I had a long talk with Mr. Moore from Prescott. Closed at 1 o'clock tomorrow.

Aug. 25. Fine day, but sultry and no wind at all. Cloudy after dinner. Some of the boys came in from the Ostrich Mine [located south of town near the Mexican border]. The stage left for Cal. Mesilla Street was crowded at night--several drunken men were about. Closed at 12 o'clock.

Aug. 26. Very sultry. Everybody is sober today. The stage came in after dark. We received news of the fight in Sonora at Altar. Leopoldo Carrillo was taken prisoner and confined until a ransom of $15,000 is paid. His wife and some others left late today to see him. There is great excitement about it. Closed at 10:30 o'clock. New Refugia--$1.75. [A revolt led by Francisco Serna broke out in Sonora against the state government controlled by Ignacio Pesqueira and his family. Leopoldo Carrillo, a wealthy Tucsonan, was in Altar, Sonora, on business and inadvertently became caught in the cross fire when fighting began on August 22. He was imprisoned by the Pesqueira forces for about a week, then ransomed by his family. This uprising was put down, but unrest and fighting continued and the Pesqueira clan was forced out of power the next year.]

Aug. 27. Fine day. The Feast of San Agustín opened splendid. Jerry and I went up, drank, ate, and walked around till one in the morning. Gambling was rather light, but *chuso*, as usual, had a big crowd. [Chuso was similar to roulette.]

Aug. 28 (San Agustín's Day). Got tight before breakfast and kept so all day. The mail came in--received a letter from Dave Davis. Went with Jerry, Bob, and Ferg to see the sights on the plaza. Had supper, drank beer, and saw everything. Had a good time. Ferg and I came home at 12 o'clock.

Aug. 29 (Sunday). Fine day. Very warm. The boys are playing cards. I took in three silver dollars this morning. Tried to take a nap but failed on account of heat and flies. Ferg is sick this morning.

Aug. 30. I was drunk early and late. Drunk all day. Very drunk. Disgustingly drunk. Everyone is drunk. Barney Connelly came in town. I went to the plaza, stayed 5 minutes, came home, and went to bed. Refugia--$1.00.

Aug. 31. Very dull in town. No news. The mail stage arrived very late.

~ ~ ~ ~ ~

September 1. Marshal Francisco Esparza shot Procopio Leivaz in the groin at 3 o'clock this morning. There was great excitement at the time. Esparza was arrested at 5 o'clock and put in jail. [According to the *Citizen*, this shooting was the result of a drunken argument at the feast grounds, and was not in the line of duty. Esparza was charged with assault and was removed as town marshal. Leivaz recovered from his wound.] Henry Schwenker was married to Refugia Jimenez today at the residence of James Hancock.

Sept. 2. Tom Ewing gave a ball at his private residence. It was a dull show on the plaza on account of rain. Clark, Jerry, and myself walked around the bull ring a few times, ate some lunch, drank a few drinks, and came home.

Sept. 3. I had nothing in the house to sell all day. Several drunken men are lying around. A telegraph message came today from the N.Y. *Herald* asking for the particulars of the outrage on Leopoldo Carrillo. I closed up early and went to the plaza. It was quite lively and pleasant. Came home early and went to bed.

Sept. 4. Pleasant day. The bummers look blue. Billy Harrison arrived. Bill Henry was bitten by a dog. I had an invite to a dance but did not go. Did not go to the plaza. Received a letter from Mark Evans and one from Dave Davis. Closed and retired early.

Sept. 5 (Sunday). Got tight. Did not go to the feast. Went to bed early.

Sept. 6. Warm and cloudy. Last day of the feast. I sent papers to J. B. Hart, Billy Bradley, C. J. Nickerson, and J. E. Roberts. Went to the plaza a short time. No whiskey or beer in the house today.

Sept. 7. Wagon loads of bar furniture and cooking utensils are leaving the plaza. I wrote to J. B. Hart and Dave Davis. The mail stage arrived--received a letter from J. B. Hart. Still no rot in the house to sell.

Sept. 8. Very dull, nothing new. We had a light rain today. The stage left. Cloudy all day and quite cool. John Clark and Jim McCaffry both have the jim-jams [alcoholic jitters]. [Clark and McCaffry were law partners and McCaffry was the U.S. district attorney for Arizona.] I was woke from sleep by a drunken Mexican serenading me. I made him leave and slept quite well the balance of the night.

Sept. 9. Fine day. There was a report that 2 horses were stolen from near Camp Lowell. James Lee, John Wood, Adam Linn, Juan Elias, and R. N. Leatherwood, mounted and armed, started out to find the thief. They found him and brought back the horses. They hung the man on a mesquite tree. Mad dogs are in town. No other news. I closed and retired at 9:30 o'clock. [The posse described by Hand was a vigilante group known as the Tucson Minute Men. They were organized with the blessing of territorial officials to help enforce the law outside of the town limits. This hanging of a horse thief without trial was business as usual in the rural countryside, and was not a cause of concern among Tucsonans.]

Sept. 10. Posters were put up this morning warning all persons to tie up their dogs. The killing of dogs running at large commences at 12 noon. Alex Wilkins, the barber, shot at John Wood. Wood knocked him down, took the pistol from him, and kicked him very bad. The marshal took the barber home. Alex told Dr. Handy he would kill Wood on sight. I bought some whiskey this evening and took in eight dollars. Closed at 11 o'clock. Jerry and I took a walk, stopped in Brown's saloon, looked at the faro game a while, and went home.

Sept. 11. Fine day. Plenty of dead dogs are lying around the streets this morning. [Andy] Nickerson came in town this morning and got drunk the first thing. Circus this evening. The mail stage arrived--received three pictures from Bradley. Closed at 9:30 o'clock and went to the circus. Came home and went to bed sober.

Sept. 12 (Sunday). Fine weather. Bedford, Henry, and Nickerson are tight--the boys are playing cards for whiskey. The circus band is playing in the streets--circus tonight. Goldberg put up a chuso table in the house. Charley Paige married Angelita Dobson today. I did not light up the house. Closed at 9 o'clock.

Sept. 13. Bill Henry, Bedford, and Shaw left today for the sawmill. Everything is quiet today. Sent papers to Bradley, C. J. Nickerson, J. B. Hart, and J. E. Roberts. The stage left for Cal. and one arrived from the Rio Grande. I closed at 10 o'clock.

Sept. 14. Stage arrived--no letters for me. Nothing new, very dull. Foster killed the fattest and finest beef of the season, 1,000 lbs. I was sick all day.

Sept. 15. The dog killing still goes on--another wagon load was hauled off today. I kept sober all day. Very dull in the house. Closed at 9 o'clock.

Sept. 16. Fine weather. The anniversary of the Independence of Mexico [from Spain, achieved in 1821] is not celebrated with as much force as in the past. Leopoldo Carrillo is mad and will not celebrate it. Nothing new, very dull. Closed at 11 o'clock. Drunken Mexicans were going about town singing nearly all night.

Sept. 17. Fine morning. Quite warm in the middle of the day. The Rio Grande mail stage arrived, the Cal. stage left. Coles Bashford [the secretary of the territory and former governor of Wisconsin] left for Prescott. Business is very dull, no gambling, no drinking--all are sitting around waiting for something to turn up. Closed at 10 o'clock.

Sept. 18. Fine weather. Very dull. Street cleaning today. Received a letter from sister Emma and one from Joe Steele--he sent me a piece of ore. The 6th Cavalry band gave a concert and ball at Levin's Park Brewery garden. I closed at 10 o'clock and went to the garden. Saw the Jews, Gentiles, officers, pot slingers, and scrubs all dancing in the same set. Came home and went to bed. [The 6th Cavalry band had been transferred to Camp Lowell to the delight of music-starved Tucsonans.]

Sept. 19 (Sunday). Very dull all day. There was some excitement at night--theatre and monte and drunken Mexicans. Closed up early and went to bed.

Sept. 20. Cool day. Rather windy and dusty. Sent papers to Bradley, C. J. Nickerson, Hart, Roberts, P. R. Brady, Morgan, and Joe Steele. Ate some enchiladas with Goldberg. Had several ladies call. [Andy] Nickerson went up to Maloney's ranch. Ferg and I were alone in the house and we closed up at 10 o'clock. Cool night, slept well.

Sept. 21. Windy and very dusty. Received a letter from the Gila River settlements. George Esslinger is on a bust again. C. O. Brown, Wheat, and Pike came up from the Gila.

Sept. 22. Fine morning. A wind came up during the day--very disagreeable weather. Sent papers to several of the boys. Some of the miners came in from the Ostrich Mine. They say the mill has shut down there. We all got tight again. Refugia--$1.00.

Sept. 23. Joe Phillips came in from the Salt River. I went to a concert on a complimentary ticket from Professor Marin, a violinist. It was the best music I have heard since I left Cal. Went to bed at 1 o'clock. [Manuel Marin was a traveling musician from Mexico.]

Sept. 24. I was tight all day. Gila Grey [horse] did not exercise today. The mail stage left as usual. Business was dull today. More fellows came in from the Ostrich Mine. Closed at 10 o'clock.

Sept. 25. There is great excitement about the horse race. The money is all up for the race and it comes off tomorrow at 4 p.m. A great many drunken men are in town. Shorty Holt and Smith Turner had a row. I was forced into two fights, and Jerry Kenny had one. Closed at 11 o'clock.

Sept. 26 (Sunday). Windy and dusty. There were more rows about the horse race. Three p.m.--people flocked to the race track. The money was taken down--no big race today, but we had several scrub races. Gila Grey ran once around the track alone for fun. Grey Eagle and Jim Lee's grey ran round to show for fun. I drank lots of beer and came home in the beer wagon. Went to hear Professor Marin the violinist. The house was so small he refused to play. Came home and went to bed sick and lame.

Sept. 27. Sick. Got tight again. Went to Bill Henry's dance.

Sept. 28. Mail stage arrived--no letters for me. Sick all day. Kept sober all day.

Sept. 29. Fine morning. The boys are getting drunk. Bedford and John Stroud are nearly fighting. The boys were all drunk at night. Bedford's woman took all her things from his house and left--he is very hostile. I closed at 11 o'clock.

Sept. 30. All the boys got drunk again. Roddick and Stroud left for the mines. I received a letter from J. B. Hart. Bedford was drunk all day--he talked several men nearly to death. I was sober all day and went to bed so.

~ ~ ~ ~ ~

October 1. Two horse thieves came in from the Gila settlements. A man following them saw them in C. O. Brown's saloon and got an officer. Cris [Constable Cresencio Rodriguez] shot one of them. The other escaped and the Minute Men failed to find him. The wounded man is in jail. Tom Bullock, a gambler, was robbed of $1,400 below Florence by road agents. All the other gamblers are glad of it. I kept sober today. Closed early and went to bed.

Oct. 2. Quite dull today. A soldier and Milt McDowell are on trial for shooting T. R. Knox at Camp Grant. [The court ruled that J. R. Mackey and Milton McDowell killed T. R. Knox in self defense.] I drank a little too much today. Tried to borrow forty dollars--could not do it. Got mad and got tight. Professor Marin gave a concert, but I forgot to go until too late. The marshal caught the other horse thief--both are now in jail. The telegraph operator got tight and someone gave him a black eye. I ate supper with him. He afterward was put in jail. Grey Eagle was raffled off this evening. Number 43 won him, Lew Elliott was the winner.

Oct. 3 (Sunday). Warm day. Very dull in the house. There were several dances in town. Theatre tonight. Jerry Kenny got full. I slept nearly all day. J. E. McCaffry was put in jail this morning for disturbing the peace. He is out and getting beastly drunk again. This evening he was carried home in the same fix. The whiskey gave out in the house this evening, but no stores are open.

Oct. 4. Fine day. The mail stage came from the Rio Grande. Clark went below to check on some stock. I tried to borrow $20--could not do it. I made out a paper to raffle off my dog Tinker, but got no subscribers. Robertson is drunk. McCaffry is drunk. Got half tight myself. A telegram says the Bank of California reopened today--there is great excitement in San Francisco about it. Very dull in all the saloons this evening. I closed at 9 o'clock and went to bed.

Oct. 5. Fine day. No news. Sold my silver watch to Julius [Berger, a jeweler] for $30--very cheap. Paid the rent. Jerry Kenny went to work papering Jim Blade's saloon today. Ferg got an order from the county supervisors to enter the hospital. Grey Eagle was taken to Camp Grant. The stage came in late. I went to Leopoldo Carrillo's home to hear Marin play the violin. I was an outside spectator. Ferg went to the hospital. I went to bed. [John Farquason (a.k.a. John "Fergy" Ferguson) first came to Arizona in 1862 as a member of the California Column. He suffered from tuberculosis, and was ordered to enter the county hospital for fear that he was infectious.]

Oct. 6. Charley Williams came to town last night from the Rio Grande. Hunt came in from the Ostrich Mine. Ed Marshall and Old Brown got drunk. Tom Jeffords came in to see me for a few moments. [Thomas Jeffords was the agent for the Chiricahua Apache Reservation in southeastern Arizona.] Professor Marin and his piano player left today for San Diego. I closed at 12 o'clock.

Oct. 7. Fine morning. The Ostrich Mine workmen got paid off this morning and nearly all are drunk. Hunt is on it big. I got full myself. Nothing new. Hunt fell into a pile of sifted lime and came down to the house as white as a miller. He got very tight afterward and Jerry put him to bed. I went to bed at 1:30 o'clock.

Oct. 8. Windy weather. Dull times. Hunt and Ed Marshall are full of rot. Hunt went to bed and slept until night. Very dull, no excitement. The stage left at 8 at night. I closed at 10 o'clock.

Oct. 9. Very windy this morning. Procopio Carrillo is drunk, and Ed Marshall is trying to get so. Nearly all the other boys were sober during the day, but got drunk at night. Dr. C. H. Lord, his wife and daughter, and Miss Williams arrived back in town. I closed at 12 o'clock.

Oct. 10 (Sunday). No business today--everybody is sick. Nothing new. I was sober all day and went to bed so at 10 o'clock.

Oct. 11. Dull and dusty. Stephenson left for the Gila. Matt Cavaness' wagon train arrived. The Cal. stage left. Jerry finished papering Blade's saloon. Old candy-man Martin was buried today. Dickey is on a small tight. Mag [George Foster's daughter] commenced going to school today. I closed at 11 o'clock.

Oct. 12. Fine weather. There is great excitement over Jim Blade's new house. Bill Linn is to run it. All hands are at work helping him get fixed up. Clark is trying to get drunk. The mail stage arrived--received papers from J. B. Hart and C. J. Nickerson. Linn's [Blade's] saloon opened with a dance--the house was full. Cooler "The Monkey" was on hand, also Shorty Holt and the whores. I went to bed early and had a good sleep.

Oct. 13. Fine morning. It rained a little. Clark was drinking all day--he sent for McCaffry to keep him company. Very dull in the house. McKey came in from the Ostrich Mine. Grant [Granville] Oury is in town. He received a telegram telling of the death of Frank Cosgrove. Very pleasant evening. Closed at 10:30 o'clock.

Oct. 14. Last night's clouds are all gone and it is quite warm today. There is great excitement over the news of Governor R. B. Hayes' re-election in the state of Ohio. 100 guns were fired on the plaza in honor of it. [Rutherford B. Hayes was a Republican and doubtless only Republicans such as George Hand were celebrating.] There was a great political argument lasting nearly two hours between Jerry Kenny and myself. I talked him nearly blind. He went home at eight o'clock, and I was left with only Ad Linn. I then went for him and talked him asleep in a short time. I went to bed full of gin and slept tip-top.

Oct. 15. Shaw, Bill Henry, and Morgan came in from the sawmill with a load of lumber. Morgan got tight the first thing. The stage left for Cal. I got tight. Went to bed early.

Oct. 16. Fine morning. Men are out cleaning the streets today. Morgan is drunk. Tom McClellan is drunk. The mail stage came--received a letter from J. B. Hart. Jerry Kenny is at work today. There was a dance at Linn's tonight--a big crowd. McClellan got licked and was taken away by a policeman. Morgan got tight. Juana's mother and sister arrived from Sonora this evening. [Juana Moreno was George Foster's common-law wife.] I took some pills this evening. Went to bed early.

Oct. 17 (Sunday). Fine morning. I saw McClellan--he has a swollen head. Says he was doubled on and cut with an instrument. Clark is sick. Morgan is sick. Very dull in the house--am out of whiskey and everyone is sober. The long-lost Charley Rice and Bill Garrett arrived from Sonora and Chihuahua in good health.

Matt Cavaness' mules and freight wagons stopped in front of the Gila Bend stage station in 1874. In the 1880s, railroads put long-haul wagon freighters out of business in the Southwest. Arizona Historical Society, Tucson, #9847.

Oct. 18. Cool weather. Tom Metzger came in from San Carlos, Charley Conwell from the Patagonia mines, and several strangers are in town, some from Pinal County. Report now says that some of the Pinal mines are a big humbug. I was sick in bed nearly all day--felt very bad, ate nothing. Hunt sold a mine for $50. Morgan is tight. Emmerson (Negro) died. I closed at 11 o'clock and slept well.

Oct. 19. Fine cool morning. Morgan is on it again. Emmerson was buried this morning. Frank Sullivan came in town and several strangers from Cal. came with him. I feel pretty well today. Very dull in the house. Went to Leatherwood's corral this evening to see the stock. Mail stage came--received a paper from J. B. Hart. Went to bed early and sober.

Oct. 20. Cloudy but pleasant. There was considerable drinking but little money received. Clark and Andy Elliott drank all the rot in the house and I got no money for it. I saw Stoakes, formerly of Company "I," 5th Cavalry. McKey won his suit against Warner. He received 200 dollars. Sol Warner had the court costs to pay. [McKey helped build Warner's new gristmill and felt he was underpaid.] Very dull during the day and evening. Cash receipts today $2.75. Closed at 9 o'clock.

Oct. 21. Nothing new, very dull. Ferg is still in the hospital and is very bad. The mail stage came--I got no letters. Garrison, Tom Gardner, and some others were drunk in C. O. Brown's house nearly all day. I closed early and went to bed.

Thirsty Tucsonans pose in front of the Gem Saloon in 1874. The man at the left in the top hat is the owner of the Gem, George Cooler. Next to the saloon, a striped pole advertises a barber shop. Buehman photo, Arizona Historical Society, Tucson, #BD-74.

Oct. 22. Cool pleasant morning. Very dull. Bob Crandall is quite sick with pneumonia. Farquason is getting worse every day. The mail stage came from the Rio Grande. Foster's daughter Maggie is sick. Court is still in session. Nothing new. Closed early.

Oct. 23. Fine morning. Called on Ferg. He is very low and out of his head. Went to see Bob Crandall also. He is quite sick. Mail stage came from Cal.--no letters for me. John Farquason died in the hospital at 20 minutes past 4 this p.m. I drank some whiskey this evening and got tight. Clark got tight and had money. I went to bed at 12 o'clock.

Oct. 24 (Sunday). We buried Fergy today. There was no funeral procession. Out of fifty or sixty old friends in town, there were only four besides the wagon driver to do him reverence. Pallbearers--Ed Marshall, John Clark, Tom Banning, and George O. Hand. I closed at 8 o'clock and went to bed.

Oct. 25. Sent papers to Bradley, home, C. J. Nickerson, and J. B. Hart. Received a letter from J. B. Hart. Wrote to Dave Davis of the death of Ferg. Called on R. M. Crandall. There are a great many strangers in town, but very dull in the house today. Did not light up the house this evening. Closed early and went to bed.

Oct. 26. Shut the door and took a walk. Called on Big Carmel--had a piece. Came home. Mail stage arrived--I read papers all day. John Wasson [editor of the *Citizen*] returned from Yuma. I caught out another girl in shutting the house. Went to bed at 10 o'clock. Big Carmel--$1.00. Little Juana--$1.00.

Oct. 27. Windy and quite dusty. The Rio Grande mail stage did not get in. I am out of whiskey today. Kelly and George Atkinson came in from the mines. A divorce case still occupies the court. Closed at 9 o'clock.

Oct. 28. Very dull. Dusty and cool. Several persons were buried today. Tom McWilliams is reported dead at old Fort Goodwin [near the town of Safford]. Nothing new. Mail stage arrived--no letters for me. Wrote to Emma and Dave Davis. Had no whiskey in the house all day. Sat around at night till I got cold, then went to bed.

Oct. 29. Cool, pleasant morning. Had fried eggs, beefsteak, and beans for breakfast. Wrote to my sister, Dave Davis, C. J. Nickerson, and Smeardon. Very dull. Did not light the house. Closed early. Big Carmel--$1.00.

Oct. 30. Windy, dusty, and disagreeable. Mail stage came in early--no letters for me. Very dull all over town. Sniffin brought in some sweet potatoes and onions. Todenworth's divorce case closed this evening. The jury demanded their fees--there was no money in the bank to pay them. No verdict until Monday. Closed at 10 o'clock.

Oct. 31 (Sunday). No business today. The bullfight was a bilk.

~ ~ ~ ~ ~

November 1. Mail stage left for Cal. Wrote letters and sent papers. Very dull. Received news that Ira Hand, my youngest brother, died in Cleveland, Ohio. Big Carmel--$1.00.

Nov. 2. Windy. Mail stage came--received a letter from Dave Davis in Prescott. McCaffry is in jail and howling like a madman. There are plenty of strangers in town. Closed at 10 o'clock. Big Jesús--$1.00.

Nov. 3. Fine morning, cloudy and cool. 9 o'clock--windy and dusty. Cady sold his saloon to Simpson. McCaffry was brought before Justice Meyer. I sent a letter to Dave Davis.

Nov. 4. Received a letter and some money from Smeardon.

Nov. 5. Got drunk today. Cady and his lady left for the Gila settlements.

Nov. 6. Got tight again. Went to a funeral. Got tighter at night. Had a great political argument with Jerry Kenny. Afterward I sat up in my room until 10 o'clock, then went to bed. Juana--$1.00.

Nov. 7 (Sunday). Quite cool this morning. Roddick and Campbell came in today with a dab of gold and some silver. Jo [dog] got married this morning. There was a bullfight this evening. I had a nice warm bath and am on my good behavior now--for how long, deponent says not.

Nov. 8. Sick today. I got full of beer and ate very hearty late last night. Went to bed and had a fearful night dreaming the most terrible dreams. Resolved to eat no more at night.

Nov. 9. Got ready to whitewash the house, but Hunt failed to come. I was sober all day and feel tip-top. Mail stage arrived--nothing for me. The town is very dull. It is terrible windy and no end to the dust. Spent the evening in sober conversation with John W. Clark. Went to bed at 9 o'clock.

Nov. 10. Awoke feeling good--no dreams last night. Went to work on the house this morning. Hunt did not come so I set Alcario to whitewashing. He finished at one o'clock. I have the pictures all hung again and things begin to look like business. The weather was quite pleasant today. I bought some rot after dark and took in $1.25. Closed at 10 o'clock. Went to bed sober and slept well.

Nov. 11. Cool morning. Up early and swept out before the boy Alcario got here. Business was dull and I read all day. Had corned beef for dinner. Andy Wall left for Florence today.

Nov. 12. Cool and windy. Neugass moved his restaurant into the new hotel yesterday at night. I closed at 11 o'clock. [The Palace Hotel had just been completed and Joseph Neugass was hired by owners Fred Maish and Thomas Driscoll to manage it. The two-story hotel was constructed of fired brick and was the fanciest building in town to date.]

Nov. 13. Cloudy. John T. Smith's wagon arrived early. Had eggs for breakfast. The mail stage arrived 12 noon--no letters for me. Quite warm this evening. There was a dance at the Wilt house [Cosmopolitan Hotel] and a bronco ball at Linn's saloon. Both broke up early, no money in either. Tom McClellan spent 50¢ in my house, the first time he has come in for many weeks. I was the last one in the street to close. Went to bed, slept well.

Nov. 14 (Sunday). Foster's folks [in-laws] cleared out last night--he had a row with the old woman. This morning they are all gone, young ones, dogs, and all. Good riddance to bad rubbish. Quite pleasant today. Had several lady callers this evening. Bedford is drunk and hunting a fight. Closed at 11 o'clock. Went to bed sober.

Nov. 15. Fine morning. Linn's house closed and was rented to another party. 12 noon--windy and very dusty. The stage left for Cal. Sent a letter to George Weston. Dull times. Bedford is still on the warpath. Brevet Major General A. V. Kautz, his wife, and staff arrived this morning. [Kautz, actually a colonel, had replaced General George Crook as commander of the Department of Arizona in March 1875.] Report says an earthquake shock was felt at Yuma and Maricopa Wells [80 miles northwest of Tucson]. Closed at 12 o'clock.

Nov. 16. Got tight today from some cause. Mail stage arrived. I met some people from Prescott. John Dawson (drunk) made a demand (in fun) with a pistol on full cock for the purses of some loafers in Cockney Jack's saloon. He was knocked down and beaten unmercifully. I closed at 11 o'clock and went to bed very much intoxicated. Awoke early in the morning with an attack of piles.

Nov. 17. Did not get up today--sick and no business. John Dawson had a hearing today, was sent to jail in lieu of $1,000 bail. My piles are getting worse. I called Dr. Handy--he put them back in and left me some medicine. Born to the wife of Isaac Goldberg, a daughter.

Nov. 18. Still in bed and no better. Born to the wife of W. C. Dunn, a son.

Nov. 19. Still sick but some better. Born to the wife of Briggs Goodrich, a daughter.

Nov. 20. Much better today. Clark was all day arguing the case of Dawson on a habeas corpus. I had three lady visitors this evening. Clark got drunk. I went to bed early. Born to the wife of E. D. Wood, a daughter.

Nov. 21 (Sunday). Pleasant morning. Feel much better. I sat up nearly all day reading and talking with Clark. Had several callers. Did not open the house. The wife and child of W. C. Dunn died. I went to bed early and rested well. Born to the wife of Henry Smith, a son.

Nov. 22. Opened the house again. I am not entirely well but much better. Had beef head roasted in the ground for breakfast. W. C. Dunn's wife and child were buried today. Very dull in the house--I read all day. Johnson came in from the Pinal mining district. Clark is full of business but is also getting tight. I was sober all day. Closed at 10 o'clock.

Nov. 23. The telegraph message in regard to the United States buying Chihuahua, Sinaloa, and Sonora proved to be a hoax. Several prominent Mexicans in town became very angry about it. Quite cool this morning. Johnson sold a mule. Billy Gale came on the stage from Los Angeles. I closed early and went to bed sober.

Nov. 24. Warm morning. The mail stage came in from the Rio Grande. Billy Gale brings Tom McClellan around quite often. Fred Myers' wagon train came in from Yuma. There is a dance tonight for the benefit of the public school. Quite a bit of excitement in town. Clark got pretty full. Closed at 10:30 and went to bed sober.

Nov. 25. Thanksgiving Day. Quite cold. When the boys began to assemble and comment on the day, there arose a difference of opinion in regard to the wording of the Lord's Prayer. The Bible was brought out to settle it. We then had a chapter read by Mr. J. W. Clark, and the meeting closed with the Lord's Prayer. News from Sonora--Pesqueira's men surrounded some of the Serna party and made quite a killing. The mail stage arrived today--received letters from Dave Davis, J. B. Hart, and P. Wheeler of Rome, N.Y. Very dull in the house. Spent the evening with J. W. Clark. Closed and went to bed at 10 o'clock.

Nov. 26. Very pleasant. Jo killed two big rats. Philomena, daughter of Teresa Sotol, was married this morning. I moved my bed and cleaned my room. Will have a fire tonight. Wrote to P. A. Wheeler, Rome, N.Y. Very dull this evening. Clark and I sat here until we nearly froze. I closed, built a fire in the stove in my room, sat and warmed. Roasted an onion to put on my throat.

Nov. 27. Very cold. More rumors of war in Sonora. Sawyer is reported killed there. They [Pesqueira's soldiers] tied him, shot him, then cut and bayoneted him outrageously. The stage arrived--very light mail. Cloudy and cold. More wagons with arms and ammunition left town for Sonora. [According to the *Citizen*, some leaders of the revolt against Ignacio Pesqueira, including Francisco Serna, had sought refuge in Tucson and were sending arms to their supporters in Sonora.] Clark got full and went home early. I sat up by a warm fire in my room till 11 o'clock and turned in. Slept well. There was a smart shower of rain after dark, and it continued to drizzle until midnight.

Nov. 28 (Sunday). Cold and damp. Very dull. Had a cold bath and put on clean clothes today. No excitement in town. Closed at 10 o'clock. I sat in my room reading old diaries until 11:30, and then went to bed.

Nov. 29. Coldest morning and first frost this season. The Rio Grande mail stage arrived, Charley White the driver. Keegan, the driver to Florence, got so drunk that the stage left without him. He is running around town getting more so on credit. I bought a load of firewood this evening. Whitey Foster drove the new army paymaster in. Clark, Charley White, and two strangers made up a game of auction pitch late and I took in $5.00 off the game. Went to bed at 11 o'clock.

Nov. 30. Cold morning. Mail stage came at noon--received a letter from Emma. Barney Connelly came to town. He was half tight when I first saw him and blowing about mines as usual. Martin Gilmartin was examined before Justice Meyer and put under $500 bond for appearance at court. [According to the *Citizen*, Gilmartin was charged with "unlawfully trying to shoot J. L. Stephenson with a Henry rifle."] Clark is tight as a brick. I closed at 8 o'clock, then built a fire in the stove and sat up till 11:30 reading Ira's old letters.

~ ~ ~ ~ ~

December 1. Very cold. I caught Alcario stealing whiskey this morning and discharged him. Barney Connelly is drunk--he is trying to get help to work his mines. John Burt came in from the Old Mine [located south of town near the Mexican border]. I had dinner at Neugass' hotel. Cloudy tonight. Closed at 9 o'clock. Read old letters for two hours and went to bed.

Dec. 2. Cold morning. Mail stage came--received papers, no letters. There are plenty of drunken men staggering about the streets, but they have no money. I paid $60 for rent today. Sam Drachman returned from San Francisco with his new wife. 4 p.m.-- the whiskey gave out--I did not light up the house this evening. Took a walk with Clark to his law office. We then came back, made a fire in my room, and I read some of Lew's [Lewis Hand's] letters to him, written while he was in the B. T. Battery from Chicago in 1861, 2, and 3. Clark went home at 10 o'clock and I went to bed.

Colonel August V. Kautz replaced General George Crook as commander of the Department of Arizona in March 1875 and served in that capacity until March 1878. Kautz was an indecisive leader, and the conflict with discontented Apaches that erupted in 1876 was poorly handled. Charles Gatewood Collection, Arizona Historical Society, Tucson, #19603.

Dec. 3. Cool day. Mail stage left for Cal. and came from the Rio Grande. Connelly still trying to get help in his mines and still trying to get tight. Clark failed to get his money from Markham. I had dinner at the new hotel. John Burt is drunk as a lord. I sent papers to Cal. and New York. Billy Harrison came to town. Closed early, made a fire, read old letters for two hours, drank a big hot whiskey punch, and went to bed.

Dec. 4. Cool morning. Got up early. Clark was the first to put in an appearance. We took a drink. I went to work and got warmed up. Had breakfast at 8. The paper came out at noon. Stage arrived at 1 o'clock--no letters for me--my friends have all gone back on me, I think. I played a game of seven-up with Charley White and another man--Charley lost. General Kautz left today. Tom Ewing gave a ball last night in honor of the General. Two wagon trains came in today. I saw Sam Drachman. Very dull today. Closed at 9 o'clock. Spent the evening (or half the night) reading old letters from my sisters and stepmother.

Dec. 5 (Sunday). Cold and very dull today. Nothing new. Connelly is tight and blowing about chlorides and oxides. He has mines on the brain and a very small brain too.

Dec. 6. Cold this morning--no stove is fired up yet. I drank a little too much whiskey today. Connelly is very drunk. Clark is sick. Hunt returned from the Santa Rita mines. Clark and myself sat up reading old letters until after 11. He went home and I went to bed.

Dec. 7. Cold and windy. The stage came in--no letters for me. Very dull. Connelly is still trying to get help and whiskey. I did not light the lamps in the house tonight. Made a fire in my room, read old letters, and talked with J. W. Clark until 10 o'clock. We then retired.

Dec. 8. Cold. Nothing new this morning. Wrote to the *Spirit of the Times*. Sent papers to John Roberts and W. F. Bradley. Charley White came in today. Drunken men are thick in town. The woman who runs the *fonda* [Mexican restaurant] next door to me was serenaded by a drunken man until she drove him away. I built a fire, read old letters for two hours, had a hot whiskey, and went to bed.

Dec. 9. Woke at 8 o'clock this morning. Had breakfast at nine. Very cold early, quite pleasant after the sun got up. The stage came from Cal.--R. C. McCormick, his wife, and E. S. Mitchell (the mail contractor) came in on it. [Richard C. McCormick was a former governor of Arizona and former delegate to the U.S. Congress from the territory.] Quite warm in the sun today. 4 p.m.-- the sun is below the houses and it is cold enough for a coat. Clark spent 75¢ in here today. Then 75¢ more. Closed at 9 o'clock. Read old letters for 1½ hours, drank a hot whiskey, and went to bed.

Dec. 10. Cold. A one-armed man was arrested for drawing a weapon on Simpson. I wrote to Emma and sent a paper to C. J. Nickerson. Received a telegraph dispatch from Prescott--"Woman dying." Let her die. Very dull in the house. Closed at 9:30 o'clock, built a fire in the stove in my room, and sat and read and talked and drank hot punches with J. W. Clark till 11 o'clock. Went to bed.

Dec. 11. Cool morning. Had breakfast early. Dull times. Connelly got drunk and started for home. Mail stage arrived--received a letter from Metzger. Andy Hall came in from Florence. Clark got a few dollars this evening but could not keep it--he spent it for whiskey. Ed Marshall was here, talking big about his fighting qualities. Puck Ryan came in town. Closed at 9:30 o'clock and went to bed at 11.

Dec. 12 (Sunday). Quite warm this morning. Opened at 8 o'clock. A soldier was buried today. The town is full of soldiers. Puck Ryan is on a drunk but has no money. McCaffry is on a tear again. Clark is with him and he is drunk. Very dull today. Hunt and John Luck were robbed last night. Another man was robbed today by a soldier. A Mormon preached in the courthouse today. Closed at 9 o'clock and went to bed.

Dec. 13. Cold. Some soldiers are changing the poles on the telegraph line. 11 o'clock--sun is very warm. Puck Ryan and others are drunk. I could not get away for dinner. Finally I ate at the Cosmopolitan Hotel with Charley White. Got a little tight and retired early.

The Cosmopolitan Hotel in the fall of 1874. A banner celebrating H. S. Stevens' election as delegate to the U.S. Congress flies from a rope stretched across Main Street. Buehman photo, Arizona Historical Society, Tucson, #93869.

Dec. 14. Cool morning. Ryan was drunk before breakfast. The mail stage arrived. A telegram says that a Mr. French is to relieve Judge Dunne--guns were fired in town in celebration of it. [President Grant appointed Charles G. W. French to replace the unpopular (but competent) Edmund F. Dunne as chief justice of the Arizona supreme court.]

Dec. 15. Pleasant day. I saw Governor McCormick--he looks well and fleshy. Clark received a letter from Judge Rush in Prescott. I got two money orders from Ryan. The stage left for Cal. I got rather full of juice. Block presented me with a plug hat [top hat]. I wore it all over town and had a big time. Took a walk with Tom McClellan and Billy Gale. Came back, sat by my fire, drank a hot whiskey, and went to bed at 9 o'clock.

Dec. 16. Got up at 8 o'clock. Had ham and eggs for breakfast. McCaffry was put in jail last night, is sober this morning. Ryan is sober also. Closed early and went to the serenade for ex-Governor and Delegate McCormick. Had a bonfire, music, and a few words from the ex-delegate. There were free drinks and cigars, nothing more.

Dec. 17. Fine weather. I felt bad and slept nearly all day. Clark and McCaffry are both sick. Ryan got drunk again. Closed early and went to bed.

Dec. 18. Fine weather. Very dull. Stage came--nothing for me. Street cleaning is going on as usual. Puck Ryan is drunk. McCaffry is drunk in bed-- Clark packed bottles of rot to him all day. McCaffry came over after dark, barefooted and pants unbuttoned, looking for more whiskey on credit--did not get it. Closed at 9 o'clock and went to bed.

Dec. 19 (Sunday). Slept till after 8 this morning. Had breakfast and fed my dogs. Built a fire and read till noon, then took a bath and put on clean clothes. I took a walk around town--went to the cockfighting pit, but was too late to see the fun. Had soup and coffee for dinner. Walked around town till dark, came home, and read old letters a long time. Went to bed at 10:30 o'clock.

Dec. 20. Cloudy all morning. Neither Clark nor McCaffry made an appearance. Got my breakfast. I opened the doors with 50¢ in the drawer after giving the washwoman $1.00 for soap. 12 noon--still cloudy and cold. Sent some papers off today. Levin opened a new place, the Telegraph Saloon, with beer at 12½¢ per glass. I think he will go broke. I kept open till 8 o'clock, then closed, read, and went to bed.

Dec. 21. Very cool. Had breakfast at 8 o'clock. Called on Clark and McCaffry--they are convalescent. Very dull times. Jim Blade is growling about selling whiskey on credit. He bought 2 billiard tables and a lot of pictures and bar fixtures, over 1,000 dollars worth. Jerry Kenny is to run his new machine, and if he don't run Blade into the ground in 6 months, I'll go hungry. Went with R. C. Brown (the printer) this evening to Levin's new place and had a drink. Went there again with Cockney Jack and took another drink. Went to bed.

Dec. 22. I stayed closed again today. Blade closed his house for repairs. Charley White came in. People commenced getting turkeys for Christmas. Times are very dull--everything looks like a very dry Christmas. Dr. Handy's dog had five pups, three of them were bob tail natural. I sat up late reading and finally went to bed.

Dec. 23. Fine morning. Nothing doing, very dull. Had a fire in my room all day. I sat reading and sleeping till dinner. Managed by strategy to fill a small bottle of stuff at Lord & Williams' store. In the evening Clark came over and I read several of C. J. Nickerson's letters to him. He left to look after J. E. McCaffry who had just returned home with a big bottle of whiskey. I ate some tamales and drank a beer. Read an hour or so and retired.

Dec. 24 (Christmas Eve). Warm this morning. A company of cavalry left Camp Lowell this morning to keep the Serna party on the other side of the Mexican line. Cockney Jack Upton is making eggnog for tomorrow, also duff [pudding]. Charles Shibell's wife died this morning. I went to a dance this evening and danced a few times. At 12 I went to the church--there was a huge crowd. I stayed over an hour, came out, and lost Jo. Went home, stayed a while, then went back at 2 o'clock, got in the church again, and found Jo waiting for me. Went to bed tight.

Dec. 25 (Christmas Day). Got up early. Had eggnog at Jack Upton's saloon. Got tight before breakfast, after which I washed, changed clothes, and at 11 o'clock went to the funeral of Mrs. Shibell. There was quite a large turn-out. I walked out to the cemetery and rode back with Levin. I slept a while, then had dinner with Jack--good food. Went to bed after dinner. Foster fell in a fit this evening--I took him home. McKenna, Hayes, and Pat O'Meara came to town. I sat in my room reading till 9 and went to bed.

Dec. 26 (Sunday). Fine morning. Had cold chicken for breakfast, with tamales, etc. There was a big time in the church today. I received some papers from Milton yesterday. Have not seen Clark or McCaffry since Friday. 2 p.m.--Clark came over for a while. Foster feels quite bad today. I stayed home all day and stayed sober. Had several callers.

Dec. 27. Cloudy, feels like rain. John Burt was fined $7. I swept out, cleaned the bar, and shut up again. Found Hayes and got $20 from him on Pat O'Meara's account. Pat owed me $41.25 and did not come to see me. After noon he came around. He had some books and papers he wanted me to keep for him. I found $5 in his pocket and kept that also. Got tight in the evening and had lots of fun. Went to bed early. Slept quite well.

Dec. 28. Got up late. Took a few drinks and felt quite well. Stayed home nearly all day sleeping and reading. The mail stage came--I received a letter from J. W. Sweeney.

Dec. 29. Pat O'Meara went home. The stage left as usual.

Dec. 30. Got tight for the want of something to do. Called on McCaffry and Clark in the evening. We sang songs and drank whiskey till two o'clock. Came home and went to bed.

Dec. 31 (New Year's Eve). Very dull during the morning. I had nothing to do and was in Foster's meat market, both hands in my pants' pockets, and suddenly fell on my face. I was perfectly sober. Was taken home and put in bed. Did not awake until 3 p.m. My left eye was considerably bruised and I felt sore and stiff. The cause was said to be whiskey, but I drank very little this morning--being broke I could not fill up. I walked around town in the evening some and went to bed at 8 o'clock.

Ad published in the Arizona Citizen *(Tucson) in 1875*

The Apache Indians were feared by other Indian tribes, Mexicans, and Euro-American pioneers alike. These Apaches, three warriors and a warrior-to-be, calmly pose for the camera. The man at the right is thought to be the noted leader Eskiminzin. Arizona Historical Society, Tucson, #46806.

Chapter Two

APACHES RESUME RAIDING IN THE SOUTHWEST--1876

"News this morning is bad. Report says that Nick Rogers and others are killed by Indians. Late in the afternoon reports came in stating that others had been killed. A meeting was called at the courthouse to resolve what to do. Nothing was done, as usual." George Hand, April 10, 1876

Customers were scarce in George Hand's saloon as the year 1876 began. Business was so bad that on many days during January and February Hand didn't even bother to open up. In March, George Foster gave up his meat market and rejoined his friend as a partner in the saloon. With Foster's capital, they refurbished the rundown barroom and partitioned off a separate card room. The saloon became popular with gamblers, and business improved.

In the countryside, an uneasy three-year truce between White settlers and Apache Indians was shattered in April when a group of disgruntled Chiricahuas took to the warpath. A decade of sporadic warfare ensued before the Chiricahua Apaches were finally subjugated.

~ ~ ~ ~ ~

January 1, 1876 (New Year's Day). Got up at 8:30 in the morning. My eye was very sore and much swollen by the fall yesterday. I carried a drink to Clark and McCaffry who are both on a spree. Took a few drinks myself. Made a few calls, mostly on saloons. Spent nearly the whole day in my room with Charley White, the mail carrier. Jim Quinlin's wagons left today and took Smith. There was a funeral this afternoon and several dances tonight. Went to bed early with a raw-potato poultice on my eye.

Jan. 2 (Sunday). Got up early. Very cold. Took a wash and a walk around. Bought a drink at Blade's. Had a breakfast of eggs, mutton ribs, and beefsteak. I built a good fire in the stove in my room, fed my dogs, and did other little chores. Washed some pocket handkerchiefs, forgetting it was Sunday. I read until my eyes gave out. The tall clerk in Lord & Williams' store got a terrible bite on his chin and lip fooling with their dog. I watched Dr. Lord sew him up. There was a Mexican funeral this evening after dark. I went to bed at 8:30.

Jan. 3. Very cold. Toole brought down the lease for the house. I got a lease for the whole corner for 2 years, and paid the rent for last month. Helped Foster make sausages. There was another funeral this evening. I sat around until 9 o'clock, then went to bed.

Jan. 4. Got up at 8 o'clock. Walked around town for an hour trying to borrow $20--no go. Think I'll remember when fortune again smiles on me. Went to breakfast and had good sausages, pork ribs, coffee, etc. After the usual chores, I went to see Clark and McCaffry and found McCaffry in a terrible state. His legs were paralyzed and he was so debilitated as to be unable to rise to take a drink--fearfully sick through the influence of whiskey. He was under the care of Dr. Goodwin. Clark was asleep and I did not disturb him. Nothing new occurred until about noon when McCaffry died. City officers were elected today--Charles H. Meyer mayor, Adolph Buttner marshal. [Meyer had second thoughts and declined to serve as mayor. A special election was held in April, and John B. Allen was chosen to replace him. Both Allen and Buttner were reelected in January 1877.] I went for a walk with Clark in the evening. Had a drink at Blade's, came home, and went to bed.

Dr. Charles H. Lord, in partnership with Wheeler W. Williams, owned the mercantile house where George Hand purchased the whiskey for his saloon. Lord was trained as an M.D. but did not practice medicine in Tucson on a regular basis. Arizona Historical Society, Tucson, #3797.

Jan. 5. Pleasant morning. Clouded up at 10 o'clock. The funeral for McCaffry was held at 3 p.m. Louis Hughes read the service and the pallbearers were members of the bar. People returned from the grave to find J. G. Phillips dead in his room. Verdict of the coroner's jury--died by his own hand, shot through the right temple. I helped lay him out. He was the agent for the new stage line, the Arizona Express Co. The funeral will take place tomorrow. Clark is very sick and unable to go out.

Jan. 6. Nothing new.

Jan. 7. Very dull, nothing new.

Jan. 8. It rained during last night and it is still rainy. Stage came in--no papers, very little mail. Had venison for breakfast. Lord & Williams are moving into their new store. Clark is still sick. Very dull in town. Blade's saloon was up and going all night. I bought two copies of the *Citizen* today. Slept very poorly.

Jan. 9 (Sunday). Cloudy and muddy. Helped Foster and the boys make sausages. Went up to look at their cattle and hogs. Kept quite sober. In the evening I went to see Clark and stayed for two hours. Came home at 10 o'clock and went to bed.

Jan. 10. Clear, cool morning. Had breakfast at 9 o'clock. Clouded up again. Went to J. T. Smith's corral to see the chickens spar. Cleaned up my room. Spent the rest of the day in Blade's saloon. Redwood Brown died today.

Jan. 11. Fine day. Redwood Brown was buried today. The sawmill fellows came in. Rooney, Brown, and Morgan all got drunk, and Brown got himself put in jail. The stage arrived at 12 noon--received a letter from the *Spirit of the Times*. Got a pup from Dr. Handy and gave it to Levin. Got tight. I bought some whiskey for the house in the evening. Went to Frank Francis' house, had coffee and a lunch, and spent the evening there till 11:30 o'clock. Went to bed at 12.

Jan. 12. Fine morning. Opened the front doors [for the first time since December 20]. [Deputy] Kelly and another man came in looking for Buckskin Alex [a fugitive wanted for murder]. Kelly got tight. I had a row with him and got tight over it. This evening J. L. Stephenson, alias "Pretty Steve," fell dead in his doorway. I sat up at his house until nearly 4 in the morning.

Jan. 13. Fine morning. Brown and Morgan made me get up very early. I feel very bad today. The funeral of J. L. Stephenson was held at 3 p.m.--quite a large turnout. The verdict of the coroner's jury was that in a fit of coughing he burst a blood vessel. Quite cold this evening.

Jan. 14. Got no sleep after 4 this morning--I awoke and found Brown and Captain Devers, and Morgan tending bar [Bill Morgan had begun rooming at Hand's place]. Had breakfast at 9 o'clock. Morgan got full. I wrote to the *Spirit of the Times*. Jo pupped 5 pups. Esslinger is still drunk, Morgan *también* [also]. Charley White came in driving the mail stage. Morgan and

McDermott had a long argument in the house on theology and politics. I closed at 9 o'clock.

James H. Toole owned the building on the corner of Meyer and Mesilla streets that housed Foster and Hand's saloon. Tucson voters selected Toole to be their mayor four times in the 1870s. He committed suicide in 1884. Buehman photo, Arizona Historical Society, Tucson, #23824.

Jan. 15. Cool and cloudy. Had breakfast at 8:30 o'clock. Morgan is full. There was a light sprinkle of rain at 10 a.m. I had supper very late. Kept open till 9:30 o'clock.

Jan. 16 (Sunday). Fine morning. Did not open the house until after breakfast. Very dull. Windy at noon. Cockfights today. It was cold in the evening--I built a fire in the stove. I closed at 7 o'clock and sat with Morgan and talked and read until after ten, then went to bed.

Cockfights were popular in the old Southwest--they are still held from time to time in rural areas. This contest took place in Tombstone. Arizona Historical Society, Tucson, #5218.

Jan. 17. Very cold--froze the water in the ollas. Sent papers to Bradley, Nickerson, and Roberts. One stage came in from the east, another left for the west. Had dinner by candlelight. Closed at 8:30 o'clock. Morgan and I sat by the fire in my room. I read an oration by George W. Curtis given at Concord on the anniversary of the battle on the 19th of April, 1775.

Jan. 18. Fine morning. Trinidad Lopez was brought before Justice Meyer for stealing goods from stores. Many thousands of dollars worth of goods were found deposited by him in different places. The mail stage arrived at 1 p.m.--received a letter from J. B. Hart from Cornucopia, Nevada. Closed at 8 o'clock. Morgan and I sat by the fire talking and reading until 11 and then I went to bed.

Jan. 19. Cold morning. Did not open the house. I called on Clark. The city marshal is going after the pawnbrokers [for dealing in stolen goods]. The sun came out very fine and warm. Saw a discharged soldier from the 6th Cavalry who served here 7 years ago in the 1st Cavalry. Received a roll of papers from my brother Mit. Morgan and I called on John Clark and spent half an hour with him. I came home, read until 11, and went to bed.

Jan. 20. Fine morning. I got a gallon of whiskey from Frank Francis. Got tight. I won all of Esslinger's pups. Mail stage came--received papers from J. L. Shipler and a letter from Mira with a Christmas present. Had dinner at Maish and Driscoll's Palace Hotel. Was tight all day. Spent the evening at home with McDermott and Morgan. Went to bed early.

Jan. 21. Opened this morning but sold nothing. Am sober and sick. Morgan tried to make some collections for me but failed. Did not light up the house this evening. We sat in my room till 11, then I went to bed.

Jan. 22. Did not open. Morgan and I sat in the back room all day reading. Robinson was on a spree and wanted to fight Dr. Goodwin. McDermott kept them apart. He took Robinson home in the evening. Esslinger is still on the spree. McDermott brought a bottle of water with a little whiskey in it. Morgan and Esslinger got away with all of it. Jack Upton's [dog] Nip was shot and killed late in the night.

Jan. 23 (Sunday). Very pleasant morning. Jack Upton is on a drunk about his dog that was killed last night. He was treating everyone to drinks nearly all day. Esslinger is trying to get sober. Morgan and I went to see Clark and spent two hours very pleasantly with him. Came home and went to bed at 10:30 o'clock.

Jan. 24. Cold. Esslinger is cleaning his tailor shop--he drinks no more. His pups opened their eyes. The buckboard from the east came in very early, Smeardon a passenger. Charley White got full of bad whiskey. Morgan and I were sober all day. Upton is still drinking. I went to bed early.

Jan. 25. Cold morning. Upton is on it yet--I had several drinks with him this morning. Mail stage came at noon--received a roll of papers from brother Mit of Joliet, Ill. Helped Foster a while in the meat market. Had dinner late. Morgan brought a bottle of whiskey. I worked nearly all day on my scrapbook, had nothing to drink. Went to bed at 11 o'clock.

Jan. 26. Warm, pleasant morning. Worked on my scrapbook until 3 in the afternoon. Morgan got some of the money Shaw owed him, then got tight as he could and went gambling. Billy Munson paid me an old bill of $3.00. Jack Upton has plenty of money and is trying to drink all of Blade's whiskey. It proves the old adage--the worse some people are treated, the better they like you. Clark and Esslinger called on me in the evening. Clark won his case in the supreme court--the blind Frenchman [Francois Forque] versus Leopoldo Carrillo. I had a cup of hot coffee in the tamale fonda, then went to bring Morgan home but he was still gambling. He came home at 10 o'clock, a loser. I went to bed but slept none until morning.

Jan. 27. Up early. Had breakfast and went to work bookbinding. Saw George Smeardon. Finished my book. In the evening I had a singing match with Morgan, with McDermott critic and sufferer. It was decided in my favor. Sat up until 10:30 at night, then went to bed.

Jan. 28. Cold but pleasant. Went out and had one drink before breakfast. Came back and found Morgan drunk again. I wrote a letter to Mit, and sent photos to J. B. Chesebro and I. W. Hand [no relation], old schoolmates of mine. Charley White came in today. Morgan bought a bottle of rot and we, with Charley and McDermott, drank it. I ate dinner at Driscoll's hotel. Went to bed at 10 o'clock.

Jan. 29. Fine morning. Stayed home all day. The mail came--received a letter from J. B. Hart. Jo was taken sick and was sick all afternoon. In the evening she showed symptoms of poison. I gave her a vomit, and oil immediately after. She was very bad. I had several callers. Morgan got very drunk and fell down and hurt his eye. He came home at 2 in the morning.

Jan. 30 (Sunday). Jo is all right--she ate quite hearty. I am satisfied that it was poison. Morgan has a black eye and feels badly. A little cloudy today but pleasant. Foster sent his lamb to Goodwin's ranch. The new Arizona & New Mexico Express Company stage leaves this evening at 10 o'clock for Cal. [This new stage service linked Tucson to California via Florence, Phoenix, Prescott, and Ehrenberg. It did not compete directly with the established El Paso-Tucson-Yuma-San Diego mail stage. The enterprise was bankrolled by Charles H. Wells, son of the founder of the famous Wells, Fargo Express Company.]

Jan. 31. The Cal. mail stage left. Epifania Rivera died today. Jack Upton is still drunk.

~ ~ ~ ~ ~

February 1. Fine day. Stage arrived--no mail for me. McDermott is getting full. Old Brown commenced drinking. Tom Banning got a team and we rode all over town, then went to the funeral. McDermott got drunk and had a row--he hit a man in the head with a six-shooter. He was arrested but Dr. Handy went his bail to keep him out of jail. Nothing new. Went to bed at 10 o'clock.

Feb. 2. Fine day. Went with Foster to see the corral and new coaches of the Arizona Express Co. Charley White, the mail stage driver to Camp Bowie, came in and quit. Billy Gale cut his foot very badly with an axe. Barney Connelly came in town from the mines, but would not take a drink. This evening I had a houseful of visitors. Bill Linn came down with his wife. The boys kept dropping in. Upton came in by chance, and left to bring all hands a drink. Singing being proposed, Mr. McDermott favored the company with an Irish song. Mr. Upton then sang a song, and we wound up the singing with Morgan who sang, to the delight of all, "Paddy McGee's Dream." The company broke up. I retired, a short time after which I was awakened by another serenading party. The night watchman made them disperse and all was again quiet.

Feb. 3. Very fine morning. Went with Charley White to see Billy Gale. Paid the rent and put a new collar on Tinker. Morgan collected a $2 bill from R. N. Leatherwood and bought a bottle of whiskey. Nothing new. We sat in my room until 10 o'clock. I helped Charley White bring his bed down to my place. Ate dinner at the Chinaman's--good meal. Went to bed at 11 o'clock. Dreamed all night.

Feb. 4. Up at 6 o'clock. Took a long walk, came home at 15 minutes after 7. Took a drink of good rot. Had breakfast. Collected $2 from Captain Devers--I let Morgan have it. Upton is still drunk. Very dull in town. The soldiers got paid yesterday, but they circulate very little money. Simpson and another breechclout opened a 75¢ *tendejón* [small retail shop] on Mesilla Street. A headache troubles me very badly today. I called at Clark's room but he was absent. Called on a lady named Carmel. Came home and slept awhile. Morgan and myself amused ourselves playing casino. Took another drink. Ate dinner at Levin's. Charley White and myself took several drinks. Went to bed early. Barney Connelly failed to get in his hotel--he slept on the floor in my room.

Feb. 5. Got up early. Took a drink at Levin's. Had breakfast. Went with Charley White to the corral of the new express company. Took Jo to Buckalew's corral to catch rats--found none. The mail coach arrived--received a letter from my sister. Took another drink at Levin's. And another drink. Bought a bottle of whiskey for Sunday. Built a big fire in the stove in my room--had to leave--too hot for comfort. Sat up until 10 o'clock. Had several visitors, Bill Linn and his wife, lawyer Clark, Jerry Kenny, and others. Went to bed. Caught several mice in traps during the night.

Feb. 6 (Sunday). Fine morning. Got up late. After the usual ablutions, I took a drink. Went to breakfast and had bacon and eggs. Charley built a big fire. We sat and drank and drank and sat and drank again until the bottle was empty. Then we drank no more. Bought some water today. Clark called on me twice. 3 p.m.--it is quite cloudy and looks very much like rain. Jim Fletcher is on a spree. Charley got half tight. Clark called on me again. Mr. William Linn and wife paid me a visit, stayed until 8 o'clock, then left in the express stage for Prescott. I wrote a letter to Dave Davis. A soldier was arrested and put in jail today. Upton is trying to get sober. I went to bed at 9 o'clock.

Feb. 7. Cool but sunshiny morning. Jo was sick last night but is better today. The stage left for Cal. I sent a letter to Dave Davis and a paper to Billy Bradley. Upton slept all day. Morgan bought a bottle of whiskey and we drank all of it. Not very good whiskey either. We sat around until evening. Jerry came down with Roach "The Unknown." He sent out for a bottle of whiskey. We had several drinks and talked of the past. Finally we adjourned. The

"Unknown" came back and left again. I went to bed. Charley came home about 2 in the morning. Morgan was sick all night.

Feb. 8. Cloudy. John Sweeney came around quite early and paid me $15. I went with him to Foster's and he paid $29 there. Then we went to the store of Velasco & Roca and got some mescal. From thence to the land office. Then we took several drinks. Went to Levin's and had a lunch. John paid for everything, he being full as well as myself. We walked out to Mr. J. B. Allen's house and looked around. The old man showed us around and treated us to custard pie. We stayed there a couple of hours, then came back and went to drinking mescal. John slept on my bed until dark. I was full. Had some female company. Finally went to bed at 11 o'clock.

Feb. 9. Fair morning. Esslinger the tailor and Jack Upton are still drunk. The stage left. Nothing interesting today. Sweeney left for home.

Feb. 10. Fine day, quite warm. The French carpenter LaFontaine died last night. Bill Henry and Andy Elliott came to town. Johnny Burt started for the Reventon Ranch [about 40 miles south of town near Tubac] to get cattle. I have to help Foster while he is gone. George Esslinger is trying to sell his pressboard to get whiskey. He stole a buttonhole cutter from Joe Ferrin and pawned it to Foster for 35¢. He wanted to sleep in my house but I could not see it. The faro game ran all night at John Toney's saloon.

Feb. 11. Very cold. Got up early. Took a long walk with Jack Upton. Came back, had a drink at the Hotel Cosmopolitan. LaFontaine to be buried today. Received $4.00 from Henry Allen. Tended shop for Foster all day--we have no beef for tomorrow. George Esslinger was taken to jail this evening for taking a pocketbook containing cash from someone in Simpson's Hole-In-The-Wall saloon. I had plenty of company this evening. Went to bed at 10:30 o'clock.

Feb. 12. Pleasant day. Foster has no beef this morning. Stage arrived--no letters for me, but got one paper. There were two funerals today. J. T. Smith came in. I took the butcher cart to the slaughterhouse. Burt came in with cattle from Tubac at 2 p.m. I had dinner at 5 p.m. Had several callers not called for this evening. Closed the door at 9 o'clock at went to bed.

Feb. 13 (Sunday). Very pleasant. Went with J. T. Smith to see the sharpening of the knives for the cockfighting this afternoon. Smith's birds won the main fight and another one. Sam McClatchy came in from San Pedro and died this morning. James Lee paid me a $14 election bet. Went to bed at 11:30 o'clock.

Feb. 14. St. Valentine's Day. Fine day. Went to the funeral of Samuel McClatchy--pretty good turn-out of Americans. Came back, drank a few drinks, and got somewhat tight. The marshal is out collecting the saloon tax levied by the city officers under ordinance 15. Most paid it, but some closed their businesses. [The Tucson Common Council had instituted a new tax of $5 per month on saloons, $10 per month on gamblers running faro, monte, or chuso games, and $20 per month on pawnshops. Cockfighting pits were taxed $5 for each day fights were held. These taxes were very unpopular with the people affected by them.] There was an auction sale today of the effects of J. E. McCaffry, all except his law library. Had dinner at 4 p.m. After dark I went to McClellan's room and ate bread and honey, and sucked eggs. We adjourned to Levin's saloon and had a lunch and beer. I walked all around town until 11 o'clock, then went to bed.

Feb. 15. Cool but very pleasant. 9 o'clock--the sun came out very like summer. Foster is discouraged--no sale for beef. Johnny Burt left for Sonoita to get cattle. I tended shop for Foster nearly all day. The mail stage arrived--received some papers from Mit. Mrs. William C. Davis died this afternoon. Young John Callahan, Arden, and another man came in from the placer mines. I had a severe headache early in the evening, was obliged to go to bed. Clark called on me as I was retiring. Went to bed at 8 o'clock.

Feb. 16. Dusty, windy, and cold. Tended shop for Foster in the morning. Morgan settled with Shaw and loaned me $30. I went to the funeral of Mrs. Davis. There was a very fine turn-out, eight American ladies and a great number of men. Davis takes it very hard. I had a few drinks after dinner. While very drunk, Abe Dunning made a trade with Swindling Simpson. Simpson gave him three old plugs of ponies and his one-horse grocery store for Abe's team and wagon worth $500. Abe has not turned over the team but has possession of the grocery. I went to bed at 10:30.

Feb. 17. Cold and windy. Abe is sober this morning. I had a long talk with him--he says he will back out of the trade, as things are not as represented. 9 o'clock--Abe sold his team and wagon to R. N. Leatherwood. Simpson threatened the law on him, but on inquiry of lawyers he found he could do nothing. He and his pimp then set to abusing Abe and all his friends. He is very sore but it serves him right. Old Brown is on a drunk--I saw him at midnight, drunk.

Feb. 18. Cold but pleasant. Had breakfast at 7 this morning. Read all the forenoon. John Burt returned but brought no cattle. I went to John Toney's saloon and took a drink with Jerry Kenny. Was summoned before the grand jury as a witness. Came home, read for a half hour, and went to dinner. Yesterday Jack Upton left for the mountains with Shaw's wagons to get away from whiskey. He came back this morning, worn out and sick. Jack talked quite like a crazy man. He commenced drinking again and at 5 this evening fell in a fit in the barber shop. He was brought home and bled by Dr. Handy. I sat with him until 12 o'clock. One-eyed Louise relieved me and I went to bed after getting my skin full.

Feb. 19. Cold. Upton is all right again. Stage came in--no mail for me. Tom McClellan was drunk all day. Upton got crazy again toward evening. Dr. Handy came to see him, and Tom McClellan, Billy Gale, and myself sat with him until 11 o'clock, during which time he made a will giving away all his property. Said he felt grim death coming. Jerry Kenny and Charley White slept in his house. I went to bed sober.

Feb. 20 (Sunday). Fine morning. Got my hair cut and got tight very early. Upton was crazy as a fool. He broke into the street screaming "murder." Said they were all trying to poison him. He went away after a while and was gone when Dr. Handy came to see him. Handy was vexed and said he would not come to see him again. Upton roamed around town and behaved himself well while no one troubled him. I had several callers in the evening, the last one was Louise who stayed an hour. She left and I went to bed.

Feb. 21. Cold. Got up early and swept out the house. Jim Quinlin and Fred Myers came in with freight from Yuma. Brown took his pup home, price--$10. Blade had trouble with Prentiss and Brown the faro dealer about a check of deposit for $100. I was sober all day. Stage left for Cal. McClellan is sober. Jack Upton is all right again. He wants to go in with me in the saloon business. A ten-dice game arrived and opened in Blade's saloon. I went to bed early.

Feb. 22. Up early. I put up my flag [in honor of Washington's Birthday]. Bought a big bottle of rot, and in running around town got tight. Had lots of fun. Charley White went on a trip for Warner with a buckboard to Point of Mountain [a stage station about 20 miles northwest of town]. I stayed tight until late. Ate dinner at the Chinaman's. I drank too much and threw it up and was sober in a moment. Read until 12 o'clock and went to bed.

Feb. 23. Fine day. Court is in session today--the trial of John Dawson [charged with robbery]. I was summoned as a witness. Dawson got off easy. I kept sober all day. Foster concluded to give up butchering and go into the saloon business with me. [Hand's saloon had been closed since January 22.] Wells' express stage left this evening with 6 passengers. The last pup left the house today. I went to bed early.

Feb. 24. Got up early to go to work, but found that [Sheriff] Bill Oury had put me on the jury list. I stayed in court all day, but did not get on a jury. Mail stage arrived--nothing for me. Had some company in the evening. Went to bed early.

Feb. 25. Warm, pleasant morning. Cloudy, no sun. Went to court at 10 o'clock. Trial of Carlotta Bullez [charged with grand larceny]. I did not get on the jury. Heard all the testimony and the statements of both the district attorney and the lawyer for the defense. The jury went in their room. Court adjourned until 9 tomorrow.

Feb. 26. Got up early, fed the dogs, had breakfast, and went to court. The jury in the case heard yesterday was hung, and they were discharged. Another case was called. I did not get on the jury and was excused until 1:30 p.m. Stage arrived--no mail for me. Back in court again, and we tried another case. John Burns was found not guilty [of grand larceny] as charged in the indictment. Court adjourned until 9 a.m. Monday. I came home and got tight.

Went to the circus. Had dinner with Briggs Goodrich [the county district attorney] and Bill Morgan. Went to bed at 11 o'clock.

William S. Oury looks peaceful enough in this studio photograph, but he was a tough customer. Oury was one of the leaders of the group of men who carried out the Camp Grant Massacre in 1871 (he was 53 years old at the time), and he served as Pima County sheriff from 1873 to 1876. He was also the first president of the Society of Arizona Pioneers. A park in Tucson was named for him. Buehman photo, Arizona Historical Society, Tucson, #1130.

Feb. 27 (Sunday). Very cold. Had a bath. Sat at home all day and read and slept. Had several callers. Foster closes his butcher shop today. I went to bed at 9 o'clock.

Feb. 28. Fine morning. Had breakfast early. I dunned a man--got nix. Hunt got the lumber to fix up the saloon. I went to court. Case of the Territory vs. Alex Wilkins. 30 jurors were excused--lacked 4 for a jury. Court was adjourned while the sheriff found more jurors. He found 7, but only 3 were accepted. Finally he found another one and the case went on. All the other jurors were excused until 10 a.m. tomorrow. The case went to the jury after dark. They soon settled it by bringing a verdict of guilty of assault with a deadly weapon with intent to do bodily harm.

Feb. 29. It rained during the night. 7 o'clock--still raining. In court again this morning. Francisco Esparza was arraigned today. The trial lasted until 9:30 in the evening. The jury went out, stayed 3/4 of an hour. They brought in a verdict of guilty of assault with a deadly weapon with intent to do great bodily harm. The defense counsel moved for a new trial. I sat up at home until 11 o'clock, then went to bed.

~ ~ ~ ~ ~

March 1. Pleasant day. Got up without a cent in my pocket. Went to court at 9 a.m. Case of murder. I was excused by the district attorney on account of conscientious scruples. Court was held until 9 p.m. The testimony was all taken and the court adjourned until 10 a.m. tomorrow. I went to bed at 10 o'clock.

Mar. 2. Fine morning. A faro game ran all night in the house. Robert M. Crandall died this morning. We commenced putting up a partition and taking down the old ceiling. I went to court. The jury in the case of Pabla Acosta, indicted for murder, brought in a verdict of not guilty as charged. Case of the Territory vs. John Burns, again for grand larceny. The testimony was all through at dark. Judge French then adjourned the court until 1 p.m. tomorrow to give all a chance to attend the funeral of R. M. Crandall. Tom Roddick came in from the mines with plenty of bullion. I went to bed at 10 o'clock.

Mar. 3. Cloudy. Wrote to Bradley, Shipler, and Nickerson informing them of the death of Crandall. The sun came out warm at 9 o'clock. Went to the funeral at 10:30. Bob was buried in the military cemetery. There were a great many people in the procession. C. H. Ott read the service. [Robert Crandall had come to the Southwest as an officer in Hand's old California Column unit, Company "G." He was said to be an uncommonly handsome man, and the 44-year-old Crandall was very well liked in the community. He made his living as a gambler.] Court opened again at 1 p.m. The jury was out only a short time. The verdict--Burns again not guilty. Court adjourned till 9 a.m. tomorrow. I had several visitors this evening, reading and playing cards. A wind came up from the east and my chimney smoked. I sat up till 10, then went to bed.

A faro game in a Morenci, Arizona, saloon. Faro is rarely played today, but in the late 1800s it was one of the most popular gambling games in the Southwest. Arizona Historical Society, Tucson, #2819.

Mar. 4. Got up at 6 o'clock. I saw Tom Roddick, and he paid Toole $90 in rent for me. I had breakfast at 7, and went to court at 9 a.m. The case of Carlotta Bullez was given to the jury--her counsel left the case to the jury without argument. The jury was in the room for 15 minutes and returned with the verdict of not guilty [of grand larceny]. Another jury was selected for the case of Tomas Valdez [charged with receiving stolen goods]. Court recessed for 1½ hours. Everyone returned and all the jurymen not on the regular panel, except those now organized, were discharged for the term.

Mar. 5 (Sunday). Fine day. Did not change clothes--worked all day fixing up the front room. Went to see the broncos start with the stage. Took a ride in Wells' buggy with Bill Gale.

Mar. 6. Tomas Valdez was tried today--not guilty. Foster and I put up the ceiling in the front room. We drank some mescal and got rather full. Morgan got tight. I went to bed at 9 o'clock.

Mar. 7. My birthday--46 years of age. Judge French gave the following sentences this morning--Alex Wilkins, $500 fine; Frank Esparza, $250 fine; the Mexican forger, 2 years in the penitentiary. Tom McClellan commenced painting the woodwork in the house this evening. Foster and I worked hard today. Jerry Kenny sized the walls. A soldier died in a Mexican mescal house this evening. His name was Michael Ryan. He had been on a spree for four days. Rufe Eldred is very bad this evening. Lots of sugarcane and oranges came in today from Sonora--the streets are full of Mexican carts. Morgan is drunk. I went to bed early.

Mar. 8. Cloudy and windy. Morgan is still on the drink. Foster and I put up the ceiling in the other room, and McClellan painted the doors and window frames. Rufe Eldred is getting worse every hour. Yank Markham is sick. Charley White left for the Gila settlements to tend stock for the mail company. A few visitors came in this evening. Foster went to bed at 9 o'clock.

Mar. 9. Up early. Had breakfast at 6 o'clock. Jerry Kenny papered the front room. The mail stage came--I received a letter from my old schoolmate John B. Chesebro of Kentville, Ind., also his photograph. Received several papers from Milton and one from J. B. Hart from which I learned that he has gone to the Black Hills. Hattie Davis, infant daughter of W. C. and the late Mrs. Davis, died today. I am very tired tonight. Went to bed at 9 o'clock.

Mar. 10. Got up and had breakfast early. Jerry worked a little while--I trimmed wall paper for him. He left us and went next door to work for Jacobs. Foster and I cleaned up the room. McClellan came and varnished. Jerry came back at 3 p.m., and nearly half of the next room was papered by 5 o'clock. We quit for the day and went to dinner. Had several visitors this evening. Morgan opened chuck [a dice game] in the house this evening. It rained all afternoon and was cold. Went to bed at 9 o'clock.

Mar. 11. Cold, damp, and still cloudy. Had breakfast early. We cannot work on the house--the paint and varnish is not dry. The monte game at Simpson's Hole-In-The-Wall saloon ran all last night. 9 a.m.--the sun is out and shining fine. Jerry came and finished papering. An express wagon went to Sahuarita [about 20 miles south of town] to bring in Schemerhorn who is sick-- he is expected to die. Very cold this evening. Went to bed at 10 o'clock. Rufus Eldred died at 11:30 o'clock at night.

Mar. 12 (Sunday). Fine morning. The church bells are going and all the stores are closed. The funeral of Rufus Eldred will be held tomorrow. There was lots of buggy riding today. Foster and I worked a little while washing bottles and glasses, and then quit for Sunday. I went to bed early.

Mar. 13. Got up early, worked until 10, then went to the funeral. Came home and scrubbed out the house--worked hard all day. Went to bed at 9 o'clock.

Mar. 14. Up early. Had breakfast. We then went at the stove, cleaned it up and blackened it. We covered the tables and put up more pictures. Cleaned the lamps and opened for business all lit up. We rented a room to Juan Borquez. Bill Johnson came in from the placer mines. Foster gave Black Jim [a dog] to Dr. Lord. I went to bed at 10 o'clock, Foster closed up at 11:30. [On March 18, the *Citizen* reported the reopening of the saloon: "George Foster has taken personal charge of and opened a nice saloon on the corner where George Hand's saloon used to be. The place has been very nicely fitted up, and now has attached to the bar room a very pleasant reading and sitting room. Everything is neat, new and tidy. Mr. Foster is an old hand at the saloon business in Tucson. He used to keep a pleasant and lively place on Main Street where Mr. Archibald's store now is, and all the boys will recollect him." Although this article implies otherwise, George Hand was a full partner with George Foster in the revitalized saloon.]

Mar. 15. Cold morning. Foster opened and cleaned up before I turned out. Sent papers to J. B. Chesebro, Kentland, Ind., and Milton Hand, Joliet, Ill. Cleaned out my room. Went to bed early.

Mar. 16. Very dull in the house. Stage came--no news. Very tired at night. Went to bed early.

Mar. 17. St. Patrick's Day. I drank a few. Whitewashed my room twice. I was tired and went to bed early.

Mar. 18. I was very sick during last night with a pain in my right side. It is hard work to breathe this morning. Cleaned my room, hung pictures, and went to McClellan's wedding party. Tom was married this morning by Bishop Salpointe. Had a good time at the dance. It broke up and I arrived home at 1:30 o'clock tomorrow morning.

Mar. 19 (Sunday). Fine morning. Barney Palm and his wife had a row and he took the children away from her. Martin Gilmartin died this morning at 7 o'clock. Clark is tight again. McClellan stayed home all day. Billy Gale is sick. I was sick all day and worse at night. Went to bed at 8 in the evening.

Mar. 20. Fine weather. Martin Gilmartin was buried today. Clark is still on the spree. McClellan put in an appearance this morning. Jerry has a sore finger and cannot work. City election for disincorporation today. Blade is very much excited over the election. The city ring is working very hard against us to carry their point. 4 p.m.--the polls closed. The votes were counted--49 for disincorporation, 139 against. We were beaten shamefully by buckfart Americans and foreign Jews, with a few lop-eared Dutch. Clark is running around in his bare feet hunting something to drink. He nearly has the jim-jams. I went to bed at 8:30 o'clock with a bad pain in my right side. [The new taxes on saloons and gamblers levied by the town council had fueled the unsuccessful drive for disincorporation (see diary entry for February 14). The council would repeal the offending Ordinance 15 in August 1876.]

Mar. 21. Pleasant morning. No sun. Feel some better today. Billy Gale is a little better. I went to see Clark, who had a secondhand paralytic stroke caused by not having mescal sufficient to reach his finger ends. Big Cleopha brought him a drink of the above named beverage and a bowl of soup. He immediately recovered. The stage arrived--I got no letters. Schemerhorn died this evening. I went to bed early.

Mar. 22. Clark is sick today and not drinking. I worked nearly all day bookbinding. The express stage left this evening. The Cal. mail stage also left. Cloudy today. Schemerhorn was buried this evening. It rained at three p.m.

and was cloudy the balance of the day. I called on Clark and found him sick in bed, still not drinking. Joe Mills is after a divorce. Another man died today. Went to bed at 10 o'clock.

John Baptist (Jean Baptiste) Salpointe was the first Roman Catholic bishop of Arizona. A cultured man born in France, he came to Tucson in 1866 and died there in 1898. A Tucson high school was named in his honor. Arizona Historical Society, Tucson, #26580.

Mar. 23. Pleasant, fine morning. I still have a heavy pain in my right side. Had breakfast early. Called on Clark, found him quite sick but not drinking. I put a cover on a book. The mail stage came--nothing for me. Feel pretty well this afternoon. Had dinner at 4 p.m. The pain got worse in the evening and I went to bed early. I was awakened in the night by the noise of a fight down the street. Went to the door and heard Carpenter say, "He bit my thumb!" The police came and stopped the row. I went back to bed.

Mar. 24. The sun came out fine. Had breakfast early. Nothing new except the fight last night between Carpenter and Miguel. The stage left today. I sent papers to Ed Gaylord and John B. Chesebro. Put a mustard plaster on my side and went to bed at 10 o'clock.

Mar. 25. Fine morning. I cut some pups' ears this morning. Clark is all right again. There was a suit today by Mrs. Palm on a habeas corpus for the possession of her two children in the charge of Barney Palm. The court adjourned until Monday. The stage came--no mail for me. Connelly and Hayes are going to San Francisco to sell mines. There was an auction today at the Wood brothers' corner--very little business. I called on Clark this evening. He was so full of law that I left. I was sick in the evening and went to bed very early.

Mar. 26 (Sunday). Fine morning. Feel quite well today. Called on Mrs. Linn and cut her pup's ears. I witnessed some papers for Barney Connelly and gave Barney some photos to take home. He and Hayes left on the stage today.

Mar. 27. Got up early. I washed up, changed clothes, and sent the washing off. Had breakfast, fed my dogs, blacked my boots, and went to court. I sat there until noon. No call for me so I went home. Late in the evening the Palm case was decided--each got one child. Clark got full and thought he had the heart disease--he sent for me in the night. He recovered and I went back to bed.

Mar. 28. Stage came--received a letter from my sister. Got full of whiskey. Went to bed early.

Mar. 29. Pleasant day. Nothing new or interesting. Sent papers to P. R. Brady, John B. Chesebro, and M. F. Hand. McDermott's boy died. I went to bed at 10 but could not sleep--coughed all night.

Mar. 30. Got up late. I rested poorly last night. Had several drinks and went to breakfast--had a good one. Came back and went to work on books. John Burt got tight. The stage came--no papers, no letters. Foster was up late playing cards.

Mar. 31. Fine day. Had mackerel for breakfast. King William could not get in his house last night--his wife must have been very sound asleep. ["King William" was the frontier nickname of German-born Otto von Reichenbach. A cultured man from an aristocratic family, the "King" was a professional gambler.] Very dull in the house. I worked on books nearly all day. Morgan got drunk. Nothing new today. I went to bed early. Foster was up till 1 o'clock.

~ ~ ~ ~ ~

April 1. The fooling commenced early. I was up early and did not get sold. Stage arrived--no letters for me. Foster was married this evening to Juana

Moreno. John Clark and Librada Palm stood up with them. Judge Osborn performed the ceremony. I got full. Went to bed at 10 o'clock.

Apr. 2 (Sunday). Very pleasant. Had breakfast late. Changed clothes today. Musicians are marching through town--theatre this evening. The boys sent up a balloon. It was a great success--it went out of sight and came down without burning. Ross is very tight. This is his birthday--30 years of age. He was born in Scotland and came to this country during the war to free the niggers. Jerry Kenny is drunk also--he is eating tamales, shuck and all. I went to bed.

Apr. 3. Fine morning. After breakfast I washed out the house. Was invited to drink several times and got full. [Deputy] Ad Linn came in from New Mexico with the man who stole James Lee's grey horse, and Sam Lauren, wanted on a charge of conspiring to commit murder. Both men were put in jail. [Sam Lauren was accused of conspiring with Ana Charouleau Woffenden to kill Tucsonan Richard Woffenden, Ana's husband. Ana had quietly slipped out of town, reportedly headed back to her native France.] A young man named Bancroft came in from the sheep ranch and gave himself up. He killed a man named Johnson. The stage left for Cal. Blade is having great money troubles and is trying to sell out. His barkeeper demanded a settlement which troubled Mr. Jim. Whiskey and more whiskey drove me to bed early.

Apr. 4. Very nice weather. Clark has been sick but is better. Nothing new or interesting today. Stage arrived--no mail for me. The boys are playing cards. Lawyer McCarty got Sam Lauren out of jail on a writ of habeas corpus. I got quite full. Went to bed early.

Apr. 5. Fine day. Everyone is tight. We are having great arguments on fish and fishing. Hunt is on a kind of spree and all is fishing and sailoring. Sanders got pretty full and struck a friend of his from Texas. Billy Gale was discharged at the stable and French John took his place. I received letters from Dave Davis and P. R. Brady. Answered Davis' letter. Went to bed at 9 o'clock.

Apr. 6. Fine morning. The boys all got up early. Quite dull in the house this morning. Stage came--no through mail from the States. Bill Kirkland came in town from Pueblo Viejo yesterday. Sanders the stage driver left for Silver City. Hand drank rather too much whiskey and got tight. Ate two lunches late. Went to bed at 11 o'clock.

Apr. 7. Fine weather. Nothing new or interesting. Dr. Mitchell was sued by Richard Woffenden for practicing medicine without a license. The doctor was fined $50, or 50 days in jail. Business was dull all day and evening. I retired at 9 o'clock.

Apr. 8. I wrote to Brady and sent him some seeds. The mail stage arrived from Cal.--nothing in the shape of letters. Got tight before I knew it. 3 p.m.--sober again. Visited Dr. Lord's sick dog. Stayed up late, closed at 12. Went to a dance for a few moments, then came home and went to bed.

Apr. 9 (Palm Sunday). The whole population turned out to church with all kinds of green twigs, and the plaza was full. Playing cards and drinking whiskey was the order of the day. Clark and McDermott gave an entertainment--Shakespeare without whiskey. Hamlet was the play. McDermott was the ghost, Clark was Hamlet. There was nothing there to drink, so I, of course, left. Later, Clark lost his dog. He was very hostile and said the man who stole his dog was a son-of-a-bitch and he would kill him. The dog had only gone for a walk around and he returned in a short time. Clark sat down, threw up, and all was right again. Hand was in all the time when the liquor was called and got full. Went to bed early.

Apr. 10. News this morning is bad. Report says that Nick Rogers and others are killed by Indians [near Camp Bowie]. Late in the afternoon reports came in stating that others had been killed. A meeting was called at the courthouse to resolve what to do. Nothing was done, as usual. Brown got drunk today. John Burt and James Lee got very tight. Clark was tight. Frank Francis was tight. I went to bed. [A group of Chiricahua Apaches had left their reservation in southeastern Arizona and gone on a raiding and killing spree. Arizonans had thought that their problems with the Apaches were over, and they reacted to the Chiricahua outbreak with hysteria. As a remedy, later in the year the reservation was abolished and Tom Jeffords, agent for the Chiricahuas, discharged. The Chiricahuas were then placed on the San Carlos Apache Reservation north of the Gila River under the watchful eye of Agent John P. Clum. However, they would cause their captors much grief for another decade.]

Apr. 11. Fine morning after a light rain was over. Stage came early. No new reports from the Indians.

Apr. 12. There are lots of stage drivers in town. Sent papers to John B. Chesebro and Mit, and a letter and seeds to P. R. Brady, Florence, Ariz. Went with Clark to call on some girls. He and his girl had a row and then closed their business. I left Clark at their house. Big Nick drove a stage out today. Billy Gale left for the Gila. I went to bed early.

Apr. 13. Fine morning. Quite cool. There is a big time in the church. Report says that Jeffords' Indians [the Chiricahua Apaches] have all left the reservation. Stage arrived this morning--no letters for me. Very quiet today. Closed and went to bed early.

Apr. 14. Good Friday. Very fine day. Very quiet this morning. Everybody is going to church. I received a letter from John L. Shipler, Port Carbon, Pa. This evening images of Christ and His Mother were carried around the plaza with singing, etc. The church was open nearly all night. Went to bed at 10 o'clock.

Apr. 15. Fine day. The Church is open this morning. Guns were fired and there were other performances. Special election for mayor today. The candidates are John B. Allen and L. M. Jacobs. The polls opened at 10 a.m., closed at 4 p.m. Allen was elected. Several of the boys got tight. I went to bed at 10 o'clock.

Apr. 16 (Easter Sunday). Got tight early. Went visiting.

Apr. 17. Washed out the house. Got tight. Got sober. Brown stole the knob off the outhouse door.

Apr. 18. Quite warm. Brown went to jail. Nothing new. Mail stage arrived.

Apr. 19. Fine day. I read and drank all day. Was tight and sober alternately. Big dance at Warner's mill. Nothing strange today.

Apr. 20. Warm. Went to Tom Ewing's to cut the tails off his litter of pups. Warm all day. Dusty this afternoon. Stage arrived--nothing for me. A man named Hank Stafford fell dead in the Gem Saloon this evening. A postmortem examination was held and the coroner's jury is to give their verdict tomorrow. Fred Hughes was married this evening to Sophia Barcelo. There was a dance at the house of Doña Bernarda this evening. I went to bed at 10 o'clock after writing a letter to Bill Bidwell. Wrote to John B. Chesebro also.

Apr. 21. Very warm. Nothing new in town. Dr. Lord and his wife and daughter left in the stage for New York. Several dances in town--I did not attend any of them. Went to bed early.

Apr. 22. Fine morning. Very warm. Stage came in--no letters for me. Ross and another fellow had a foot race--75 yards. Ross was beaten by 5 yards. I went to a dance, came home, and sat up reading till 4 tomorrow morning.

Apr. 23 (Sunday). Very warm this morning. Did not get up until 10 o'clock. Constable Andy Hall tried to arrest a Mexican. For fun he struck at the Mexican with his stick, and the Mexican took the stick away from him. Bryson tried to help him, but the Mexican got away from both of them. Circus this evening and a dance at the house of Doña Bernarda. Went to bed at 9 o'clock.

Apr. 24. Cool morning. Captain Smith Delos and his wife came in to town with Whitey Foster. Doc Rogers, O'Meara, and another man came in from the mines today. Very dull. Went to bed at 9 o'clock.

Apr. 25. Cloudy and cool. Stage arrived early--no mail for me. I got too much whiskey today. Made several calls. Was sober at night. Went to bed at 9 o'clock.

Apr. 26. Cool and pleasant. Whitey Foster from Yuma left today, and Bill Walker went with him. Nothing new today. Wrote to William F. Bradley. Went to bed at 9 o'clock.

Apr. 27. Fine day. Mail stage came in--received a letter from J. B. Hart, Eureka, Nev. Got tight today. Blade rented his saloon to Toney and [Andy] Nickerson to run as a dance house. They moved the billiard tables, but had no dance. I went to bed at 10 o'clock.

Apr. 28. Good weather, but very warm. Wrote letters to Bradley and Bidwell. I drank a little too much and went to Blade's dance. Had a couple of dances, came home, and went to bed.

Apr. 29. Cool morning. Mail stage arrived. Heard that Dave Davis killed a Mexican in Prescott. Got my hair cut. Tom McClellan got very tight and slept until dark. I had a big time at Levin's saloon. Went to bed early.

Apr. 30 (Sunday). Fine day. Excursion parties were going out all morning. I got full of gin. Went to Levin's. Called on several ladies. Went home and to bed.

~ ~ ~ ~ ~

May 1. Put up the new licenses. Was sick all day--slept nearly all day. Ate no dinner. Received 2 telegrams from Camp Grant. Received three more telegrams from Grant. Clark was on a spree and spent seven dollars in here. I went to bed at 10 o'clock.

May 2. Mail stage came--received a letter from Dave Davis. Went to bed early.

May 3. Clark is still drunk. Ed Marshall is drunk. G. O. Hand is drunk. John Burt and Bill Morgan left for the mines, both sober. Bill Matlock got a sore head put on himself by John Bryson. I went to bed early.

May. 4. Got my watch back from Toole. Very warm today. Mail stage came in, Big Nick the driver. Dr. Harvey arrived from Sonora. Clark quit drinking. I took a walk with Jerry Kenny to Levin's Park Brewery. Nothing much doing, so we came back. I went to bed.

May 5. Windy and dusty. A pain in my side forced me to lie down all afternoon. The stage left. Nothing new today. Went to bed at 9:30 o'clock.

May 6. Cool morning. Stage came early. Very light mail, no letters for me. There was a dance at Levin's Park. Very pleasant in the evening. Foster played poker for whiskey till 2 o'clock.

May 7 (Sunday). Very cool morning for this season. Lovejoy took Tinker [dog] home. John, alias "Puck," Ryan came to town--he got tight of course. Every Jew and c. s. in town went to a picnic. I went to bed at 9 o'clock.

May 8. Ryan is still on a bust. He bought some new clothes and has lots of money. Very windy and dusty today. Ed Marshall is drunk. Stage left--I sent papers to Cal. and other states. I am sick with a pain in my side. Clark is quite sober.

May 9. Fine morning. Got up early. Stage came at 9 o'clock. Ryan moved his blankets form my place to McClellan's house. Nothing strange today. Sat up till 9 o'clock and went to bed.

May 10. Fine day. Ryan was walking around in front of the house at 4 o'clock this morning, forgetting that he had moved. Nothing new today. Wrote some letters and sent some papers. I hung out my banner for the opening of the centennial celebration.

May 11. Stage came--no mail for me. Got tight today.

May 12. No excitement, very dull. Wrote a letter to Lew [Lewis Hand].

May 13. Sick this morning. Started drinking early and got full sooner than usual. The stage came and brought the wife of Judge French. Governor Safford also returned on it. Clark and Goodrich left for Pinal County to attend court at Florence.

May 14 (Sunday). Very cool morning. Had breakfast early. Kept sober until three o'clock, then had dinner. Think I'll go to bed sober. Commenced wearing linen clothes for summer. Big Nick and Cramer had a row. Tom Banning and Cramer also had a growl. Banning got very drunk. I was sober and went to bed so.

May 15. Fine morning. The Arizona Express stage arrived. Foster's boy is very sick. The Rio Grande stage came late. The mail coach left. Jim Blade and another gent left for Florence. Foster's boy died at 4 p.m. I got full. Shut up the house at 12 o'clock.

May 16. Cold morning. Nothing new. We buried Foster's boy in the Catholic churchyard. I got tight late at night and went to bed so.

May 17. Got up early. Kept sober all day. Stage left for Cal. Several men got drunk today. Went to bed at 9 o'clock.

May 18. Cold morning. Quite cool all day. Kept quite sober. Covered the mirrors with gauze. Rooney left for White's ranch [near Camp Grant]. I went to a dance at Hovey's saloon. Did not like the movements and came home at 10 o'clock and went to bed. The dance went on until several got tight and fighting commenced. Marshall, Nickerson, Carpenter, and a Mexican had a sore head put on each. The dance wound up at 4 in the morning tomorrow.

May 19. Very cold. Got up early. The city marshal is looking after the fighters at the ball last night. Carpenter and Bryson were arrested for assault and battery and brought before Justice Neugass. The case was put off until 10 a.m. tomorrow. Nickerson, armed with a fine shooting pistol, went to get some satisfaction of Bryson who took his gun from him and kicked him out the door. Things are now quiet. Not as cold this evening as last. Went to bed at 9 o'clock.

May 20. Not só cold this morning, but a coat is comfortable. Stage arrived--very little mail. Received a letter from Dave Davis. Very dull in the house. Walked around town until 10 o'clock, then went to bed.

May 21. Fine morning. Warmer than yesterday. There were musicians in the gambling houses today. Express stage came in. I kept sober all day. Nothing new or interesting. Lovejoy went on a picnic. I retired at 10 o'clock.

May 22. I was awakened by the sound of music and singing. People formed a procession and marched from the church, singing and praying to the Patron Saint to stay the ravages of the fever now killing children every day. Quite warm today. Cool in the evening. Walked around after sundown and went to bed at 10 o'clock.

May 23. Now warmer than usual. Had a good breakfast. Took a ride with John Bartleson to Soloman Warner's mill. There was a picnic there today. It is a fine cool place to spend a few hours. Lots of ladies there, few men. [Solomon Warner's water-powered flour mill was located at the base of Sentinel Peak (now called "A" Mountain) about a mile west of town.] McDermott and Shibell returned to town. Hand got pretty full this evening.

Solomon Warner's home and water-powered flour mill as seen from Sentinel Peak ("A" Mountain) ca. 1880. The fields in the background have long since been urbanized. Arizona Historical Society, Tucson, #18233.

May 24. Warm morning. After breakfast I went to call on Mrs. W. W. Williams to show her my little dog Vic. Had a good time looking at the trees, flowers, and shrubbery. Mail stage leaves today. Bryson sold his saloon. Nothing new worthy of note. The water cart commenced sprinkling the streets today. [Adam Sanders delivered household water to customers around town with a mule-drawn cart. He recently acquired a new outfit, a 200-gallon metal tank mounted on a two-wheeled cart custom made at Yuma, and used his old rig to sprinkle the streets, on contract with the village government.]

May 25. Stage came in--no letters for me. Stockton is in town. I kept sober until night, then filled up. Ate some tamales. Very warm night. Went to bed.

May 26. Very warm--cloudy and sultry. Tom Roddick and Stroud came in town and both got drunk. I kept tolerably sober. Big things tonight--an Apache war dance. I went in company with Mr. O'Reilly to see the dance at 8 o'clock in the evening. It smelt so strong and wild that we only stayed a few moments. I came home and went to bed. Very hot. [The war dance was held by a troop of Apache police from San Carlos who were camped at the edge of town. These Apaches, organized and led by John P. Clum, were on their way to southeastern Arizona to try to capture renegade Chiricahua Apaches. Michael O'Reilly was nicknamed "Well-digger Riley" because he specialized in that craft. Many wells at stage stations in southern Arizona were dug by him.]

John P. Clum (foreground) and a contingent of Apache police on the outskirts of Tucson in 1876. They were on their way from San Carlos to southeastern Arizona to chase Chiricahua Apaches who were on the warpath. Arizona Historical Society, Tucson, #924.

May 27. Cloudy and very warm. Stage came--no letters for me. Got some *chile verde* from Sonora. John Luck cut his thumb off today. Whipple licked Fred Miller. A circus is marching through town--they are to perform this evening. 8 o'clock--commenced raining but lasted but a short time. The circus performance went off. I went to bed at 10 o'clock.

May 28 (Sunday). Very warm. The clouds have disappeared and it is hot as blazes. Jim Caldwell came in with a wagon train. The circus is out in the streets again, playing music. There was a high-toned dance at Hovey's place this evening--the dancing was free. I went to bed at 11 o'clock. The dance ran all night. There was a big monte game there all night--Blade lost his shirt.

May 29. Warm day. Several drunken men came around this morning. They got so at the dance and game at Hovey's. I went to bed early.

May 30. Mail stage arrived--no letters for me. Windy and cool today.

May 31. Pleasant day, windy and cool. Clark's dog Pericles died in a fit this morning at 7 o'clock. Dull in the house all day. Some soldiers came in who knew us 4 years ago. They called me out at 2 in the morning to drink with them. Hovey moved into Jim Blade's old place. Jack Long arrived from the Salero Mine [in the Santa Rita Mountains]. We buried Pericles this evening.

~ ~ ~ ~ ~

June 1. Cloudy and pleasant. The stage came in as usual, Big Nick the driver. No mail for me. Nothing new until night when Foster and McDermott had a growl. Marshall and Hunt also had a row. Closed up at two o'clock.

June 2. Fine morning. Closed the old privy. Sent papers to P. R. Brady. Pancho Gomez' child was buried. Quite warm this evening. Went to bed at 9 o'clock.

June 3. Fine day. Street sweeping commenced early. Lots of soldiers are in town. Stage came in--no mail for me. Nothing new. There was a concert and ball at Levin's Park garden this evening, $1.00 admittance. Went to bed at 9:30 o'clock.

June 4 (Sunday). Warm but pleasant morning. I went to see my dog Tinker. Col. James Biddle, Inspector General of Arizona, and George H. Tinker arrived from Yuma. White-headed Foster drove them in. The circus musicians are promenading through town today. George Tinker drank some whiskey in our house. I kept up with him all day. He then went to sleep. Night came--circus and ball at Levin's Park. Went to bed early.

June 5. Very warm. Nothing new. Stage left for Cal. Sober today. Went to bed at 9 o'clock.

June 6. Fine morning. A little breeze this morning. Streets all wet from the sprinkling wagon. Stage came in at 9 o'clock. Warm day.

June 7. Warm. The stage left--I sent papers to the States and the Gila settlements. Jo took sick this morning. I caught a scrub son-of-a-bitch fast to Jo and pounded him off double quick. Hand got tight and tighter. There was a

dance at Levin's Park this evening. Went to Levin's and drank some beer.
Came home at 11 o'clock and went to bed.

June 8. Cool morning. Water in the olla is cool and fine, good enough
without ice. Stage came in late, 10:30 o'clock. Received a letter from Dave
Davis. Nothing new, very dull. Warm later in the day. Went to bed early.

June 9. Warm morning. John Bartleson left for Phoenix. I got a little
tight today. Ate some ice cream this evening. Sent a letter to my sister and to
the Utica *Herald*. Moved my bed out in the yard. Went to bed at 10 o'clock.
[A man named Francois Forque had opened an ice cream parlor in town. How
he chilled his product is a question--he may have had a steam-powered
refrigeration system. A steam-powered ice plant was installed in Tucson in
1879.]

June 10. Slept well last night. Jo is still sick. There was an auction of the
furniture at the Cosmopolitan Hotel today. [The owners of the Cosmopolitan
Hotel were going out of business. It would reopen under new management.]
Stage arrived at 15 minutes to 10 a.m. I was sober all day. 5 p.m.--went with
George Tinker in the Inspector General's ambulance [carriage], Whitey Foster
the driver, to Camp Lowell for the first time. It is a very nice post. We stayed
there half an hour and came back before sundown. In the evening I found a
ticket for a concert and dance at Levin's Park. I stayed there an hour, but did
not dance. Came home and went to bed.

June 11 (Sunday). Warm day. Slept well last night. It was very sultry
until 1 p.m. when a light breeze sprang up. The boys played cards all
afternoon. Nothing new. Warm evening. Went to bed at 10 o'clock.

June 12. Warm. 9 a.m.--warmer. 12 noon--hot, no breeze. This is George
Foster's 44th birthday. The Inspector General left with George Tinker.
Charley Conwell got tight. Cal. mail stage left. 1 p.m.--mercury 105 degrees.
2 p.m.--very hot. Nothing strange happened today. Went to bed at 10 o'clock.

June 13. Pleasant morning. Stage arrived from Cal.--no letters for me.
Very warm. Mercury 105 degrees at 1 p.m. Very warm after sundown. Hot all
evening. 10 at night--comfortable. Went to bed.

June 14. Warm. 9 o'clock--hot. 12 noon--hotter. The mail stage came
from the east. The express stage from Cal. brought some [San Francisco]
Chronicles. Mercury 105 degrees at 1 p.m. Received a telegram telling of the
sickness of Blains. Went to bed at 10 o'clock.

June 15. Corpus Christi Day. Big time in the church. Very warm
morning.--97 degrees at 9 o'clock. Took a walk up town with Conwell and
came near melting. John Day and Captain Devers came to town. Big Nick was
discharged by the stage co. Mercury 110 degrees at 1 p.m. Received a N.Y.
Herald from William Bradley that came from New York to San Francisco in
Jarrett and Palmer's fast express train. Went to bed at 10 o'clock.

June 16. Very warm. Munson came in town. Mercury 111 degrees at 1
p.m. Mercury 112 degrees at 2 p.m. Mercury 108 degrees at 6 p.m. After

sundown the breeze made it quite pleasant. Received a photo of Mrs. J. B. Chesebro and her little child. Went to bed at 10:30 o'clock.

June 17. Warm. Flies made me get up early. Had breakfast at 6:30 o'clock. 8 a.m.--hot. A telegram reports the nomination of Hayes and Wheeler by the Republican convention in Cincinnati. Mercury at 1 p.m.--109 degrees. Nothing more new. Went to bed early.

June 18 (Sunday). Fine morning. The boys commenced drinking early. Hand got drunk and had a row with Rebel Jack. In the row we broke two of the biggest and best ollas in the house. Day, Shaw, and everyone got drunk. Hand stayed up very late, walking around town to get sober before going to bed. Went to bed at last.

June 19. Was sick nearly all day. Day and the others got drunk again. I kept sober until night. Foster was sick and went home. I was obliged to stay up until I got full, then had no desire to retire. Singing songs, etc., took up the time until 3 in the morning when I closed.

June 20. Sore-headed this morning. Bill Gale came to town. I took a walk around town with him. We drank a few drinks. Billy got full, went to bed, and slept till 5 p.m. I went to bed at 9 o'clock.

June 21. Warm morning. George Fields' wagon train arrived. Wrote a letter to Dave Davis. John Day is sober. Mercury at 2 p.m.--102 degrees. There is a fine breeze today. Jack Long brought his dog Spot into town. Jo killed 12 rats this evening. Tom McClellan got drunk. The boys played Pedro until 12 o'clock. I then went to bed.

June 22. Cloudy and sultry. Jack Long's Spot is lying in the street, dead from poison. Stage came in--no mail for me. Billy Gale leaves today with stock for Wheat's [stage] station [50 miles north of Tucson near Florence]. Mercury at 1 p.m.--99 degrees. It rained very lightly all evening. I slept in the house.

June 23. Cloudy this morning. We had a little sprinkle of rain and a cool breeze. Sent papers to Mit, J. B. Chesebro, C. J. Nickerson, and J. B. Hart. Mercury at 1 p.m.--77 degrees. Puck Ryan came to town to get a woman. He got blind drunk in 30 minutes. We had quite a rain shower this morning. 2 p.m.--cleared up a little. 4 p.m.--commenced raining and rained all evening. Ryan had a row in the drugstore with Carpenter. He came back fearful drunk and fell down in front of my door. I put him in the back room. After a while he got up and went away. He came back and went to bed on a table. I went to bed early.

June 24. San Juan's Day. No work, no business, no nothing. Among Mexicans there was much dancing, drinking, riding, and a general holiday. Rain kept the dust down and made it much more pleasant than usual on this day. There were several arrests for fighting. Puck Ryan left on the express stage. Billy Gale returned from the Gila. Circus tonight. I went to bed at 9:30 o'clock.

June 25 (Sunday). Pleasant morning. The horses are all sick from the hard riding yesterday. The church was busy today. All the whores in town went to get Holy Water and pray off the sins of yesterday. Mercury at 1 p.m.-- 99 degrees. No one killed today. Circus this evening. Went to bed early.

June 26. Fine day. News came of the failure of the Arizona and New Mexico Express Co. The mail stage leaves for Cal. today. I wrote to Rush and sent papers to M. F. Hand and John Shipler. George Esslinger is on a bust. Mercury at 1 p.m.--101 degrees. Dr. Handy brought back my black and tan dog. I went to bed at 10 o'clock.

June 27. Cloudy and pleasant. Lots of the fellows are tight. I got tight by some means, I suppose by drinking whiskey. Toole cleaned out the corral and cut a ditch under the door. I ate some ice cream--sweetened snow. Mr. Schwenker, bookkeeper for Tully & Ochoa, shot himself accidently and died in a very few moments.

June 28. Very warm. The funeral of Henry Schwenker was to be held at 11 a.m. but, the grave not being finished, it was put off until 3 p.m. He was buried with Masonic honors.

June 29. Warm and a little cloudy. The stage came with news of the nomination by the Democrats of Tilden of New York and Hendricks of Indiana for president and vice president. More clouds in the afternoon. Mercury at 1 p.m.--104 degrees. Sam Wise came to town from San Pedro and is going at the whiskey furiously. Nothing extraordinary today.

June 30. The last day of June. Rent to pay and stock to buy with no money is very hard. Mercury 103 degrees at 1 p.m. Went to bed sober and early.

~ ~ ~ ~ ~

July 1. Fine day. Warm. Mail stage came from Cal.--received letters from my sisters Mira and Emma. They also wrote one to the postmaster inquiring of me. I also received a letter from Dave Davis, Phoenix. Circus tonight. Sweeney is tight. Hand is tight also. We slept in the corral.

July 2 (Sunday). Great preparations are being made for the celebration of the Fourth of July. Very warm this morning. Hand and others got tight. Went to bed at 11:30 o'clock. [This was the centennial of the signing of the Declaration of Independence and the Fourth was being celebrated with special vigor throughout the country.]

July 3. Worked all day fixing the decorations for the Fourth. A telegram from San Francisco says the town is decorated in every part splendidly. We put up our flags crossing the street. The American flag is in the center and those of other nations on the sides. Went to bed at 10 o'clock.

July 4. The day broke with the firing of guns, including a 12-pounder [cannon] from the post. A procession formed in different parts of town and came together at the courthouse. They marched through town very fine. One large wagon carried 100 little girls, each with a flag. The band from the post played, and a Mexican band also. They all went to Levin's Park. There we had music and the usual order of exercises for July 4th. It was the finest celebration I ever saw in this town. Tom Jeffords and the district attorney [Briggs Goodrich] got very full. I kept sober all day. Went to bed at 9 o'clock.

July 5. Warm morning. No water cart sprinkling the streets today. Windy, dusty, and hot. Tom McClellan got tight and wound up by getting on the warpath. Billy Gale put him to bed in Leatherwood's corral. 4 p.m.-- threatened rain. The wind blew terrific and the dust was so thick that I was obliged to shut all the doors. After filling everyone with dust, it rained a little. I sat up till quite late--it was too hot to sleep. Went with Billy Gale to call on a lady. Came home, ate some tomatoes, and went to bed.

July 6. Warm. Could not sleep late--flies are very thick. Worked hard for two hours. Mr. Glasco is on a drunk. Foster is sick. Someone tore my flag down last night. I took all the flags in this morning. 3 p.m.--very warm, clouding up. 5 p.m.--commenced to blow--fearful dusty, almost unbearable. 6 p.m.--commenced raining. The house leaked rain nearly all night. The streets were running water like a river. Jacobs' store leaked in every part. [Lionel and Barron Jacobs' general merchandise store was next door to Hand's saloon.] Went to bed at 10 o'clock.

July 7. Muddy, cloudy, and quite cool. A little drizzling rain is falling--the storm is not over yet. I was very busy cleaning up the mess caused by yesterday's rain. No mail stage from the Rio Grande today. A telegram says that General Custer was killed. [General George Custer and his command were wiped out by Sioux warriors on June 25th on the Little Bighorn River in Montana.] Cloudy in the evening. It was so cool at 9 o'clock at night that I was obliged to put on a coat. Went to bed at 10 o'clock.

July 8. Warm, a little cloudy. The Rio Grande mail stage is a long way behind time. It arrived at 11 a.m., but should have been in yesterday. The Cal. mail stage came in at three p.m. The roads are very muddy. Very dull times. Went to bed early.

July 9 (Sunday). Warm morning. I took a bath, changed clothes, and feel tip-top for one who has been drunk for 6 years. I beat Lovejoy twice throwing dice. George Foster and Lovejoy are both mad at the Chinaman [probably Wong Tai, the new owner of the Celestial Restaurant]--it is all about vegetables. George Esslinger and the nigger barber [Charles Glasco] were here after a free drink. I took Esslinger's blankets from him to keep him from pawning them at another saloon for whiskey. Very warm today. Col. [Thomas] Dunn, 8th Infantry, and Lt. Ross, formerly of the U.S. Army, with the Honorable Thomas Banning dropped in my house and took several drinks. Nothing new in the evening. Went to bed early.

July 10. Very warm and sultry. No breeze during the whole day. George Esslinger is still drunk, begging whiskey everywhere. The Rio Grande mail did not come in. The stage left for Cal. Mercury at 1 p.m.--104 degrees. Very warm in the evening and after dark. Went to bed at 10 o'clock.

July 11. Warm and sultry. Mercury at 1 p.m.--104 degrees. The mail stage came from Cal.--received a letter for F. M. Hodges by mistake--returned the letter. I was very sleepy all day. Went to bed at 10 o'clock.

July 12. Today is the anniversary of the Battle of the Boyne. No one noticed it here. Very sultry day. Garrison is drunk. John Davis is drunk. Esslinger is trying to get sober by putting on a clean shirt and bumming more whiskey. There was a dancing party tonight at Major [John] Lord's residence. [Lord was the U.S. Army quartermaster in command of the Tucson depot.] I slept in the yard--very warm.

July 13. Cloudy and hot. 9 a.m.--a little sprinkle of rain. Very sultry all day. Stage arrived with five passengers.

July 14. Cloudy. Flies made me get up too soon. Dick and the black dog were poisoned this morning and died. There was a court-martial today at Camp Lowell. It threatened rain all day. Very sultry. The Rio Grande mail stage came with a big load of mail. Received a paper from J. B. Chesebro and a roll of papers from Milton. Went to bed at 10 o'clock.

July 15. Cool morning. Had breakfast early. Returned to the saloon just in time to miss a shower of rain. 10 o'clock--cleared up for a while. The stage from Cal. came in at 10:30. C. H. Meyer arrived in today's stage. Oscar Buckalew came in from Florence. I received a Utica *Herald* from J. E. Roberts. Nothing very new. Went to bed at 10 o'clock.

July 16 (Sunday). Fine morning. Warm all day. Went to see the goldfish at Meyer's drugstore. [Meyer's goldfish, brought from San Francisco, were the first aquarium fish to be kept in Tucson.] Got tight towards evening. Very warm at night. Had a lady call on me. Slept pretty well.

July 17. Got up early and had a few drinks. Went to breakfast. Called on some lady friends. I am sleepy this morning. Kept quite sober all day. Rooney came to town. Cool in the evening. I slept in the corral.

July 18. Cloudy at sunrise--quite pleasant. Received the news of the death of Toddenworth and Cadotte, killed by Indians. [Renegade Chiricahua Apaches killed these men while they were prospecting in southeastern Arizona.] Stage arrived--no mail for me. Very sultry--cloudy and hot at night. Went to bed at 9 o'clock.

July 19. I was drunk all day. Puck Ryan and Tom McClellan were drunk.

July 20. Stage came--received a letter from Rush. Ryan started for home but lost his horse. I got drunk in the afternoon and went to bed so.

July 21. We had a little rain last night, with heavy thunder. Very warm today. Ryan spent all last night looking for his horse. He did not find him and is going out in the stage. Ryan's horse came in after he left--everything is now all right. I kept sober all day. The Rio Grande mail stage came in very late. Big Jesús and Teresa came back from Camp Grant. There is a big dance at the post tonight--ambulances were running out there all night. A small shower of rain laid the dust well. I went to bed early.

July 22. Cloudy, cool, and pleasant. Dave Burroughs came in last night. I had a talk with him this morning about the fight in which George Toddenworth and Joseph Cadotte were killed. Stage from Cal. arrived--received several papers. Nothing new or interesting. It rained in the evening. Went to bed early.

July 23 (Sunday). Rooney left with Yankee Joe for Pinery. I had a long talk with Pete Kitchen and Col. Dunn. [Pete Kitchen came to Arizona about 1854 and established a farm south of Tucson near the Sonora line. He became famous for stubbornly defending his place against frequent Apache raids.] Jimmy Andrews got tight and played off $110. Hand was slightly drunk this evening. Took a bath in the *acequia* [irrigation ditch]. Went to bed. Very warm--could not sleep.

Women do their laundry in the spring-fed acequia *(irrigation ditch) near Tucson. Buehman photo, Arizona Historical Society, Tucson, #B-187.*

July 24. Warm morning. Sent papers to J. B. Chesebro and J. E. Roberts, also to Billy Gale and Charley White. Very warm and sultry. Jim Douglass was playing monte in the house. He was a 200 dollar loser at one point, but played out a winner. I went to bed at 10 o'clock.

July 25. Warm. Mail stage came in--got several newspapers, very little news. Hand got a little tight. Shorty Holt came to town on business. George Wasley and Sherman had an examination before a judge today and were bound over on 500 dollars bail. We had a sharp shower this afternoon. Went to bed early.

July 26. Sober all day. Very warm--mercury 106 degrees at 1 p.m.

July 27. Warm day. Stage came--brought a *Harper's Weekly* with a picture of the double-headed Democratic tiger, inflation and contraction. Bill Johnson and Lew Elliott came to town in search of Johnson's mule. We had a terrific wind and sand storm late in the evening. Went to bed at 10 o'clock.

July 28. Fine morning. News came by telegraph stating that Indians had run off Morell's stock at Point of Mountain [stage station]. Johnson and Elliott left for Camp Grant this morning. The stage left for California. Col. Dunn left for Yuma with several other officers. Now the report of stock being run off by Indians at Pt. of Mountain is said to be false. Very warm this evening--very hard work to sleep.

July 29. Yankee Joe came down before light this morning and brought our flagstaff. Charley White came in by stage--he looks very thin. I entertained him as well as I could. We had whiskey, soda, and ice cream. Went to bed at 11:30 o'clock.

July 30 (Sunday). Cloudy and warm. 9 a.m.--sunshine and warm. 12 noon--hot as the devil. I went with Charley White to a dance given by Mr. Drumm and his lady. On the way home we met the marshal, who was looking for a man who cut the barber. After resting awhile I saw the marshal again. He told me who was cut--Francisco Martinez. I went to see him--his head was nearly cut off. I helped Dr. Handy fix bandages on him and came home. Went to bed.

July 31. Warm morning. Mail stage left for Cal. Charley went on it to Desert Station. The young fellow who was cut last night is very bad--think he will die. I slept in the yard.

~ ~ ~ ~ ~

August 1. Pleasant morning. Bill Henry came in from [Henry] Hooker's ranch [near Camp Grant] with some cattle. Yankee Joe left for the mountains. I went to see the injured man, Frank, then took a long walk. Called at Sanders' house to see his dog Paddy. Called at several other houses. Passed the evening very well and went to bed in the yard.

Aug. 2. Very warm, cloudy, and sultry. No news today. Stages left and came. There is a petition in circulation to have the feast. [Some stuffy citizens had urged that the San Agustín feast no longer be held, objecting to the many nights of noise and dust. A petition in support of the feast was being circulated by another faction. The traditional celebration was held, but this year the town council moved it from the courthouse plaza to the old military plaza, the former site of Camp Lowell, on the eastern edge of town.] Foster is sick and went home early. Had several ladies call, all wanting to bum a drink--no go. Closed up at 11:30 o'clock.

Aug. 3. Fine morning. Flies drove me up early. I took a working fit and washed everything. Mail stage came--nothing for me. Tom Banning and Staples left this morning to meet some army officers and their wives and take a trip into the Rincon Mountains. Captain Jeffords called on me, and with two others we kept Mr. Foster behind the bar a short time. We had a light sprinkle of rain at 5 in the afternoon. Mrs. Hall called on me this evening. I sat up till 10:30, then went to bed. Very warm.

Aug. 4. Very warm and the flies are terrific. Ate a very hearty breakfast. Lula, John Moore's girl [friend], died today. The stage left. I sent papers to Bill Gale and Charley White. Abe Dunning was released from jail this morning. I went to bed early.

Aug. 5. Flies are very troublesome--I was obliged to get up early. John Moore's girl, Lula, was buried today. Bill Elliott came in town from Florence with his woman to get married by the priest. The stage came--no mail for me. Lovejoy went with his wife to Van Alstine's ranch [at Tanque Verde near Camp Lowell]. I took a long buggy ride this evening with Jack Long. He was full of rot and drove like the devil over brush, adobes, holes, and people. Bill Elliott got a big shanty put on his *cabeza* [head] by John Hovey. Verdict--served him right. Abe Dunning got drunk and was talking in his sleep all evening. I retired at 9 o'clock.

Aug. 6 (Sunday). Fine morning. All are busy going to church. Abe Dunning went to work for Major Lord [the army quartermaster]. It clouded up after noon, but is still very warm. 5 p.m.--the wind commenced blowing. It was quite windy at dark. 8 o'clock--the wind blew all the lights out and we had to shut the doors. 9 o'clock--it is raining good. I went to bed. Foster closed at 10 o'clock.

Aug. 7. The clouds cleared off. Puck Ryan is in town again. Very warm today. Dunning got drunk and got discharged. Puck is decently sober. Bill Elliott left for the Gila. Hand was sober all day. The Rio Grande mail stage arrived at 5:30 o'clock. Cloudy and windy this evening--no rain.

Aug. 8. Still cloudy and quite cool in the morning. No rain yet. Very warm later in the day. Stage from Cal. came in--received a Monterey paper from Billy LaRose, editor and proprietor. Very cloudy and dark in the p.m. I went with Ryan to see his girl. He fell down two or three times on the road. Came home, took a drink, and went to bed. Very hot. Had a nap and a lady in black called on me, after which I slept well all night.

Aug. 9. It rained hard today. Puck Ryan left for Desert Station. Cloudy and cool in the evening. Went to bed early.

Aug. 10. Cool, pleasant morning. McDermott came back from Adamsville [on the Gila River near Florence] yesterday. Jo had five pups this morning. Lovejoy went to get his wife at Van Alstine's ranch. Hayes returned to Tucson. Stage arrived--received a letter from Charley White with money for medicine. Tom Roddick came in from the Yellow Jacket Mine. We all got full. Nigger Jim, who stole Fields' watch, broke out of jail late this evening. Very warm night. Went to bed at 10 o'clock.

Aug. 11. Cloudy. Wrote to Charley White and sent him some medicine. I also wrote to my sisters. The Rio Grande mail stage came in at 1:30 p.m. It rained a little today. Nothing new. No business. Went to bed early.

Aug. 12. Cool morning. Very dull in the house. Stage arrived at 10 a.m.-- received a letter from Hog Davis. He refused to acknowledge receiving the $100,000 sent by myself to him. Charley Conwell came to town. Shorty Holt got a sore head put on himself by a six-footer named Holden. I managed to get drunk by night and went to bed. A lady called on me but I was too drunk to do anything.

Aug. 13 (Sunday). Got up late. Felt bad. Ate a good breakfast. We had several fine showers today. It was cool and cloudy all day. Nothing new or interesting. Went to bed at 9 o'clock.

Aug. 14. Cool and cloudy. We had a light sprinkle of rain. I put up the flagstaff today and raised the Stars and Stripes. Nothing more new today. Went to bed early.

Aug. 15. Fine day. I raised the flag at sunrise in honor of the return of Delegate Stevens. We started out in buggies to meet the Delegate, and met him this side of Whipple's [stage] station [Nine Mile Water Hole, nine miles northwest of town]. He looks well. We all returned. I received a letter from Milton with the news of the death of Emma. Nothing more of note. Went to bed early.

Aug. 16. Jo killed two rats this morning. Still cloudy--it rained very hard last night. Foster is sick and he went home. I closed up at 11 o'clock.

Aug. 17. Mail stage arrived--no letters for me and not much news. The Honorable Hiram S. Stevens called on us. He looks well but is very tired from his long journey [from Washington]. It is cloudy and looks much like rain. No rain until 9 in the evening, then it rained hard nearly all night.

Aug. 18. Warm and cloudy. No rain today. Stage left at 2 p.m. There were rainstorms all around us. Nothing interesting today.

Aug. 19. Still cloudy. I received a roll of papers from Mit, Joliet, Ill. The Rio Grande mail stage arrived late last night. The Cal. mail stage came in-- nothing for me. Still cloudy. Nothing new or strange all day.

Aug. 20 (Sunday). Still cloudy. Very dull and quiet this morning. Report says there is high water and mud everywhere on the roads. Mrs. Drumm and another lady had a fight in the street. Mrs. Drumm was put in jail and fined $8. I went to bed at 10 o'clock.

Aug. 21. Fine morning, clear and pleasant. There was a nice breeze, but it was warm later in the day. Went to bed early and sober.

Aug. 22. Fine cool morning. Stage came in--received a letter from Charley White. Jim Cowan came to town. Steele arrived from the mines. We received the news of the first race between the *Madeline* and the *Dufferin*. Duffer got beat. Went to bed early. [The American yacht *Madeline* defeated the Canadian challenger, *Countess of Dufferin*, in the first race of the fourth America's Cup regatta. The American yacht went on to win the cup.]

Aug. 23. Jesse Aubrey came in from Sonora. I sent a paper to Hog Davis.

Aug. 24. Got up early, had a bath, and put on clean clothes. Had to sew half an hour on a shirt. After breakfast I called on Mr. Ross and borrowed some books. Called on Mrs. Speedy. Mail stage came early--no letters for me. John Burt and Jim McQuinn came in from the mines. Joe Fugit is in town. Tom Roddick also came in town.

Aug. 25. Warm and cloudy. People are still coming to town for the feast. Nothing new.

Aug. 26. Stage arrived--received a letter from Charley White. Jesús Maria Flores shot himself in the forehead and died instantly. I went to bed early and full.

Aug. 27 (Sunday). Attended the funeral of J. M. Flores. Was obliged to walk out to the cemetery and back--very warm. The St. Augustine feast started by the firing of a cannon on the [military] plaza. I took a walk out there in the evening and stayed on the feast ground for two hours. Came home and went to bed.

Aug. 28 (San Agustín's Day). The feast is running red hot, but it is very dull in town. Went to bed early.

Aug. 29. Dull in town. Some horse thieves were arrested today. I went to bed early.

Aug. 30. Nothing is happening in town--very dull. Everyone is on the feast ground.

Aug. 31. Fine morning. Dull in town. Stage came--no letters, no arrivals. I went in company with Jim Douglass to see the performances on the feast ground. Saw a balloon start up. Came home and went to bed.

~ ~ ~ ~ ~

September 1. Drunk.

Sept. 2. Drunk.

Sept. 3 (Sunday). Drunk.

Sept. 4. Drunk. Went to the feast. W. W. Williams won a wagon with no. 47. Joe Phy won a gun with no. 44.

Sept. 5. Very warm. The soldiers were paid and the town is full of them. Mail stage came--no letters for me. John Burt got tight. I went with him to the feast plaza, had supper and some drinks, then came home. The store of Borquez was broken into and some money taken.

Sept. 6. Fine cool morning. There were drunken fellows in the house all day. Bill Morgan and Riley Dunton had a fight in Leatherwood's corral-- Morgan bit off a piece of Riley's ear. Tom Roddick arrived from the Yellow Jacket Mine. Bill Johnson, Jim Hart, and Casey came in from Camp Grant. I went to the feast, had several drinks, came home, and went to bed.

Sept. 7. Got drunk early and kept so all day. Went to the feast ground with Jim Hart. Came home and went to bed.

Sept. 8. Sick. Went to bed.

Sept. 9. Fine day. Kept sober all day. Mail stage came--no letters for me. S. H. Ramsey was shot by a man named Brady at San Carlos. Puck Ryan came to town. I went to the feast plaza with Jim Caldwell at night, stayed an hour. Came home and went to bed.

Sept. 10 (Sunday). Fine morning. Very dull all day. Last night of the feast--I did not go. Went to bed after a bath.

Sept. 11. Got up early. Lovejoy is drunk. I made some calls. Wrote to J. B. Chesebro and sent papers to several people. Puck Ryan is still drunk. The feast people are moving out. Jack Upton is on a bust. Foster has a headache. Fred Myers and Boley came in with the wagon train. Hand was sick and sober all day. Went to bed at 8 o'clock.

Sept. 12. Mail stage came and left for the Rio Grande. We got news of the Hartford horse races. Puck Ryan went home. The gambling was terrific in Hovey's house. Went to bed early.

Sept. 13. Warm morning. 9 o'clock--very warm. Stage left for Cal. Nothing new. Sick. Went to bed early.

Sept. 14. Fine day. Cloudy in the forenoon, then a little rain. Received news of the killing of S. H. Ramsey at San Carlos by Brady. I was sick and took some pills. Went to bed at 8 o'clock.

Sept. 15. Sick all day. Received a telegram reporting that the American rifle team beat everybody [at an international match held at Creedmoor, Long Island, part of the centennial festivities]. Conwell came to town. The Mexican Independence celebration commences this evening with flags flying and other demonstrations, such as firing illuminations [fireworks] and music. A rain commenced in earnest and broke it all up.

Sept. 16. Cloudy. The Mexicans are making great preparations to celebrate. All their stores closed at noon. The big wagon for carrying the little girls turned over. The next misfortune was a very heavy shower which put an end to all pleasure and so closed the day.

Sept. 17 (Sunday). Sick. The independence celebration is bound to come off sooner or later and did come off. The procession marched through town and to Levin's Park. Then there was singing and speech making. They had quite a time but again it rained very hard and wet everyone. Lovejoy had a row with Robertson in our house. Then Charley Conwell got on a high horse and wanted to kill anyone who would say his name was not Conwell.

Sept. 18. Conwell and McQuinn left. The Rio Grande mail stage brought news of 2 men killed at old Camp Wallen [near Camp Huachuca] by Indians. A Mexican was shot in the street after dark--he is thought to be one of the men who killed Sawyer [in Sonora in November 1875].

Sept. 19. Fine morning. Stage came early--no mail for me. Charley White and Billy Keegan came in. I ate very little dinner. Went to bed at 9.

Sept. 20. Lovejoy leaves for the mountains today. He brought Tinker [dog] back--he is very thin.

Sept. 21. Sick in bed nearly all day

Sept. 22. Sick in bed.

Sept. 23. Some better. Still in bed.

Sept. 24 (Sunday). Sick all day.

Sept. 25. Getting better. Billy Keegan left with J. T. Smith. Wiley, Hovey, Judge Mabbitt, and others left for the Feast of Magdalena. [The town of Magdalena, Sonora, 50 miles south of the border, held its own annual celebration beginning a few days before October 4, the feast day of San Francisco de Asís (Saint Francis of Assisi). Like the feast at Tucson, the Magdalena celebration was an amalgam of religious observances and riotous merrymaking, attracting both revelers and pious pilgrims from many miles around. While Tucson's annual feast has withered in modern times, Magdalena's continues undiminished.]

Sept. 26. Feel much better this morning. Stage came in--got some papers but no letters.

Sept. 27. Fine cool morning. Wrote to J. B. Chesebro and Mit, and sent papers.

Sept. 28. The stage brought 11 passengers, no mail for me. Went to bed sick.

Sept. 29. The games ran all night at Hovey's. Jim McNabb and Ike Brokaw had a row there during the night. Hopkins and Cooler had a fight in the Gem Saloon.

Sept. 30. Everyone got drunk. I received no mail today. Whipple took his dog home. Van Alstine got drunk and lost his boots and hat. I went to bed early.

~ ~ ~ ~ ~

October 1 (Sunday). Ate quite hearty. Took a bath. Went to bed early.

Oct. 2. Warm day. Very dull in the house. The politicians are getting awake. [A general election was scheduled for November 7 and political campaigning was getting underway.] Old Gay is drunk. Jim Douglass and John Miller are very tight.

Oct. 3. Fine morning. Got up very early and took a long walk. Felt well all day--drank very little whiskey. Goodrich started out electioneering. Stage came--no mail for me. Very dull. Went to bed at 9 o'clock.

Oct. 4. Got up early and had a long walk. Felt quite well.

Oct. 5-11. Nothing of interest.

Oct. 12. Cloudy. No telegrams--the wires are down. Oury's saloon opened yesterday. Stevens is in town. Politics is getting warm. I had a talk with Hiram Stevens. Spent the day moving my bed and fixing up my new room. Went to bed early.

Oct. 13. Worked all day fixing up my room. My fingers were sore from lime. Slept in the new room for the first time.

Oct. 14. Fine day. Stage came in early--no letters for me. I fixed the doors and hung curtains. Tom McClellan took Tinker home with him. There was a dance tonight at Brown's woman's private house. I did not go.

Oct. 15 (Sunday). Fine morning. 9 a.m.--cloudy. 4 p.m.--rain. It rained very hard from dark until late at night. It is very uncommon to see such rain at this season of the year. Foster got full and slept from 6 to 9:30 at night. I shut up the house and went to bed.

Oct. 16. Cloudy and cold. There was a little rain this morning. The Honorable John Titus died at 11 a.m. [Titus was chief justice of the Arizona supreme court from 1870 to 1874. He died of typhoid fever which was making its rounds in Tucson.] The mail stage left for Cal. I sent papers to Mit, J. B. Chesebro, and P. R. Brady, and wrote to John Bartleson. Went to bed at 9 o'clock. Gamblers and drunkards filled the street all night.

Oct. 17. Very cold this morning. The funeral of Judge Titus was held at 10 a.m. The chaplin from the post performed the service which was held at the courthouse. He was buried in the military cemetery.

Oct. 18. Cool and pleasant. I am fixing and cleaning.

Oct. 19. The stage came--no mail from Cal. Nothing new.

Oct. 20. Cold morning. Nothing new except more candidates for county offices.

Oct. 21. Cold. Nothing but politics.

Oct. 22 (Sunday). Politics, nothing more.

Oct. 23. Very cold morning. Nothing but electioneering.

Oct. 24. Colder. The stage came in with some passengers. Nothing new. Van Alstine is full of politics but gives up on the election. Jim Quinlin arrived. I went to bed early.

Oct. 25. Ross has been sick but is getting well. Esslinger is still drunk. Roddick, White, and Stroud arrived from the mines. I got a letter and a photograph from Hog Davis.

Oct. 26. The stage came. Politics is getting warm. H. S. Stevens arrived from Florence. I got drunk and retired early.

This is the earliest photograph known of a Tucson scene. It was taken by an itinerant photographer in December 1871 in front of the Pima County courthouse. The men in the photo are the defendants, jurors, and court officials involved in the Camp Grant Massacre murder trial (all of the defendants were acquitted). The tall man in the foreground is John Titus, then chief justice of the Arizona supreme court. The adobe courthouse, built in 1868, was replaced with a two-story brick one in 1882. Arizona Historical Society, Tucson, #654.

Oct. 27. The candidates are out walking around today. Captain Gay is electioneering hard. Hand got full as a goose. I left for a walk early in the evening and went to all of the saloons. Drank and ate several lunches at Levin's. Got fuller and drunker. Made a contract in fun with Maloney for a bull, he to get a pup. I started for home, then followed a lady home. I arrived at my room very late and very full of rye.

Oct. 28. Cool. The stage arrived and brought some passengers. Stroud got drunk as a fool. There was a big dance at Chata's tonight. I was sober all day. Went to bed early.

Oct. 29 (Sunday). Fine morning. Very dull in the house until noon. Then Jerry Kenny and Bill Kirkland came to town. A few candidates came around and Jerry, Hand, and Co. got full. Circus this evening. There is free lunch at the Palace Saloon. Went to bed at 10:30 o'clock.

Oct. 30. Quite cold. Very dull all day. Had a lunch at night. Van Alstine sent in 5 gals. of buttermilk from his ranch.

Oct. 31. Colder. There was a funeral today of a child who was burned to a crisp in bed. Several telegrams came today--one says Oury will win, another says Stevens, the next one says Hardy will carry everything. [The race for delegate to the U.S. Congress was a hot one. Granville Oury (Phoenix), Hiram Stevens (the incumbent from Tucson), and William Hardy (Hardyville) were running and each had considerable support.] Roddick left to look at some mines. I put up the stove this evening. Went to bed at 10 o'clock.

~ ~ ~ ~ ~

November 1. Very cold. The boys are beating Hovey's faro game down the street. Sam Hughes says that Stevens will come out O.K. A few candidates came in here this evening. I went to bed early.

Sam Hughes' home on north Main Street. Hughes owned one of the first windmills for pumping water to be installed in southern Arizona. The man on the right is Hiram S. Stevens, and Hughes is second from the right. They were brothers-in-law. Photo taken by Henry Buehman in 1874. Arizona Historical Society, Tucson, #BD-144.

Nov. 2. Cool and pleasant. The stage came. Nothing new. Went to bed early.

Nov. 3. Very lively for talk, but no money in the till.

Nov. 4. The stage arrived--no letters for me.

Nov. 5 (Sunday). Everyone is drunk. It is a very busy time. Van Alstine is drunk.

Nov. 6. Van Alstine left for San Pedro. Business is quite lively. Telegrams about the election are coming all the time. Everyone is jubilant or drunk. There were shouts, music, and parading through the streets all night.

Nov. 7. The ball opens this morning in earnest. Some are vexed, others are in a good humor. The polls closed at sundown. I went to bed at 11:30 o'clock. It took until 3 o'clock tomorrow morning to count the votes here.

Nov. 8. All sorts of rumors are afloat. Some telegrams say that Tilden carried several northern states, others say Hayes has got them all.

Nov. 9. There was great excitement today. Telegrams were coming all day. It was reported this evening that ballot boxes were broken into in Florida, stopping the counting of the election returns there. [Voting irregularities in Florida and other states threw the 1876 presidential election into a state of chaos. The winner was not determined until March 1877.]

Nov. 10. All is quiet this morning. A report now says that Hardy is leading, Stevens 2nd, and Oury sucks the hind teat. Nothing definite is heard.

Nov. 11. Warm and cloudy. The stage came in--no letters for me. Telegrams were coming all day but nothing reliable. Red Brown got put in jail. Roddick and others left on the track of Dimmett [an outlaw]. Stroud left for Globe City [120 miles north of Tucson]. It was dark and very cloudy at 9 in the evening. I went to bed at 10 o'clock.

Nov. 12 (Sunday). Damp and muddy. It rained from 12 last night till morning, stopping at daylight. A woman brought her new baby in the house this afternoon. I went to bed at 10 o'clock.

Nov. 13. Cloudy and rainy. The telegraph wires are down--no news.

Nov. 14. Fine morning. Vic took on another dog for the first time. John Clark and Melvin came in from Florence. Roddick came back--they did not find Dimmett. Stevens is reported elected, also Hayes and Wheeler.

Nov. 15. Worked nearly all day on my scrapbook. The election returns reported from Yavapai County this evening say Oury is elected. *Quien sabe?* [Who knows?] I went to a dance and came home full.

Nov. 16. Warm and pleasant. Stage came in--no news. None of the telegrams about the election is reliable. No one knows who is in and who is out. There is lots of talk of trouble in the States. Sidney Carpenter married Tomasa Meyer this evening. I kept sober all day and went to bed so.

Nov. 17. Very cold this morning, but when the sun came out it was warm enough. The stage left for Cal. No returns yet from many election precincts. I went to bed early.

Nov. 18. Stage came in--no mail for me, the news is all old. Nothing new. Dull times.

Nov. 19 (Sunday). Cold, clear, and pleasant. A report now says Hayes and Wheeler are elected. Stevens also. It was warm in the middle of the day, cold at night. Went to bed early.

Nov. 20. Sent a money order for $3.00 to Currier & Ives in N.Y. for a picture of Rysdyk's Hambletonian [the great trotting horse]. Tom McClellan had a row with Ike Brokaw and got licked. Everyone got drunk today. I went to bed at 12 o'clock.

Nov. 21. Fine morning. 12 noon--windy. Stage came in--no election news. I received two letters from J. B. Hart. L. C. Hughes arrived on the stage, also Fatty Curtis. I kept sober all day. Felt sick and went to bed early.

Nov. 22. Sent papers to J. B. Hart, Virginia City, Nev. Fine day but windy after 12 o'clock, and very dusty all evening. There was a dance at Hovey's saloon tonight. It rained all night till 3 in the morning.

Nov. 23. The stage came in with several passengers. I received a letter from sister Mira Roberts. Gibson came in. Nothing new.

Nov. 24. Cold. Nothing new about the election. Dull in the house today. I got pretty full of stuff. Stayed up till midnight.

Nov. 25. Very cold morning. No election news yet. The stage came in at 10:30 a.m. Jerry Kenny left for Camp Grant. Lazy Bob came to town. The monte game ran all night at Hovey's saloon.

Nov. 26 (Sunday). Fine morning. Took a bath and put on clean clothes. Took a few drinks. Went to the circus with Gibson. Went to bed at 10:30 o'clock.

Nov. 27. Fine day. Wrote to Tom Britton, Altar, Sonora. Willis B. Morgan came in with his crutches. Tom McClellan came up looking well--he was sober all day. Lovejoy arrived from Sonora this evening. I went to bed at 10 o'clock.

Nov. 28. Cold. Morgan went to work keeping books for Smith the butcher, but he got drunk first. We received news that Hardy is elected. Lovejoy was arrested and placed under a 6,000-dollar bond to appear tomorrow. [Charles Lovejoy, the assistant postmaster, was accused of embezzlement.]

Nov. 29. Cold morning. Got some buttermilk today. Jeffords, Stevens, Sweeney, and Ad Linn left for home. Lovejoy was around this morning, waiting for 10 o'clock to make his appearance before Judge Osborn. There was an auction sale at the store of E. N. Fish & Co.

Nov. 30. Thanksgiving Day. The stores are all closed. No excitement. The mail coach came--no mail for me.

~ ~ ~ ~ ~

December 1. Very dull in the house. Hovey and Mabbitt left for Yuma. I got full and went to bed early.

Dec. 2. Had an introduction to Jack Swartz. John T. Smith came in from his farm with vegetables. The U.S. mail stage arrived--no mail for me. The Feast of San Xavier commences today. [The San Xavier del Bac church was located about ten miles south of Tucson. The mission was established in the 1690s by the Jesuit missionary Eusebio Francisco Kino to serve Papago (Tohono O'odham) Indians living nearby. The magnificent church so familiar to present-day Arizonans was erected in the late 1700s by the Franciscan order. It had fallen into a state of disrepair in Hand's day, and had no clergy. Nonetheless, the structure was a noted landmark, and the annual feast of San Francisco Xavier (December 3) was still observed by the people in the area. San Xavier del Bac church has since been refurbished and is used as a place of worship by the Tohono O'odham.] I was sober all day, sick at night. Went to bed early.

Dec. 3 (Sunday). Fine morning. Everybody is getting ready for the feast at the mission of San Xavier. 12 noon--the town is empty. Very dull. Went to bed early.

Dec. 4. Fine day. The stage from the Rio Grande came in--received some papers. Stage left for Cal. Dull all day. Butler married the daughter of T. G. Rusk--they held a dance in the evening.

Dec. 5. Stage came in early--received a letter from J. B. Hart, and several papers from others. Nothing important today except the arrival of John Wasson and his wife. The Feast of San Xavier closed today. Hayes and Wheeler are reported to be elected for sure.

Dec. 6. Cold morning. No excitement in town. Nothing new but the surety of the election of Hayes and Wheeler, also Stevens as delegate. [Hiram Stevens was confirmed the winner of the race for delegate to the U.S. Congress from Arizona. Rutherford B. Hayes would have to wait several months before he assumed the office of president.] Stage left--I sent papers to Bill Gale.

Dec. 7. Fine day. Stage came--no mail for me. Hayes is elected sure thing. Smith opened a monte game in our room this evening. Foster was up all night. Van Alstine brought in a jug of buttermilk from his ranch. I went to bed at 10 o'clock.

Dec. 8. Cold. Van Alstine is still in town and is full of mescal, talking politics and mourning the fate of Tilden and Hendricks. Henry Hooker and his family came to town. Nothing new today. Went to bed at 10 o'clock.

Dec. 9. Fine day. Cold. The stage came in very late--no letters for me. There was a dance tonight at Kendall's club (whore house). I went to Levin's, heard some very good singing, drank a few glasses of beer, came home, and went to bed at 11:30 o'clock.

Dec. 10 (Sunday). Fine cool morning. Everyone is going to church. Nothing new except some boys playing marbles in front of the church door. I took a bath and took cold. At night I went to Levin's, from there to a dance. Came home and went to bed.

Dec. 11. Very dull. The monte game opened early in the house--Smith had a good game all day. Hand got drunk. Went to bed at 11:30 o'clock. Smith's monte game ran nearly all night.

Dec. 12. The stage came in and brought two hungry ladies from Prescott. I received a letter from J. B. Hart.

Dec. 13. Nothing new. Van Alstine came in with butter and buttermilk. Very dull all day.

Dec. 14. Stage came in. Nothing new.

Dec. 15. Sober. I drank buttermilk all day, no whiskey. The monte game ran till 4 in the morning. Charley White's girl [friend] died.

Dec. 16. Fine morning. The stage came in early--no through mail. A gun was raffled off at Sanders' saloon--Jerry Kenny won it. I went to bed at 11 o'clock. The monte game ran all night.

Dec. 17 (Sunday). Fine morning. We had some excitement--Buttner's team ran away with him, and a horse pulling another buggy ran away out of control. No damage. Smith's monte game lost last night. Very dull in the house this evening. Went to bed at 10 o'clock.

Dec. 18. Very dull. No papers to read. Puck Ryan arrived from Sonora. Stage left for Cal.

Dec. 19. Stage came--no through mail. Jim Simpson got on his gin, knocked a Mexican down, and a short time after he was shot in the back by someone from outside the house. We took him home--he was very drunk. I went to bed at 1 o'clock.

Dec. 20. Simpson is doing very well. I wrote to H. S. Stevens today. Got full of whiskey. Went to bed at 11 o'clock.

Dec. 21. Stage came from Cal.--no through mail.

Dec. 22. The mail came from the east and I received my picture of Rysdyk's Hambletonian, also a letter from my sister Mira Roberts.

Dec. 23. Stage came in--very little mail. I washed out the house. Got quite full at night. Called on Pancha a few moments ($10.00). Went to bed early.

Dec. 24 (Sunday, Christmas Eve). Fine day. Very dull in the house until night when everyone got full of whiskey. Fighting was then the order of the day--there were several fights and more fighting talk. I went to church at midnight. The streets were full of drunken men all night. Went to bed at 1:30 o'clock.

Dec. 25 (Christmas Day). Lots of eggnog. Everyone got drunk again but there was no fighting. All was quiet in the house. Very dull. Sent to Currier & Ives for two more pictures.

Dec. 26. Coldest morning of the season. The mail stage came in early--not much mail. Lish is drunk. Everyone is drunk. No fights.

Dec. 27. The weather is moderate. Got the picture of Hambletonian in a frame and hung up. Went to Levin's with Jerry Kenny. Called on a lady. Came home, went to bed.

Dec. 28. Moderate weather. Stage came--very little mail. Several people arrived from Prescott--Bob P., Johnny Dobbs, and others. Dull day. Went to bed early.

Dec. 29. Nothing new.

Dec. 30. Stage came--brought very little mail.

Dec. 31 (Sunday, New Year's Eve). Fine day. There were several dances this evening. Went to bed tight at 10 o'clock. So closed the old year.

~ ~ ~ ~ ~

Dr. John C. Handy stands in the doorway of his office. He led the battle against the smallpox epidemic that ravaged Tucson in 1877. Arizona Historical Society, Tucson, #28383.

Chapter Three

SMALLPOX COMES TO TUCSON--1877

"William Teague died today of black measles--called smallpox by the doctor."
George Hand, January 31, 1877

The year 1877 saw continued attacks by Chiricahua Apaches on settlers and prospectors in Arizona, but a far more deadly foe appeared in the territory. Smallpox swept through the Southwest taking a terrible toll. Many of the victims were children, but the pioneers were used to disease outbreaks and bore their grief stoically. It will never be known how many Native Americans died, but their losses were undoubtedly very large. The number of people killed on both sides during the Indian wars was tiny compared to those carried away by disease epidemics.

~ ~ ~ ~ ~

January 1, 1877 (New Year's Day). Fine day. We stuffed a wild turkey and baked it in the baker's oven. Jerry Kenny ate dinner with us. The legislature met and adjourned. [The ninth territorial legislature, the last one to meet in Tucson, was getting underway.] I went to a dance in the evening. Went to bed at 10 o'clock.

Jan. 2. Stage arrived--no mail for me. The N.Y. papers are 3 weeks behind. Everyone is blue today. The legislature met and did some business. Hand got full at night.

Jan. 3. Very windy, terrible dusty, and cold. A new dance house started up. I drank nothing but buttermilk all day. Went to bed sober.

Jan. 4. Fine day. Stage came in--brought some mail. Many drunken men are around. Lovejoy is drunk. I went to bed early.

Jan. 5. Warm and pleasant. The gambling was plenty in the house-- Smith's faro game was busted. Blade and others were drunk.

Jan. 6. Cold. Stage arrived early--L. M. Jacobs came in on it. 10 o'clock-- very pleasant and warm. I was sober all day. Judge Mabbitt arrived today. I received the Christmas no. of the *Spirit of the Times*. Went to bed at 9 o'clock.

Jan. 7 (Sunday). Fine morning. Mollie Monroe was arrested for wearing men's clothes and put in jail. [Mollie Monroe was one of the most fascinating women to enliven the Arizona frontier. She first came to the territory in 1864 as the 18-year-old bride of a young army officer stationed at Fort Whipple near Prescott. Despite her cultured New England upbringing, Mollie soon left her husband and took up with a rough prospector named George Monroe. She used his last name thereafter, although she had numerous other consorts. Over the years, Mollie become a singular figure in the territory--prospecting, fighting Indians, and drinking and gambling in the saloons with the boys. She always dressed in men's clothes (but did not impersonate a man) and was as tough as any male frontiersman. However, in the late 1800s many communities had ordinances prohibiting the wearing of clothes typical of the opposite sex. In many places it was not until the early twentieth century that laws were amended to allow women to wear pants or overalls in public. Of course, the wearing of women's clothes by men remained against the law until recently, the practice universally being regarded as perverse.] 12 noon--I called on Sam Hughes but he was not at home. I came home and raised the American flag in honor of the anniversary of the Battle of New Orleans.

Jan. 8. At daylight my flag was seen at half-mast. People were astonished to see it so. On inquiry they found that General Andrew Jackson was dead. Nothing new today. Mollie Monroe called on me twice. I went to bed early.

Jan. 9. Matt Bledsoe was killed this morning in Hovey and Brown's Ohio Saloon by Tom Kerr. He was shot through the body and above the right temple--lived over an hour. Sheriff Shibell took Kerr and lodged him in jail. Our house was open all night--Foster did not go to bed. I made several calls around town with Mollie Monroe and retired at 11 o'clock.

Jan. 10. Fine morning. Jo ran off on a jamboree. I found her in a field behind the flour mill with some other dogs. Brought her home and locked her in the dog jail. Bledsoe was buried at 10 o'clock. The stage left. Lew Davis and some others left for Phoenix. I went to bed at 9 o'clock.

Jan. 11. Warm and cloudy. Stage came in--I got some papers, no letters. Kerr's trial is continuing today. 12 noon--the trial is not through yet. 4 p.m.-- the court adjourned--Kerr was cleared and turned loose.

Jan. 12. Nothing new except the arrest of William Forney on suspicion of beating R. C. Brown. He was put in jail. [Newspaper man Rollin C. Brown was attacked from behind on a dark street and savagely beaten. He did not see his assailant. Brown was Forney's boss.] Cuff came in from Camp Grant.

Jan. 13. Stage came in--lots of passengers, very little mail. Forney's examination began at 5 p.m. [William Forney, a printer employed by the *Arizona Citizen*, was ordered held in jail pending trial. His bail was set at $500.] There is a dance at the Club House this evening. Justice Neugass' court adjourned at 9 o'clock. I went to bed at 10.

Jan. 14 (Sunday). Fine day. It rained in the morning, cleared off at 11 a.m. Several of the boys got drunk. I went to a dance in the evening--no one killed. Went to bed early.

Jan. 15. Cold and windy. Stage left for Cal. Vic had three pups. Jo is still in the calaboose. I went to court again this evening. A suit of Williams against Sanford is now being tried. Sullivan came in from Camp Grant. I went to bed at 10 o'clock.

Jan. 16. Stage arrived--no mail for me. Everyone is drunk. Bill Gale arrived from Florence. Hand was drunk all day. Went to bed early.

Jan. 17. The Rio Grande mail stage came in. Many of the boys are drunk. No fights, no one killed. The Cal. stage left. Mollie is very crazy today. [Later in the year, 31-year-old Mollie Monroe was declared insane and sent to the Langdon and Clark Asylum in Stockton, California. She was the first Arizona woman confined because of insanity. Upon completion of the territorial insane asylum in Phoenix in 1887, she was transferred there. Mollie was never released and died in Phoenix in 1902.]

Jan. 18. The stage came in from Cal.--no mail for me. Nothing new.

Jan. 19. Got up early. Feel bad. Ate no breakfast. Bill Munson came into town. I kept sober all day. Received some papers from M. F. Hand. Joe G's monte game closed in the house at 8 o'clock. I went to bed.

Jan. 20. Cloudy. Street cleaning makes it dusty. There was some heavy drinking today down in the two-story house [the Palace Hotel]. There was a musical concert all night in our house. Principal singers--C. V. D. Lovejoy, W. B. Morgan, and Tom Roddick. I got no sleep until 2 in the morning.

Jan. 21 (Sunday). Fine morning. Very dull in our house. The new skating rink is going full blast. There was dancing there in the evening--I had a few dances. Came home at 12 o'clock. Slept well. [A man named F.G. Wentworth had opened a roller-skating rink on Meyer Street. The venture failed and Wentworth left town in March.]

Jan. 22. My father's birthday. Fine morning. Roddick is drunk again. The Rio Grande stage came in. I wrote to my sister Mira. Bill Gale, Joe Elliott, and Charley White got on a drunken spree. Billy went to bed. Charley was very hostile and got on the warpath. He said he could lick any man or other son-of-a-bitch in the world. He wrote and sent a challenge to Bill Gale to mortal combat.

Jan. 23. Fine day. Mail stage came--received only papers. Tom Roddick got bulldozed today. The duel between White and Gale did not go. Dull day. Went to bed early.

Jan. 24. Very quiet and dull. Moderate weather. Nothing new.

Jan. 25. Fine day. Roddick got drunk again. Kirby left for the mines. Stage came in--no mail. Early to bed.

Jan. 26. Jerry Kenny and Charley White got me up very early--they were up all night and are drunk this morning. Very pleasant day. John Fitzgerald-- "Jack the Nailer"--came in from Florence this afternoon. Charley White got drunk again and got mad at me. He left the house in disgust. I hope he will stay away.

Jan. 27. The stage came in from Cal.--not much mail. There is a dance at the skating rink and several other dances in other parts of town. There was a show in back of Hovey's saloon this evening. Jack the Nailer is drunk. Morgan also. I went to bed early.

Jan. 28 (Sunday). Fine day. There were both Catholic and Protestant church services this morning. [The first Protestant congregation in Tucson (Presbyterian) was organized the previous month, with the Reverend John E. Anderson as pastor. Their services were held at the county courthouse prior to construction of a church building in 1879.] There were chicken fights in the middle of the day, a circus in the evening. [Don Severo Murillo's "Grand Spanish Circus" had come to town from Sonora.] I took a walk in the evening with Linn and Marsh. There was a high-toned Mexican dance upstairs in the brick house [Palace Hotel]. There were several other dances in town. Went to bed at 9:30 o'clock.

Jan. 29. The first news this morning is the killing of a girl in the upper part of town. It rained this morning. Someone stole Foster's horse. The sheriff has gone after the thief. The coroner's jury only found the girl dead. The sheriff did not find the thief or the horse.

Jan. 30. Cloudy and damp. 9 a.m.--the sun came out quite pleasant. Stage arrived--very little news. I was sober all day.

Jan. 31. Holt and Sander's saloon commenced moving. William Teague died today of black measles--called smallpox by the doctor. [Teague had recently come to town from Los Angeles, apparently bringing his infection with him. This was the first death from smallpox in Tucson since 1870.] There was a meeting of the Democrats this evening at legislation hall. They adjourned until Saturday, to meet then at the courthouse. [The Democrats were struggling to reorganize and revitalize their party within the territory.] I went to bed early.

~ ~ ~ ~ ~

February 1. The stage came in very early bringing the notorious Hog Davis and Mr. C. O. Brown. I went to hear Mr. Autrim lecture and show his trained horse, Little Fred. He is a very pretty horse and well trained. Mr. Autrim is, in my opinion, a smart man, but I think his education is very limited for a veterinarian. Jim Blade had a hearing today. He is accused of shooting Simpson [in Hand's saloon in December]. He did not do it. I went to bed early.

Feb. 2. Cloudy. Mr. Dave Davis is still here. He has a little business with the governor and legislature about a divorce. [The territorial legislature had the power to grant divorces.] He will perhaps return to Florence in a few weeks. Very dull today. A telegram says that the U.S. Congress met and counted the Alabama vote--Tilden is ahead so far. Jeffords is very drunk. Sweeney also. I went to a dance this evening. Got to bed at 9 o'clock.

Feb. 3. Received a letter from Currier & Ives stating that they had sent the picture of Lucy [a racehorse]. Dave Davis is still here. Fine day, very warm.

Feb. 4 (Sunday). Church services today, both Catholic and Protestant. Also chicken fights and a circus. Davis had a fit.

Feb. 5. The stage left. Fatty Curtis, Col. Boyle, and others left on it for Cal. The Democrats are meeting at the courthouse. There was so much wrangling and talking that they were obliged to adjourn till Thursday evening. Bill Morgan came in exhausted, his horse very much fatigued. He tells of the massacre of a number of people on Sonoita Creek by Indians, and the running off of their stock. Dave Davis had a fit again today.

Feb. 6. Mail stage came--nothing for me.

Feb. 7. Mail stage came from the Rio Grande. I got drunk today. The Democrats are getting scared, the Republicans are in good spirits.

Feb. 8. Stage came--no mail for me. I was sober all day. The Democrats are to meet this evening.

Feb. 9. The stage left--several passengers are going to Prescott. [The legislature had adjourned and legislators were going home.] Sam Miller bought a big load of wood and piled it in the street. He set fire to it after dark and placed a quarter of beef on it. We had roast beef with music and singing. The evening passed off fine. Went to bed at 10 o'clock.

Feb. 10. It rained and it is cold and muddy. More people left for Prescott today. Stage came--very few letters. Rainy this evening. I went to bed.

Feb. 11 (Sunday). Rainy and very muddy. Davis still under the influence of liquor. I refused Lovejoy a free drink and he went off mad. I took a hot bath. 2 p.m.--still cloudy and a little rain. 6 p.m.--it rained like thunder. Went to bed early.

Feb. 12. Very muddy but pleasant. A telegram came from Cal. stating that the Florida vote was counted for Hayes. The Democrats talk of war. I went to bed early.

Feb. 13. Pleasant day. The mud is drying up. Lovejoy was arrested and put in jail [charged with embezzling from the post office]. Forney was released from jail--the [assault] charges against him were dropped. The stage came in at 8 o'clock in the evening. I closed at 2 o'clock.

Feb. 14. St. Valentine's Day. Lovejoy is still in jail and is very disconsolate. Nothing new today.

Feb. 15. Yankee Joe is still drunk. Stage came--no mail for me. Dave Davis is drunk. Foster was up all night.

Feb. 16. Cloudy. The Rio Grande mail stage came--I got lots of papers, and a picture of Lexington [a racehorse] from Currier & Ives. Dr. Lord took his pup home. I went to bed at 10 o'clock.

Feb. 17. Windy, cloudy, and cold. Stage came in--no mail for me. Davis and others are drunk. I went to bed early.

Feb. 18 (Sunday). The church is busy today. Circus in the evening. The house was open all night.

Feb. 19. Pleasant morning. Lovejoy is on trial today--he came down to the house. Roddick and Puck Ryan arrived. Puck is very lame.

Feb. 20. Fine morning. Stage came in from Cal.--I got no mail. Roddick and others got drunk. Dobbs beat a fellow at seven-up--won $10. Lovejoy's trial is still going on. Mr. Favorite lost a due bill and a Mexican found it and drew some of it. He sold the balance to Jim Andrews who sent Forney to draw the balance. Forney was then put in jail for having the money order, but was immediately released.

This Currier and Ives portrait of "Lexington, the great monarch of the turf and sire of racers," helped brighten the interior of George Hand's saloon.

Feb. 21. Fine weather. The case of Lovejoy is still in court. Puck Ryan left for Sweeney's stage station [at Picacho, 50 miles northwest of town]. Dobbs left on the stage also. Lovejoy's case went to the jury at 4 p.m. 5 p.m.--the jury went to supper. The knowing ones say that they stand 11 for conviction, 1 for acquittal. The jury sent out for blankets. Green Rusk is drunk and gambling, has more money than he knows what to do with. I give him 2 weeks to get broke. Dave Davis is drunk. I went to bed early.

Feb. 22. Washington's Birthday. Fine morning. I put up the flag at daylight. The Stars and Stripes spread beautifully. The jury in the case of Lovejoy is still in their room, still 11 to 1. Mr. John Bedford arrived this morning.

Feb. 23. Nothing new. The trial of Lovejoy on a 2nd indictment resulted in his conviction. The jury was out only 5 minutes this time. Dave Davis opened a monte game in the house.

Feb. 24. Stage came in--received a letter and a fine specimen of Silver King silver ore from Col. Boyle. Also received news of the counting of the Oregon vote in favor of Hayes and Wheeler. Frank Sullivan arrived. Davis and McDermott had a fight. There were big dances at two places tonight. I attended one and danced till 11 o'clock. Came home and went to bed.

Feb. 25 (Sunday). Got up early and felt bully. Ate a good breakfast. Drank very little today. Church services were held at the courthouse. There were chicken fights in the afternoon. Green Rusk's birds won three fights. He then got full of beer. McDermott shows a queer mug--he is scratched all over his face. There were several rain showers today. Another dance tonight at the house of Little Jesús.

Feb. 26. Cloudy and rainy. Several of the boys are intoxicated. The trial of McDermott [charged with assault] was very short. Verdict--acquittal. John Bedford and several others got drunk. I found myself a little under the influence of the extract. T. G. Rusk left for San Francisco by stage--he says if he likes the town he will buy it. I went to bed at 10 o'clock.

Feb. 27. It rained nearly all last night. Still cloudy and very muddy. A Mexican was found guilty of stealing mules. 12 noon--the sun shines a little. The stage arrived--very little mail. Dave Davis is very drunk. Jim Blade is on the warpath. Esslinger is on a spree. Charley Conwell came back from San Carlos. It rained nearly all day. I went to bed early and sober.

Feb. 28. Pleasant day. The jury is excused for the term. The boys are all sober. The Rio Grande mail stage came in. I bought a dog from Esslinger for one drink.

~ ~ ~ ~ ~

March 1. Fine cool morning. Thomas McClellan left for Adamsville. Tom Roddick is sober. The stage came in--very little mail. The first number of the *Tucson Daily Bulletin* was published today. [Founded by Carlos Tully, the *Tucson Daily Bulletin* became the *Arizona Weekly Star* in a few months. The *Star* was Democratic in political orientation, the *Arizona Citizen*, founded in Tucson in 1870 by R. C. McCormick and John Wasson, was Republican. The *Star* was acquired by Louis C. Hughes in June 1877, and ownership transferred to A. E. Fay in August 1877. Hughes re-acquired the paper in December 1878 and ran it for many years. John Wasson was still owner and editor of the *Citizen*, but now in partnership with Rollin C. Brown.]

Mar. 2. Fine morning. A telegram brings notice that Hayes and Wheeler were finally declared elected [president and vice president] at 3 o'clock this morning. Flags went up immediately on several houses. There was some little drinking and talking, and several cases of bulldozing, Marsh and Morgan particularly. Dave Davis went in with them.

Mar. 3. Fine morning. Roddick and Sullivan left for the mines. The stage arrived--Paige came in from San Francisco. Jerry Kenny was appointed deputy jailor by the U.S. marshal to watch Lovejoy. Dave Davis is drunk. Hand was sober all day. A paper was circulated for subscriptions to buy powder to celebrate the election of Hayes and Wheeler on Monday. I went to bed at 10 o'clock.

Mar. 4 (Sunday). Pleasant day. The church was open in the morning. There were cockfights and a circus in the afternoon and evening.

Mar. 5. Guns commenced firing at 9 o'clock this morning and continued until sundown. There were some cases of intoxication. I wrote to my sister Mira. No news today. Went to bed early.

Mar. 6. Fine morning. A *Citizen* extra came out early giving the proceedings at the inauguration of Hayes and Wheeler. It included Hayes' inaugural address. That settles all the trouble.

Mar. 7. My 47th birthday. Fine morning. 10 a.m.--it commenced blowing hard and dust and papers fly every way. One little boy killed another yesterday with a pistol by accident. Jerry Kenny, Ad Linn, and Charley Conwell left for the mines. A telegram says that Matilda Heron [a famous actress] died today in New York.

Mar. 8. Fine morning. Dickson came in from Picacho Station and had a good drink. Bedford had a drunken fight with Frank Francis. I received a letter from J. B. Hart.

Mar. 9. Very quiet this morning. Some of the boys got on the drink toward noon. Mr. Bedford, being full of liquor, made a row with old Dick. Foster hit Bedford in the neck and put him out of doors. I was sick all day with a sore throat. Went to bed early.

Mar. 10. Fine morning. Stage came early--received some papers and a letter from Mira with a photo of Emma. Went to bed at 9 o'clock.

Mar. 11 (Sunday). Fine warm morning. My cough is better. The church bells are ringing very loud. The circus band and animals are parading through the streets. There is a Presbyterian church service today. Also a Mormon service in the evening. Wrote to J. B. Hart. Bill Warford won $80 at monte last night beginning with only $2.00. He lost it all this morning just as easy. Dave Davis is drunk. I paid Berger $2.50 to fix Jerry Kenny's watch. Rather dull today. Marsh is drunk. I retired at 9 o'clock.

Mar. 12. Very warm today. Dull in the house. Mr. Crocker, a friend of Marsh, left town for somewhere--bilked me for $5.75. Jerry Kenny went to work for James Moore as a stage driver.

Mar. 13. Fine day. Davis is sick, says he had a fit during the night. Stage came in--no through mail. Some Mexicans are drunk and talking very bad in the streets. Ross got pretty tight at night and was anxious to make a row with Brokaw, but did not.

Mar. 14. Fine weather. Nothing new or extraordinary. Jo had pups.

Mar. 15. Fine morning. Received no mail. Wash Evans came to town. Gibson is in town. He was arrested and charged with jumping Garrison's ranch. There is a dance this evening.

Mar. 16. Cloudy this morning. Nothing new today. Sam Drachman's wife and child left by stage for Cal. to get the boy circumcised. Very warm day. I kept sober all day. Went to bed at 10:30 o'clock.

Mar. 17. St. Patrick came in this morning but did not set them up for the boys. He says times are too hard and corky. Stage arrived at 9 o'clock--very little mail.

Louis C. Hughes owned the Arizona Star *newspaper in Tucson for many years. He served as governor of Arizona from 1893 to 1896. Louis Hughes was the brother of Tucson pioneer Sam Hughes. Arizona Historical Society, Tucson, #139-A.*

Mar. 18 (Sunday). Fine day. Church services were held in both denominations. There was a circus performance in the evening--one acrobat was badly hurt by falling. Frank Sullivan came in from Roddick's mining camp. Nothing extraordinary today. Davis is intoxicated. I went to bed early.

Mar. 19. Fine day. Davis and Sullivan both got drunk. I was very sober all day. Went in the evening to the flour store with my dogs to kill rats--could not find any. Morgan is drunk. I went to bed at 10 o'clock.

Mar. 20. Fine day. Stage came--no mail for me. Davis got drunk early. A woman was prosecuted and fined $25 today. I was sober all day. Went to bed at 10 o'clock.

Arizona Star *office in Tucson ca. 1880. Arizona Historical Society, Tucson,* *#2881.*

Mar. 21. Fine weather. The stage came in from the Rio Grande--no mail for me. Doña Felipe took two pups home. A report says John Day was married at the Trench Mine [located southeast of town near the Mexican border]. I went to bed at 11:30 o'clock.

Mar. 22. Fine morning. Foster bought a new lot of ollas for the house. W. W. Williams' dog Dick had 5 pups. Sullivan is drinking with a man named Baker from California. Warm day. Very dull.

Mar. 23. Pleasant day but dull. Sent to Currier & Ives for some pictures.

Papago (Tohono O'odham) women carry ollas down Congress Street in the 1880s. The ollas were popular with Tucsonans for storing drinking water. Moisture would bleed through the porous pottery and evaporate, cooling the contents. Arizona Historical Society, Tucson, #2911.

Mar. 24. Stage arrived--nothing for me. There was a dance tonight. I kept sober.

Mar. 25 (Palm Sunday). Pleasant morning. I took a bath. Some soldiers are in town--they were paid yesterday. There was music at Levin's Park this afternoon and evening. Went to bed at 10 o'clock.

Mar. 26. Fine day. Mail stage came from the Rio Grande. Cloudy today. Tom Banning is very drunk. Davis is drunk and was up all last night. I went to bed at 11 o'clock.

Mar. 27. Cloudy, a little sprinkle of rain. Dave Davis is drunk. He says he will leave town today and hopes lightning will kill him if he ever starts to come back to Tucson again. Sergeant Corn left for Camp Bowie in the stage.

Mar. 28. Ed Hudson, Sullivan, and Joe Elliott started for the mines. Joe came back to bid the boys good-bye and got so drunk he could not get off. Frank Francis was complained of by his woman and the marshal took him from the house. He is very drunk. I went to bed at 10:30 o'clock.

Mar. 29. Moore came in on the stage. Dave Davis did not go to Camp Bowie. Waldo is drunk. I bought a can of caviar from Levin--Foster cannot eat it. Went to bed early.

Mar. 30. Good Friday. The church is full of people. It rained this morning and was cloudy all day. Tom Gardner, Francis, Evans, and McQuinn left for the sawmill. The stage left for Cal. A church procession marched around the plaza after dark. It rained this evening.

Mar. 31. Cloudy and cold. A fire is pleasant. I worked on my scrapbook and covered some bound volumes of the *Spirit of the Times.* Stage came in--little mail today. Went to bed at 11 o'clock.

~ ~ ~ ~ ~

April 1 (Easter Sunday). Cold and windy. Went to W. Williams' house for some eggs to set a hen on. Easter Sunday--a big time in church. There is no gambling, but all are drunk. There were church services in two places. I went to bed sober.

Apr. 2. Stage arrived--no mail. Very dull. Closed early.

Apr. 3. No stage came in today. Very dull in the house. Charley Norris, while driving the stage out, was thrown from the coach and hurt badly. Gale, Davis, and myself made some calls around town.

Apr. 4. Mail stage came in--very little mail. Dr. Lord arrived from Yuma with a lot of government money [$625,000]. His escort was 1 captain and 25 soldiers. [Dr. Charles Lord was in charge of the U.S. Depository at Tucson, part of a banking system organized in the territories by the federal government to pay soldiers and government contractors.] Jack the Nailer came to town. The soldiers are all drunk this evening. I went to bed early.

Apr. 5. Cool morning. Jack the Nailer got drunk before I got up. Davis had a good thing for whiskey all day. In the drinking, somehow I got full also, but walked it off in the evening and went to bed sober.

Apr. 6. Cold enough for a fire this morning. Davis awoke and found himself sleeping out of doors. He and Jack the Nailer were both drunk before breakfast. The mail stages came in this morning from both ways. Mr. Dave Davis, while sleeping on a bench on the sidewalk, rolled off onto the ground and was covered with the bench. He kept drunk all the evening. John Sweeney came to town today. Judge Osborn's child died of smallpox. I retired at 9 o'clock.

Apr. 7. Fine day. Davis is drunk. Mail came in--nothing but a few letters. Davis was out all night and slept in a corral. J. W. Clark is also drunk. I retired at 10 o'clock.

Apr. 8 (Sunday). The stage ran away and smashed up. Fine morning. Very dull. I took a bath and read all day. Nothing strange occurred. Went to bed at 10:30 o'clock.

Apr. 9. There was a sandstorm last night and the air is still full of dust. The mail was brought in on horseback. I went to Levin's at night and drank several glasses of beer and whiskey with Dickey and Neugass.

Apr. 10. Quite cool this morning. The stage came in early--I got some papers, no letters. Sweeney is trying to get sober. Davis and Jack the Nailer are sober. Mr. T. G. Rusk arrived from San Francisco today. Very windy--dust and sand and a terrific time out of doors. I called on Mrs. W. W. Williams and got my little dog. I named him Bill. He sucks Jo as well as any pup could. Sweeney had a light touch of the jim-jams. He was in a fearful state, walking around and praying to the Almighty. 9 p.m.--the wind subsided and it rained a little. Very dull. Went to bed at 11 o'clock.

Apr. 11. Cool and cloudy. Sweeney is some better. He stayed in my room all day. I got a little full. In the evening I went to Levin's, ate some caviar, drank a big mug of beer, and had a whiskey straight. Paid the bill and then called at the Gem Saloon and drank with Shorty Holt. Came home and went to bed. I was taken sick in the night, ran out in the street, and threw up all that I had eaten during the day. Went back to bed and slept well the rest of the night.

Apr. 12. Cold enough for a fire. Sweeney has recovered. The stage arrived. Charley Norris came down this morning. He is recovering from his injuries quite fast. The immortal Hog Davis left this morning with Sweeney and Jack the Nailer for Florence. Oranges and lemons from Sonora were brought in today. The stage left this evening. Dr. Lord, his wife, and her mother went with Sniffin to the country for a few days. A telegram says that a hotel in St. Louis burned down, killing over one hundred people. Nothing more of importance today. Went to bed at 10 o'clock.

Apr. 13. Cool this morning. Fine weather until 10 o'clock when the wind blew up, throwing dust around something terrible. Very dull. I kept sober all day. Went to bed at 10 o'clock.

Apr. 14. Cold but pleasant. Both papers came out early. The wind commenced blowing at 12 noon--plenty of dust again today. The stage left for Cal. Very dull in the house. A court injunction was served on Secretary [of the Territory] Hoyt to restrain him from moving any territorial property to Prescott. [The ninth territorial legislature passed a bill moving the capital from Tucson to Prescott in Yavapai County. Officials in Tucson were contesting the move in court. Their protests were in vain, however, and the injunction was lifted and the capital moved in a few weeks.] There was a cold wind at night. I went to bed at 10 o'clock.

Apr. 15 (Sunday). Pleasant morning. Had ham, eggs, and corn cakes for breakfast. Kept sober all day. Foster, Caldwell, Gale, and Moore sat down at 9 o'clock in the evening to play one game of Pedro. They played until 3 in the morning. They all got tight and some of them wanted to fight. I went to bed at 4 o'clock tomorrow morning.

Apr. 16. Woke up and got out of bed at 10 o'clock. Had breakfast at Hucke's chop house. Charley Conwell and Ad Linn arrived in town. I received a book from Delegate Stevens. Tom Roddick came in town this evening and got drunk in one hour. It rained after dark. I went to bed at 9 o'clock.

Apr. 17. It rained all last night. The stage arrived this morning--I got a few papers. Quite cold and rainy. Cloudy all day. Quite dull. Some of the boys came in from the mines. I went to bed early.

Apr. 18. Cold morning. Tom Banning returned from Smith's ranch at Calabasas [about 50 miles south of town near the Mexican border] and brought a letter from Maloney saying that Indians had killed two Mexicans, shot

Captain Devers, and stolen some stock. [Ben C.] Parker went crazy today and put his head under a wagon wheel, trying to kill himself. He was taken in charge by a constable. George Hucke had a dance tonight.

Apr. 19. Got up early. Raised the flag before sunrise in honor of the anniversary of the Battle of Lexington and Concord in 1775. Parker got out of jail by paying $5. Conwell was up all last night gambling. He is drunk and broke this morning. The stage came in--no mail for me.

Apr. 20. Cold and windy. T. G. Rusk went on a bender and was arrested. Stage left for Cal. Bill Gale took his pup away. Nothing new or interesting. Went to bed at 9:30 o'clock.

Apr. 21. A cold wind blew early today. Court Commissioner S. W. Carpenter sustained the injunction on the removal of the capital to Prescott. Conwell is drunk this morning. I called on Dr. Lord to see his dog and had a glass of ale. The nigger brought his pup down and I cut her ears. I was sick at night and went to bed.

Apr. 22 (Sunday). Fine cool morning. Three young girls took the veil today at the [Sisters of St. Joseph] convent. Many people went to see the ceremony. Manuel Vasquez fell dead this afternoon. A man was brought into town dead, shot through the head. Verdict of the coroner's jury--killed by his own hand.

The seven members of the Sisters of St. Joseph of Carondelet who established an outpost of their order in Tucson in 1870. Left to right, Sister Ambrosia, Sister Maxima, Sister Hyacinth, Sister Martha, Sister Monica, Sister Euphrasia, Sister Emerentia. The order founded St. Mary's Hospital in Tucson in 1880, the first private hospital in the town. The Sisters of St. Joseph have provided comfort and healing to sick and injured Tucsonans ever since. Arizona Historical Society, Tucson, #62509.

Apr. 23. Fine day. Stage came in--received a letter from my aunt and papers from Bradley and my brother Lew. Also got my Currier & Ives pictures from New York. Times are very dull. Treanor's new stable outfit and buggies arrived from San Diego. There were six funerals today. Tom Roddick is drunk. I went to bed at 9 o'clock.

Apr 24. Fine cool morning. Stage left for Cal. Roddick and Britton left for the mines. Mr. O'Reilly came to town and got tight very soon. I went to bed early.

Apr. 25. Cold, windy, and cloudy. The stage came in early with six passengers. O'Reilly is still drunk. He slept in a chair from 2 to 7 p.m. and finally walked away. Very cold tonight.

Apr. 26. Cold this morning. O'Reilly is duly sober today. John Burt is drunk. Cloudy, windy, dusty, and looks like rain. I got pretty full, but stayed around the house and finally went to bed sober.

Apr. 27. Cold this morning. Nothing new. Stage came in at 8:30 a.m.-- received a letter from my sister. 9 o'clock--the sun is out and it is warm. Very cool and cloudy after sundown.

Apr. 28. The *Citizen* and *Star* are both out early. I met a representative of the Prescott *Miner* [newspaper] who is writing up our town. He has not made a favorable impression on people so far. The mail came in from both ways-- received papers from Bradley, Shipler, and my brother Milton. Went to bed at 10 o'clock.

Apr. 29 (Sunday). Posters in town say that some camels are here and will have a show this evening, 50¢ per head. Nothing else new. Went to bed early.

Apr. 30. Fine cool morning. Had a good breakfast. Wrote to San Francisco for a [hernia] truss. Also wrote to J. B. Hart and Joe Shipler. Sent papers to my brother Mit, Shipler, and John Chesebro. Nothing new or interesting. Went to bed at 10:30 o'clock.

~ ~ ~ ~ ~

May 1. Paid the new [federal] revenue licenses today. Fine morning. Stage arrived--no passengers. [Deputy Sheriff] John Miller and Jerry Kenny left on an assessing tour. Hopkins, Dr. Goodwin, and Horton left for Port Libertad [Sonora] for their health. [A number of Tucsonans went to Sonora and elsewhere to escape from the smallpox outbreak.] Cold and windy this evening. Went to bed at 10 o'clock.

May 2. Fine morning at sunrise. 9 a.m.--the wind blows fearful and dust is everywhere. Daly, the agent for the [Prescott] *Miner*, was relieved of his horse and equipments by a government officer. [The reporter for the *Miner* was being harassed by Tucson officials because of the impending move of the capital to Prescott. A number of government jobs were at stake, and tempers were hot.] Cold and windy after sundown. Went to bed at 8:30 o'clock.

May 3. Fine morning, quite cool. 10 a.m.--very warm. The stage came and brought Mr. Sweeney, Col. Boyle, and others. No letters for me. Very dull all day. Went to bed at 9 o'clock.

May 4. Fine morning. Nothing new. A telegram reports the death of William G. Brownlow. I put my flag up at half mast. [Brownlow, a well-known Methodist clergyman, had fought strenuously to keep his home state of Tennessee out of the Confederacy. Even though he failed, he became a Union hero.] 10 a.m.--very warm. Windy and dusty in the afternoon. Sweeney left for home.

May 5. Fine morning. Levin brought us some bock beer--not good. The stages came from both ways--no letters, received some Chicago papers. There was a dance at Levin's Park this evening. I went there with Sniffin. We enjoyed ourselves looking at the dancers and drinking beer until the dance broke up. Came home and went to bed.

May 6 (Sunday). Fine morning. Many people have gone to a horse race. Very dull today. Lopez won the race. John Hovey and Ike Brokaw returned to town. Smallpox broke out in the hospital--Jim Cowan has it. Pleasant evening. Went to bed at 10 o'clock.

May 7. Nice morning. Had ham and eggs for breakfast. I called on Mrs. Williams and saw the shade trees, the flowers, the chickens, puppies, and horses. The stage came in--received a bundle of papers from J. B. Hart, no letters. Nothing new. Went to bed early.

May 8. Warm. There was a light wind in the early part of the day. The *Star* came out.

May 9. Fine weather. Stage came in--brought my picture frame molding, but the side pieces are too short. John T. Smith is reported to have died at his ranch. S. W. Carpenter and his wife left for Sonora, and Tom Banning went with them.

May 10. Shorty Holt opened a new saloon yesterday. The *Star* came out today. It says that John Clum was sent for by the Czar of Russia to put the Turks out. [The *Star* was now being printed three times a week, but would soon become a weekly. The Russians and Turks were at war and the editor of the paper facetiously suggested that the brash but capable Indian agent at the San Carlos reservation might help the Czar subdue his Turkish enemies--John Clum had had notable success in controlling Apaches.] One of C. O. Brown's children died of smallpox. Quite a number of other deaths today. Went to bed as usual.

May 11. Quite cool. The funeral of Clara Brown was held at 9 a.m. Stage arrived--not much mail. Received a letter from my brother Milton with the news of the death of my stepmother. [George Hand's mother, Sible, died in 1854 while George was in California. His father, Ira, subsequently married a woman named Amelia. George never met Amelia, but referred to her as his stepmother. His father died in 1867.] Charley Conwell went to work for E. N.

Fish. 11 persons are said to have died of smallpox today. [Smallpox was the only disease for which vaccination protection was available in the 1800s. The procedure had been discovered in the 1790s by the British physician Edward Jenner. It was not known why the vaccine worked, only that it did. George Hand received a smallpox vaccination upon his induction into the Union Army in 1861, but the protective inoculation was not readily available on the frontier and most Tucsonans were vulnerable to the disease. While the 1877 smallpox epidemic was in progress, the Tucson newspapers made almost no mention of it. Disease outbreaks were bad for business and the commerce-oriented newspapers were loath to discuss them in print.]

May 12. Fine morning. Both papers came out early. Dave Horton, who left with Hopkins, Goodwin, and Co., came back from Sonora all broke out with smallpox. There was a dance at Levin's Park tonight. Went to bed at 10 o'clock.

May 13 (Sunday). Cool morning. Stage came in--got some papers, no letters. Foster sent a telegram to H. B. Smith. Very dull indeed. Treanor's carriages are all rented out today-- people are riding around. The boys are all in from the Yellow Jacket Mine.

May 14. Quite cool. Smallpox seems to have somewhat abated--only a few deaths reported in the past few days. James H. Toole and his family left for San Francisco. Two more cases of smallpox were reported this evening. I went to Levin's, came home, and went to bed at 10:30 o'clock.

May 15. Cloudy and warm. The Cal. stage arrived at 8:30 o'clock--no mail for me. The Rio Grande stage came in at 9 o'clock. Windy and dusty until 2 p.m., then it commenced raining and the rain continued until late in the night. Only a few people were buried today. Went to bed at 9 o'clock.

May 16. The sun arose as usual but soon became covered with clouds. No wind or dust. 10 a.m.--the sun comes out at intervals but clouds still hang over us. No mail today. Nothing to read. Very dull.

May 17. Cool and cloudy. There were several funerals this morning before 9 o'clock. The stage came in at 9:30--no letters for me. Received a [hernia] truss from San Francisco--no good. The wind started up and it got quite cold. 3 p.m.--a light rain. Some petty thief stole three papers from the table after dark. Went to bed at 9 o'clock.

May 18. Moderately cool. C. O. Brown's youngest child died this morning, is to be buried at 4 p.m. Farley and Pomeroy [attorneys] were arrested by order of Justice Neugass for contempt of court. Johnson the saddler is drunk. Farley and Co. were released from jail on a technicality. I went to bed early.

May 19. Very cold, damp, and disagreeable. There is snow on the mountains. Both the *Star* and *Citizen* are out early. Stage arrived at 7:50--no mail for me. News arrived this morning of the death of John Hopkins in

Sonora [of smallpox]. 9 a.m.--the sun came out warm. Dr. Goodwin and Keene came in today from Sonora. I went to bed early.

May 20 (Sunday). Quite cold early. The sun came out hot at 8 a.m. Took a bath and changed clothes. Wallace and a soldier started for Florence. John Miller and Jerry Kenny came in town today. There was a dance at Levin's this evening. Went to bed at 10 o'clock.

May 21. Warm today. Stage came in early--not much mail. Received a letter from Dave Davis and papers from Milton. Bill Gale was on a jamboree today. He went to both San Xavier and Camp Lowell. The stage left at 4 p.m. Very dull. Nothing new. Went to bed at 9 o'clock.

May 22. 5 a.m.--quite cool. Warm after sunrise. There was a fine breeze at 9 a.m., no dust. A man died of smallpox in the hospital today. Mrs. Briggs Goodrich left for Cal. on the stage. Andrews got drunk and shut up his saloon. George Fields' wagon train arrived. Very pleasant after dark. I went to bed at 10 o'clock.

May 23. Fine morning. The stage came in at 8 a.m. No wind and dust this morning. Dan O'Leary and 30 Hualapai Indian scouts arrived this evening. [This was a contingent of Indian police on the trail of renegade Chiricahua Apaches.] Very pleasant after sundown. Closed at 10 o'clock.

May 24. Fine morning, cool and very pleasant. Several smallpox patients in the hospital are getting well. Foster has a pain in his side. Puck Ryan came in and got drunk in 15 minutes. I was obliged to get full drinking with him to make him spend money. In the evening we went to Levin's and had a lunch and beer. I found Mansco there and got him to pay an old bill. Came home and went to bed.

May 25. Fine morning. Mail coach arrived--not much mail, no letters for me. The stage left for Cal. Dr. Handy, [Coroner] H. B. Smith, and [District Attorney] Briggs Goodrich went to Calabasas to get the stomach of John T. Smith for analysis. [Smith died at his Bosque Ranch at Calabasas on May 9. Rumors were circulating that he had been poisoned by someone, and the county officials were going to the ranch to investigate.] Puck Ryan is drunk. I went to bed early.

May 26. Fine day. The *Citizen* and *Star* both came out early. Some mail and papers came today. Ryan is drunk again. The mail came in from Sonora.

May 27 (Sunday). Nice morning. Stage came in--no letters for me. Ryan was sober for a short time. There was some wind this afternoon. Dr. Handy, Smith, etc., arrived home today. I went to bed at 11 o'clock.

May 28. Fine morning. I moved the stove out and washed out the house. Puck Ryan got mad and left with his blankets. Tom Roddick arrived this morning with more ore specimens.

May 29. Nothing suspicious was found in the stomach of J. T. Smith. Very dull.

May 30. Fine day. Roddick and Buck left for the mines. Frank Sullivan came to town.

May 31. Corpus Christi Day. The usual celebrating and foolery was done in the streets. I bought a pair of shoes today. An adopted child of Ad Linn and his wife died this morning.

~ ~ ~ ~ ~

June 1. Ad Linn and John Hovey came to town. There was a funeral for Linn's child. This morning was cool enough for a fire. It was very warm later in the day. Pleasant in the evening. Went to bed early.

June 2. Fine cool morning. Both papers came out early. Stage came in-- no mail for us. 10 a.m.--very warm.

June 3 (Sunday). Warm today. Guns were fired in front of the church this morning in honor of the 50th anniversary of Pio Nono's [Pope Pius IX] appointment to the bishopric.

June 4. Very dull. Nothing new.

June 5. Fine day. Plenty of drunks around. I got drunk also. Got no letters today.

June 6. Fine morning. 9 a.m.--quite warm. 12 noon--hot and got hotter until sundown. A child of James Lee died.

June 7. Warm to start with, and warmer every hour. Stage arrived--no passengers. There will be a funeral for the child of James Lee today. No drunken men about this morning--the boys are all sober. Puck Ryan scrubbed the floors. Nothing new.

June 8. Quite warm. Sweeney received a letter from home [Florence] saying that his little child is very sick. He will go home today. The stage left at 4 p.m., taking Sweeney and Ryan. I cut Williams' dog's ears. Some discharged soldiers are in town, all drunk. Prentiss and Brokaw had a fight in Brown's saloon. I went to bed at 10 o'clock.

June 9. Pleasant before sunrise. 9 o'clock--windy, very dusty, and disagreeable. Nothing new but a lot of drunken discharged soldiers in town. There was a dance at Levin's Park this evening.

June 10 (Sunday). Fine morning. 9 a.m.--commenced blowing dust terrific and we had it all day. The soldiers are still on a spree. There was a dance at Levin's again. Very warm today--104 degrees on the thermometer at the drugstore.

June 11. Warm but quite pleasant. Nothing new today. The mail came in from both ways--no letters for me. Very warm--109 degrees at 2 p.m. The Mexican who stole one of our chairs was sent to jail for three months. The Arizona Militia returned today. Governor Safford and Robert Leatherwood came in yesterday. [A volunteer militia had been raised by Governor Anson P. K. Safford in February to chase down outlaw Apaches. Safford himself had joined the scouting party in May. Their efforts were fruitless, however, and no

Apaches were captured. John P. Hoyt had replaced Safford as governor of Arizona on May 30.]

Anson P. K. Safford served as governor of Arizona from 1869 to 1877. He was one of the most able governors Arizona has ever had. Safford took a special interest in public education and a middle school in Tucson was named for him. Arizona Historical Society, Tucson, #13757.

June 12. Warm. Nothing new except lots of discharged soldiers in town on their way to Cal. The mercury at Meyer's drugstore was 111 degrees, at the military weather office 105. I was sick all day.

June 13. Very warm morning. More soldiers came in to town. Miles [Michael] O'Reilly is still on a spree. I wrote letters to Mit and Lew. Meyer's thermometer showed 111 degrees, the weather office had 105. I was sick and went to bed early.

June 14. Warm. Sullivan and O'Reilly are drunk. Morgan is drunk. Jerry Kenny is sober. 11 a.m.--mercury 110 degrees at the drugstore. James Lee and Ad Linn came in. After calling the drinks, Captain Gay mixed in the party which adjourned to the reading and sitting room. Shortly thereafter, Linn and Gay got into a row. Shirts were torn but no blood was spilled. Lee and Linn

144

stayed and kept drinking, and finally at 4:30 p.m. they had a row. Linn was very wild and very much to blame. He was arrested and taken away by a constable, but was released and returned in a short time. He was very angry and was about to take over the house. Linn used very bad language, but after getting a little sober he was somewhat ashamed and went home. O'Reilly is very drunk. Roddick is very drunk. Sullivan is moderately drunk.

June 15. Warm. No breeze until 9 a.m. Lee and Linn came in this morning, drank together, and settled their difficulty. An officer came by and arrested them for the disturbance yesterday. They were fined $12.50 each. They got pretty full and went to Lee's [flour] mill. Then Linn went around town looking for Constable Buttner and talking about whipping him. Mercury 108 degrees today. Very pleasant after sundown. Went to bed at 10:30 o'clock.

June 16. Fine morning. Fred Myers got tight and kept so all day. Quite dull. Mercury 108 degrees. I raised the flag this evening. Went to bed at 10 o'clock.

June 17 (Sunday). The anniversary of the Battle of Bunker Hill. The flag blows out free this morning. Hundreds of people want to know what it is up for. Fred Myers is still tight. The streets were full of horsemen and vehicles all day. Nothing new today. Went to bed early.

June 18. Warm morning. Myers is still on a spree. Dr. Lord left for San Francisco. [Eli B.] Gifford and Ike Brokaw opened a monte game in the house- -no players. I went to bed at 10:30 o'clock. [Isaac Brokaw had recently replaced Adolph Buttner as town marshal, and Buttner was then appointed constable. On the frontier, it was perfectly acceptable for a law enforcement official to work as a gambler on the side. Brokaw would soon resign as marshal and Buttner would again take the job.]

June 19. Fine day. Nothing new. Very warm. Myers is still on a spree. He sent Sullivan off with his wagon train to Whipple's stage station. Morgan left for Yuma. A new law firm has been established--Clark & McDermott. Principal business--drinking whiskey. The monte game won $201 today. Went to bed at 10:30 o'clock.

June 20. Warm morning. Received a letter from J. B. Hart. Dr. Goodwin's boy died. Fred Myers is still on a spree.

June 21. Very warm. Fred Myers left this morning. Clark got tight and had a row with Buttner. Jimmy Andrews, Marsh, and others were quite drunk, Hand not far behind. A funeral was held for Goodwin's boy. I sent to San Francisco for a flag. Went to bed at 10 o'clock.

June 22. Fine day. Very warm. Nothing new. Very dull. Jonesy came in town. There was some singing in the house late this evening, but I was already in bed.

June 23. Fine morning. Got up at 4 o'clock and found five men asleep on the floor. Street cleaning today. 10 a.m.--very hot. Tom Banning, Carleton, Meyer, and Welisch returned from Sonora. I went to bed at 10 o'clock.

German-born Adolph Buttner served as Tucson's marshal and chief of police during the 1870s and 1880s. Buehman photo, Arizona Historical Society, Tucson, #7538.

June 24 (Sunday). San Juan's Day opened as usual, windy, dusty, and hot. There is singing all over town. Went to bed early.

June 25. Warm morning. Tom McClellan fixed the sidewalk in front of the house. All the boys are tight. A Mexican was killed below town. Foster got pretty full. We sat up singing all night.

June 26. Cool morning for a change. Went to see the man killed last night. His name is Geronimo Morales. On the way I called on Mrs. Stevens and Mrs. Hughes. Frank Sullivan arrived in the stage coach. The coroner's jury adjourned till tomorrow.

Petra and Hiram Stevens (left) and Atanacia and Sam Hughes (right) were friends of George Hand. Petra and Atanacia (Santa Cruz) were sisters. Stevens represented Arizona in the U.S. Congress from 1875 to 1878. Sam Hughes was a strong supporter of public education and a Tucson elementary school was named for him. Arizona Historical Society, Tucson, #1867.

June 27. The coroner's jury met in our monte room and found the man dead. He was buried yesterday. I received a paper from John Chesebro. Morell died of smallpox and was buried this evening. Charley Norris was taken to the hospital with smallpox also. Jonesy and Hudson left for the mines. Sniffin brought me a piece of gooseberry pie. I went to bed early.

June 28. Warm and cloudy. Received some papers from William F. Bradley. Ad Linn and Marsh left for the Yellow Jacket Mine. There is a special meeting of the city council and the citizens this evening at the courthouse. [This meeting was held to discuss additional measures that might be taken to fight the smallpox epidemic, and how to pay for them. Dr. John Handy had obtained a small supply of "vaccine matter" from San Francisco and was inoculating as many people as he could, free of charge. After the meeting, the community redoubled its efforts to identify sick people and quarantine them, and to fumigate infected houses and rooms.]

June 29. San Pedro's Day. People were playing music very early this morning. Quite warm today. A Mr. Evans left owing me $4.00. He disputed the bill and gave me a very short answer. I sued him, and McDermott was deputized as a special constable to go after him. Very few drunk men around this evening. I went to bed at 9 o'clock.

June 30. Pleasant cool morning. Stage came from Cal. and brought me a letter from William F. Bradley, the first in over a year. He also sent a photo of his boy. McDermott returned--he did not bring Evans but did bring his horse. Foster sold the horse for $30.

~ ~ ~ ~ ~

July 1 (Sunday). Fine morning. The monte game is still running and has been going all night. Jim Blade is tight as a boot. I had ham and eggs for breakfast. 10 a.m.--the monte game is still going. Clark and McDermott are drunk. The monte game closed a winner at 4 p.m. and opened again immediately after. I went lame and was obliged to go to bed early with a sore toe.

July 2. Fine morning, and quite cool for this time of year. There is a small monte game this morning--the game ran all night. I cleaned up the house and sent out the washing. We got our flag from Sam Hughes. Everyone is drunk. The monte game was a winner.

July 3. The monte game is still running. John Hovey has won $200 since 4 o'clock this morning. Brokaw and Gifford closed the game at 10 a.m. Foster bought some fireworks for the boys. Bill Gale quit working at the stable today. No monte game in the house this evening. We closed early. [George Hand sent the following note to his friend John W. Clark on July 3: "Dear Sir: Having been appointed a committee of one to get up a programme for the celebration of the Fourth of July, I hereby order and direct you to bring to my office on the morning of July 4 a book containing the Declaration of the Independence of the United Colonies. You will therefore make your appearance at an early hour prepared to read the above to the rising generation. Fail not to perform the above under the most fearful penalty."]

July 4. Fine morning. Got up early and raised the flag. Foster fired off 13 bombs for the 13 original states. Rickman died this afternoon. We made a bonfire in the street in the evening. The town was all noise with bombs and crackers until a very late hour.

July 5. Very dull today. All the boys have the blues. Rickman was buried this morning.

July 6. Very warm all day. Mercury at 12 noon--106 degrees. Nothing new. Bill Gale left for Florence. Very warm this evening.

July 7. Very warm last night. All quiet today. The stage came in--no letters for me, and the papers were all wet. 4 p.m.--cloudy and commenced blowing. We had a terrific sandstorm for nearly 3 hours, but no rain. Very dull. Went to bed at 9 o'clock.

July 8 (Sunday). Fine, warm morning. Captain Barry arrived from Cal. Very warm all day. The wind blew from 4 p.m. to 7 and the dust was almost insufferable.

July 9. Cloudy and pleasant before sunrise. Hot as the devil at 9 a.m. Still hotter at 11. 3 p.m.--a light rain laid the dust nicely. 6 p.m.--the wind sprang up again. It got very cloudy and dark but no more rain.

July 10. Pleasant morning. [Deputy Sheriff] Miller is rushing around quite fast. He says that Fat Man Moore escaped from jail last night. [Deputy] Ad Linn started on the trail of the fat man this morning. A little cloudy today but very warm. Some strangers came in from San Diego. Esslinger is on a spree.

July 11. Warm and very sultry. 11 a.m.--the stage is not in yet. It has been detained on account of high water. It clouded up at 3 p.m. and commenced raining at 6 p.m. We had a fine rain, just enough to wet the ground. Frank Francis returned to town.

July 12. Cool and pleasant after last night's rain. 9 a.m.--very warm. 2 p.m.--the stage arrived, no mail for me. Pacheco shot another Mexican, and [Marshal] Brokaw arrested him. The justice of the peace ordered him to jail in lieu of 3,000 dollars bail. A Mexican woman robbed a soldier today. I went to bed at 9:30 o'clock.

July 13. Sheriff Shibell came back from Sonora with the fat man. Pacheco was discharged from jail. We fixed the faro table, served up some belly-wash, and worked quite hard. All the boys got drunk. No faro game in the house tonight.

July 14. Very warm. Dull day, no excitement. Esslinger is still drunk. He beat the faro game for $6 and won a few dollars at monte. Marsh returned from the mines.

July 15 (Sunday). Warm. Everybody is in church. Faro and monte are both open in the house. Shibell leaves today for Cal. with Fatty. Very warm this evening. Shibell, Goodrich, and the fat man left on the stage. [Fat Man Moore was a big-time swindler and a $500 reward was offered in California for his capture. Thus it was well worth Sheriff Charles Shibell and District Attorney Briggs Goodrich's time to take him to California for trial. Shibell had caught up with Moore a few miles below the Mexican border--the international boundary did not often stop U.S. officers in pursuit of fugitives in the 1870s.]

149

July 16. Pleasant morning. Smallpox is getting worse in town. Several men got drunk in the house this morning. I raffled off a picture--it was won by Brokaw. I went to Levin's, had a Dutch lunch, and drank 4 glasses of beer. Came home and went to bed. Very warm. I got up in the night and lay on the sidewalk.

July 17. Very warm. Not much mail today. Nothing new. Frank Sullivan is drunk. I was sober all day. Went to bed at 10 o'clock, and went out and slept on the sidewalk after the house closed.

July 18. Warm. Dull. Williams' dog is sick--got into some poison. I went up to see her. She got over it. The stage came--no mail for me. Francis and Sullivan went to the army post to get work. Mercury at 2 p.m.--112 degrees.

July 19. There was a high wind last night and terrific rain and hail. It blew off corners of houses, broke windows, blew down flagstaffs, and played sad havoc with gardens, fruit trees, vines, and watermelons. Men were almost blown away and the streets were full of water. It is cloudy and very sultry today. My little dog Bill died.

Ad published in the Arizona Star *(Tucson) in July 1877. Ideas about appropriate advertising gimmicks have changed since the 1870s.*

Sam Drachman's store on Main Street in the 1880s. The short man with his left hand raised is Sam. Arizona Historical Society, Tucson, #16525.

July 20. Very close and sultry. The streets are full of debris from the high wind and rainstorm. Very warm all day. It rained after dark.

July 21. Warm morning. Dull day. Nothing new.

July 22 (Sunday). Cloudy and very warm. It rained at night.

July 23. Warm and sultry. Windy in the afternoon. Dr. Handy left for San Francisco. It rained quite hard after dark and in the night. I had to sleep in the house.

July 24. Cool morning. The streets are muddy. Foster is sick. Parker is taking oil. John Hovey got the contract to fix the old racetrack near the feast grounds [the military plaza on the southeastern edge of town]. I received a letter from Milton in Joliet informing me of the death of brother Lewis in Chicago. Carmen Lopez died today. We had rain this evening, with some wind.

July 25. Warm. There was a funeral for Carmen Lopez.

July 26. Not so warm today. Dull, nothing new.

July 27. Fine morning. Tom Roddick came to town and got drunk. Edward Sampson died in the hospital. He owed me $20--he settled his bill and left for a better world. No rain today. I retired at 9 o'clock.

July 28. Warm today. Washed out the house. The stage came in early-- received a letter from my sister Mira. The molding for my picture frames came in. Bill Gale came in to town. Williams' dog had fits and died last night. Foster is sick--had a light chill. I got rather full. Spread my bed on the sidewalk at 11:30 o'clock and slept well all night.

July 29 (Sunday). Nice cool morning. Got up early. Some horses and mules were stolen last night. Mr. Woffenden's house was robbed--there is no trace of the thieves. I got tight today. Went to bed late.

July 30. Fine day. Moderately warm. The faro and monte games ran nearly all day. Old Kentuck, from the stage station between Camp Grant and here, is in town. Roddick, Stroud, and others are drunk. John Brown and Parker are sober. Hand is quite sober.

July 31. Warm morning. The house was quite lively today. The stage came in--no letters for me. Jonesy came to town. Nothing important happened today. I stayed rather sober and went to bed so.

~ ~ ~ ~ ~

August 1. Tom Gardner and Wallace came in this morning. 12 noon--very warm and no breeze. I saw Mr. Payne who was talking about me in Brown's saloon. He took back what he said and I left him. Went to bed early.

Aug. 2. Warm, cloudy, and sultry. Very dull. Nothing new.

Aug. 3. Warm morning. The flies are very bad. The stage came in a 7 a.m. Our Indian helper got arrested this morning. A complaint was made against Dr. McLaughlin and a warrant issued for his arrest. Very dull.

Aug. 4. Warm day. Nothing new.

Aug. 5 (Sunday). There was a horse race today. Buttner's horse won it.

Aug. 6. Sick all day and taking medicine. Ate nothing. I took more pills this evening. Was up and down all night.

Aug. 7. Ate some breakfast. Feel some better. I met a man named Greene from Nevada City--had a long talk with him. Very dull day. Went to bed early.

Aug. 8. Quite cool this morning at last. Feel some better--ate a little. There was a raffle for Franklin's mare. She was won by Clark the telegraph operator with no. 43. The rights to the feast plaza were sold to John Hovey for $371.25. [Each year, the town council leased the San Agustín feast grounds to the highest bidder. The lessee was responsible for organizing the festivities and keeping things reasonably orderly. He would recoup his expenses and hopefully turn a profit by subleasing booth space to food and drink vendors, gamblers, and various hucksters.]

Aug. 9. Fine morning. I was sick all day. The stage came in late. Nothing new. Cloudy and windy at night.

Aug. 10. Strangers are coming to town very fast. I feel some better today. It is very hot--the mercury was 112 degrees at 2 p.m. Clark is tight.

Aug. 11. Fine pleasant morning. I feel pretty well. Wheeler Williams and his family left on a trip to the mountains. Bill Gale went to work for Jim Carroll at his livery stable. Mr. Wheat arrived from Florence.

Aug. 12 (Sunday). Warm day. Smith Turner came to town with a race horse. Very dull all day and night. Felt sick and went to bed early.

Aug. 13. Very warm, no breeze. Feel some better today.

Aug. 14. Very warm. [Deputy Sheriff] John Miller was arrested and placed under a bond in the sum of $500 to appear before the grand jury. [Miller was suspected of helping Fat Man Moore escape from jail the previous month.] Lots of drunken soldiers are in town. W. W. Williams and his family came back to town. Cloudy, windy, dusty, and looks much like rain. Went to bed at 8:30 o'clock.

Aug. 15. No rain last night but still cloudy this morning. The soldiers are still on a spree. Very warm. The stage came early. Pat O'Meara came to town to work on the boiler at the flour mill. He got drunk in a very short time. Joe Phy came to town. He saw John Hart at Whipple's stage station. Cloudy nearly all day. I feel tip-top and ate hearty. Went to bed at 9 o'clock. There was a very heavy wind and dust about 11 o'clock.

Aug. 16. Cloudy and warm. Monte and faro are both going quite lively. No mail for me. J. B. Hart arrived at 5 p.m. I saw him at 7 and we had drinks and a long talk--same old John. [John B. Hart had lived in Tucson in previous years and he and Hand were old friends. The *Citizen* noted his return to town and referred to him as "the great American hunter and prospector."] Very lively in the house this evening. I stayed up till after ten, then went to bed.

Aug. 17. Still cloudy. Had another talk with Hart. He is the same old John, happy as can be. The boys beat the monte game badly. A man was hung at the Point of Water [about ten miles south of town near San Xavier] for stealing a mule. We had a little rain this evening. I talked with Hart until after 10 and then went to bed.

Aug. 18. Pleasant morning. Very warm. Jack Barry found his missing horse. Juana's mother [George Foster's mother-in-law] came in from Florence last night. A circus is advertized for tonight. It was very windy after sundown. Went to bed at 9 o'clock.

Aug. 19 (Sunday). Pleasant day. The stage came in--very little mail. 12 noon--the mercury is at 111 degrees. The circus troupe has been parading through town again. There are lots of soldiers in town. Wiley and Bryson came in from the Gila. There is a circus performance tonight so our games closed early. Went to bed at 10 o'clock.

Aug. 20. Fine morning. The soldiers are all broke. John Hart went to San Xavier and lost Joe Phy's saddle horse there. He came back, got another horse, and started out to find the lost one. Hart finally returned with everything all right. Very warm this evening. I went to bed at 9 o'clock.

Aug. 21. Fine cool morning. Slept well last night. Stage came--very little mail. I wrote two letters, one to my sister Mira and one to Milton's wife. Very warm today. George Fields came in today and Murphy came with him.

Aug. 22. Fine morning. John Dobbs came in town early. Bill Morgan came in. Strangers are beginning to come in town for the feast. Very dull and hot. Parker opened his roulette wheel in the house today.

Aug. 23. Warm day. Strangers are coming to town very fast.

Aug. 24. Fine morning. The water in the ollas is cool. Charley Ashton and Dave Wilson came in from Silver City. Copely arrived from Phoenix. Smith and Prentiss opened a faro game in the house and went broke. Circus and theatre tonight.

Aug. 25. Cool morning. Kelly's wife had an apoplectic fit this morning. No mail for me today. Went to bed at 9:30 o'clock.

Aug. 26 (Sunday). Fine morning. Hovey hired Jerry Kenny to run a drink stand at the feast. All the rounders and bums are on the [military] plaza this morning to see Jerry and get a free drink. Jerry got drunk and filled up several other fellows--Hovey discharged him. Wagon loads of melons came in town this morning. Mercury at 1 p.m.--114 degrees. Charley Ashton beat the faro game again today.

Aug. 27. Everyone is moving to the feast plaza. Jonesy is helping Foster get set up. [George Foster set up a booth for selling drinks at the feast.] At dark, rockets and other fireworks were sent up and set off. I did not light up the house--went to see the sights on the plaza. There were more gamblers and games than people to play them. Came home and went to bed at 10:30 o'clock.

Aug. 28 (San Agustín's Day). Dull in town. I saw L. B. White, son of Mr. William White of Oneida Co., N.Y. I had not seen him for 28 years. He showed me a picture of his father who was an intimate friend of my father. I did not light up the house. Went to bed at 11:30 o'clock.

Aug. 29. Dull in town today. I went to the feast at night. Went to bed at 10 o'clock.

Aug. 30. Warm and dusty. Dull in town. Everything was running red hot on the plaza at night. I had supper there. Came home and went to bed at 10 o'clock.

Aug. 31. Dull and hot day. Went to the feast ground at night and had supper. Came home and went to bed.

~ ~ ~ ~ ~

September 1. The month opened hot. No rain. Charley Conwell and Button-Head Joe had a fight. Joe knocked Conwell on an olla, broke it, and spilled all the water. Then they both got drunk. Marsh is drunk. I went to bed early.

Sept. 2 (Sunday). Fine morning. The stage came in early. I slept poorly last night and feel bad this morning. Foster is sick. I went to bed early.

Sept. 3. Fine morning. Stage came--very little mail. Sorghum Smith arrived with his horse Pumpkins. Very windy and dusty today. There were rain showers later. I went up to the feast plaza and bought some pools for the horse race. Got drunk today, the first time in my life. Came home early and went to bed.

Sept. 4. Dull in town. Racing pools are selling on the feast ground--I bought some more. The race comes off tomorrow. Came home and went to bed.

Sept. 5. Very dull in town--everyone went to the horse race. I closed up and went to bed. Dudley beat Pumpkins in the big race. I opened again after the race, then closed at 6 p.m. and went to the feast plaza. I turned in my pool tickets--won $5.30.

Sept. 6. No race today. I went to the feast grounds and won $14. Got drunk and made a fool of myself. Came home and went to bed at 9 p.m.

Sept. 7. There is a one-mile horse race today at 2 p.m. I have nothing bet on it. Fred Myers left today for Yuma. Wheat's horse won the race. The feast is still running strong.

Sept. 8. Fine weather. Still very dull in town. I spent an hour on the feast ground. Came home and went to bed.

Sept. 9 (Sunday). Fine day. Everyone was in church in the morning, and from church they went to the horse race. A one-mile race--the Gila horse won. This is the last night of the feast. A faro game ran all night at the plaza--everyone lost.

Sept. 10. Very warm. All commenced moving from the feast plaza. A very busy time. Smith is getting ready for a trip to Hermosillo [Sonora] and John Hart and others are to go with him. Kendall and Bob Wood opened a faro game in our house. It rained this evening and Smith did not get off. It was raining hard when we closed the house.

Sept. 11. Smith and Co. left early for Sonora. It rained all last night and is cloudy this morning. We had some light rain today. Ashton beat the faro game in our house this evening.

Sept. 12. Cloudy this morning. Foster and Hovey settled their feast business. Red Hart and others left for Sonora. Wiley left also. Tom Roddick leaves this evening for the mines. 2 p.m.--the sun shines, and the stage is not in yet. 4 p.m.--the stage came--no mail for me. Dull day. Went to bed early.

Sept. 13. Cool morning. Nothing new. Closed early.

Sept. 14. Very cool. Telegrams came in telling of yesterday's shooting match--the Yanks won the first day. [American and British rifle teams were holding a two-day match at the National Rifle Association's range at Creedmoor, Long Island. The Yanks went on to win on the second day as well.] 12 noon--quite warm again. I sent for some pictures and a binder.

Sept. 15. Fine morning, cool and pleasant. Very dull day. Tomorrow is the real celebration of the Independence of Mexico, but tonight there were illuminations and fireworks and speeches at Levin's Park. Music was played all night. I went to bed at 10 o'clock.

Sept. 16 (Sunday). Fine morning. The day opened with the firing of 21 guns. The town is full of flags of both countries. The same proceedings of our Fourth of July were performed, and at night the illuminations at Levin's Park were very nice. The singing by the girls was good. The speakers were very poor--they could not be heard. I went to bed after filling up with tamales.

A troop of traveling theatrical players at Levin's Park. Arizona Historical Society, Tucson, #15583.

Sept. 17. Warm and sultry. Eight cases of Milwaukee beer came today--had quite a run on it this evening. Went to bed at 11 o'clock. [On September 22 the *Citizen* reported that "The justly famous Milwaukee beer can be had at the Old Stand. Foster & Hand also deal it out to appreciative customers. It is the best beer made." The Pasteurization process for preserving beer was introduced in 1873. This allowed bottled beer to be shipped long distances, and the railroad, having reached Yuma from the west, brought beer made outside the territory to Arizona for the first time. The imported brews became stiff competition for the local product. In July 1879 the *Citizen* noted that "Alex Levin is on the warpath on the beer question. He says he intends to make better beer than any importation...." Of course, the imports eventually triumphed.]

Sept. 18. Warm. The Milwaukee beer tasted good today--sent for 5 more cases. Worked a little today. Very dull. Went to bed early.

Sept. 19. The anniversary of the First Battle of Bunn's Heights. Warm. No news of importance. Ate some tamales and went to bed at 11 o'clock.

Sept. 20. Fine cool morning. Foster's mother-in-law and brother-in-law left for Sonora this morning.

Sept. 21. Good day--quite lively in the house. Parker, McClary, and company left for Sonora. One Mexican shot another this evening. I went to bed at 10 o'clock.

Sept. 22. Fine morning. Rather dull. Hovey and Brokaw left for Sonora. Nothing new. [A number of Tucsonans were going to Sonora to attend the Magdalena feast held in early October. Others were heading south to check out recent reports of promising mineral discoveries below the border. It didn't take much, only vague rumors would do, to send these frontiersmen off into the hinterlands looking for mines.]

Sept. 23 (Sunday). Tom Banning returned from Sonora. Speedy, Fairbanks, Lyons, and Jack the Nailer are to leave for Sonora today. There was a dance at the park this evening.

Sept. 24. I moved my things and we commenced taking the old roof off of the house. I got tight. Slept in my new room tonight.

Sept. 25. Sorghum Smith, Wall, and Murphy came in from Florence, bound for Sonora. Hand got tight. Went to bed.

Sept. 26. The house is full of dirt and dust. I was sober all day, but got quite full in the evening. Went to bed at 10 o'clock.

Sept. 27. Cool morning. Murphy, Wall, Sorghum Smith, and Kendall left for Sonora. Very dull. I was sober all day. The new roof on the house is finished. Went to bed early.

Sept. 28. Nothing new, very dull. Got full today. Went to bed early.

Sept. 29. We are still fixing on the house--waiting for the varnish on the floor to dry. I got drunk again.

Sept. 30 (Sunday). Nothing new. Church services are going today. Very dull. Went to bed early.

~ ~ ~ ~ ~

October 1. I had a fit last night and bit my tongue and lamed my arm. Ming and Burt had their monte game attached by the marshal, but he returned half of their money. I went to bed at 9 o'clock.

Oct. 2. I feel better this morning. King William was arrested by Constable Martinez this morning. He was released on bail. The arrest caused no little talk in town. Very dull in the house today.

Oct. 3. Fine morning. John Miller's wife beat up Ott's wife--nothing was said about it. Louise got drunk and was out all night with the gang.

Oct. 4. We finished up on the house and made a fine room of it. Nothing new in town but an extra of the Yuma *Sentinel* [newspaper] telling of the rail cars crossing the new Yuma bridge. [The Southern Pacific Railroad was completed from Los Angeles to the Colorado River across from Yuma in May 1877. A bridge bringing rail cars into Arizona for the first time was now in operation. The line would not reach Tucson until March 1880.] I went to bed at 9:30--slept very little--the streets were full of barking dogs and drunken whores.

Oct. 5. Very dull. Drank all day and all evening.

Oct. 6. Got up early. Feel well today. Scrubbed the door screen, mopped the boards, and washed the safe and counter with soap and water. Tom Roddick left for the mines. I kept sober all day and went to bed so.

Oct. 7 (Sunday). Fine cool morning. Ate a hearty meal of baked beans. Went to bed sober.

Oct. 8. The grand jury meets today. Pete Kitchen returned from Sonora. Voisard, Holden, and others arrived from the mines. McIntee sold a claim.

Oct. 9. Went to court this morning. [Deputy Sheriff] Miller was suspended from office. Jerry Kenny was put in his place as jailor for the present. King William was put in jail--got out on bail. Levin, Fairbanks, and Speedy returned from Sonora. I went to bed at 9 o'clock.

Oct. 10. Cold this morning. Very dull. John Ming sold out [sold his meat market] to John Burt. Some smallpox patients were removed to the pesthouse. I received a binder for the *Spirit*. [On July 30, Tucson Mayor John B. Allen prematurely told the town council that the smallpox epidemic was over. At that time he reported that there had been about 500 cases of the disease in town, with about 150 fatalities, mostly among children. However, smallpox cases continued to appear and deaths continued to occur, and October saw a vigorous resurgence of the killer. Then, mercifully, the disease abated. In all, some 200 Tucsonans died of smallpox during 1877, about 5% of the population. Today, such a loss of life would be regarded as a calamity of immense proportions, but in the 1870s an outbreak of a deadly disease was viewed as a sad but normal part of life.]

Oct. 11. Cloudy. Stage came--no mail for me. Telegrams from Silver City say Tom Bow shot and killed a gambler in that place and escaped. Holden and Sullivan started for the mines and were brought back by a constable. 12 noon-- still cloudy. Holden went out again. Shiner arrived from Sonora. Jim Blade's little girl Rosa was taken to the pest hospital today. I went to bed at 11 o'clock.

Oct. 12. Windy. Smith, Ike Brokaw, and Blade arrived in town. Parker, Antoine, and others also came in. Jim Blade's little boy died this evening of smallpox. Mud Spring Steve beat Parker's game for $300. John W. Clark was taken with smallpox and went to the hospital.

Oct. 13. Quite cold. Stage came in early. Blade's boy was buried this morning. There were some more arrivals from Sonora today. I sent for a picture of a double team. Went to bed at 9 o'clock.

Oct. 14 (Sunday). Cold and cloudy. 9 a.m.--rain and a very cold wind. 12 noon--still raining. It rained all day and hard after sundown. Very cold evening. Closed early.

Oct. 15. The clouds cleared off. Pleasant, cold, and muddy. Very dull day. Clark is very low and it is not thought possible for him to recover.

Oct. 16. Fine cold morning. John W. Clark died during last night of smallpox. He will be buried today. The stage from the west came in early. Red Hart, John Hart, and others came in from Sonora. W. J. Ross was appointed undersheriff and jailor by Sheriff Shibell. The jail keys were turned over to him this morning. Nothing new today. Went to bed at 10 o'clock.

Oct. 17. Got up early. Raised the flag to commemorate the surrender of Burgoyne at Saratoga in 1777. Cloudy and quite cold today, very cold after dark. Went to bed at 9:30.

Oct. 18. Cool morning. There was an auction sale today of saloon fixtures at Levin and Braun's house. Stage came in--very little mail. There is a synopsis of President Hayes' message in this morning's *Star*. Cold all day. Dobbs opened a faro game in the house this evening. I went to bed feeling quite sick.

Oct. 19. Raised the flag this morning--it is the anniversary of the surrender of Lord Cornwallis at Yorktown, Va., in 1781. Cold and windy today. Lew B. White and another man left for Texas. Cold at night.

John Wasson helped found the Arizona Citizen *newspaper in Tucson in 1870. He sold the* Citizen *to John Clum in 1877. Arizona Historical Society, Tucson, #23793.*

Oct. 20. Cold and windy. There were two auctions today. The games in the house ran till 3 in the morning.

Oct. 21 (Sunday). Fine morning. Very dull all day. Nothing new. The games were lively in the evening. Stayed open until after 12.

Oct. 22. Cold morning. I ran the flag up--the anniversary of the Battle of White Plains in 1776. Went to court and was excused from the jury by Judge French. The mail came from both east and west. Johnny Hart put a sore head on King William and landed in jail.

Oct. 23. Cloudy this morning. King William and John Hart were fined $10 each. William's other case is being tried today. No evidence was presented against him, so the jury acquitted him. Very dull today. Jim Caldwell got drunk and got discharged by his boss. I went to bed early.

Oct. 24. Pleasant day. The stage came in early--nothing for me. Very dull. John Dawson [charged with grand larceny] was tried and acquitted this evening. Mayor Allen turned over the ground to the Southern Pacific Railroad Company for their depot today. John B. Hart backed the cards out of the box and says he wants no more faro games in Tucson.

Oct. 25. Fine morning. Dull all day. I stayed up all night.

Oct. 26. Fine weather this morning. Nothing new. Wrote to Currier & Ives for some pictures, sent them $2.00. George Fields came in this evening. Our Indian helper, Charley, got a terrible beating late in the night. Closed at 1 o'clock.

Oct. 27. The *Citizen* came out very early today--it has been sold and will be moved immediately to Florence. [John Wasson and R.C. Brown sold the *Arizona Citizen* to John P. Clum, the former agent at the San Carlos Indian Reservation.] 12 noon--George Fields' freight wagons are in and now unloading. After dinner, Noriega's wagon train came in--we received 5 cases of beer from Yuma. Shaw is tight and on the warpath. Sanders knocked the stuffing out of John Brown's monte game. Everybody is drunk tonight but Dobbs and myself. I went to bed at 10:30.

Oct. 28 (Sunday). Windy. Dull. I was sick all day with a bad cold. Nothing doing today until night. The faro game ran till 3 o'clock--it lost $200. There was a dance tonight given by Hucke.

Oct. 29. Pleasant morning. 11 a.m.--terrific wind and dust. Dobbs got drunk and his faro game went broke.

Oct. 30. Pleasant in the daytime, cold at night. I was sober all day. Went to bed early.

Oct. 31. Cold morning. Commenced bookbinding. Foster's cook left this morning.

~ ~ ~ ~ ~

November 1. Cold. The stage arrived--very little mail. There was a dance at Meridith's saloon. Speedy and Co. opened a faro game in the house and made a winning the first night. Charley Paige is very tight. A telegram says that Senator O. P. Morton died this evening. [Oliver Morton of Indiana was a well-known Union patriot during the Civil War.] No more news today. Went to bed early.

Nov. 2. Very cold and windy. The stage came in early--no mail for me. My flag was at half mast all day. Very dull.

Nov. 3. Cold and windy this morning. No *Citizen* today. Several fellows came in from the mines. There were two fights in the Ohio Saloon. Very dull in our house. Closed early.

Nov. 4 (Sunday). Cold, windy, and dusty. Dobb's faro game at Dill's saloon was taken for a loss. Very dull. Went to bed at 10 o'clock.

Nov. 5. Cold morning. Prentiss and Caballero had a row in which Mr. C. was badly cut. I received some papers from brother Milton. 12 noon--very pleasant. John Ming got drunk and got on the warpath. He had a fight with McIntee and was worsted. In the evening, McIntee was jubilant over his performance and talked too much, in consequence of which he got a sore head painted on his shoulders by Brokaw. When he got a chance to run he made good his escape by the fastest running this year. All is quiet now. Closed at 12 o'clock.

Nov. 6. Very cold. "Duke" George [McIntee] has not been seen since last evening. I received a picture by mail. Wrote to William White. Very dull all day. Tom Roddick came in and went out sober. 6 p.m.--Duke George put in an appearance. He has two black eyes, a swelled nose, and looks like a defective p. f. There was a faro game in the house this evening. Mr. Redfield went in for several dollars and soaked [pawned] his pipe, watch, and field glasses. I went to bed early.

Nov. 7. Cold. The Sonora stage arrived at 6 p.m. Dull all day. Lew Burton got discharged and got tight. The faro game lost.

Nov. 8. Fine cold morning. The stage came--nothing for me. Nothing new today.

Nov. 9. Fine weather. John Brown and Parker left for Florence. John Ming got drunk and had a boxing match with a Negro. He struck a window and cut his hand very badly. Billy Wood came to town. I received a letter from A. T. Garrison. Went to bed at 9 o'clock.

Nov. 10. Fine morning. 9 o'clock--windy and dusty. Stage came--received some papers from Mit. I wrote to Garrison and Samuel Jones. Billy Wood had a fight with Sam Hughes and got licked. The first number of the *Citizen* from Pinal County arrived.

Nov. 11 (Sunday). Fine morning. I had a hot bath. Windy and dusty at 11 o'clock. Ross and a prisoner started for Yuma [site of the territorial prison, completed in July 1876]. Harry B. Jones, [three-year-old] son of Buckalew's brother-in-law, died today.

Nov. 12. Warm this morning. 9 a.m.--windy and very dusty. The stage from Cal. arrived at 11:30--I received a letter from my sister. There was terrific wind and dust all day. Lew Burton left for Maricopa Wells. Harry B. Jones, son of Mr. H. C. Jones, was buried today. The monte and faro games both ran nearly all night in the house. I went to bed at 10 o'clock.

Nov. 13. Cold and clear. Very pleasant. Stage came in--no mail for me. Old Brown (Brumfield) is in town--he is drunk and singing Methodist hymns. Foster is dealing faro. I went to bed at 11 o'clock.

Nov. 14. Cold but pleasant day--no wind or dust. No one killed. No one lost. Very dull. Not a cent to be seen. McIntee got drunk in the evening. Johnson the saddler got drunk--very drunk. The faro and monte games ran late--faro lost, monte won. I went to bed at 10:30 o'clock.

Nov. 15. Very cold morning. The boys call for hot drinks. The stage came in--very little mail. Very dull all day. McIntee is drunk. I commenced to read the memoirs of General W. T. Sherman. The faro and monte games ran till 1 o'clock. I retired at 9.

Nov. 16. Cold and windy. Lew Bailey came in on the stage. Very dull all day. There were only a few faro and monte players. We had one fight tonight. Closed up at 12 o'clock.

Nov. 17. The stage came in early. Quite cold. Street cleaning today. Cold, dull, and dreary. There was a dance at the Palace Hotel at night.

Nov. 18 (Sunday). Cold morning. Cold all day. Very dull. James Fitzgerald came to town broke, but got a job in half an hour. I went to bed early.

Nov. 19. Fine weather. The stage came in early--nothing for me. Very cold this morning. Fitzgerald left for the mines. Very dull. Went to bed at 9:30.

Nov. 20. Cold. Dull. Sullivan has gone three days without whiskey. Cold tonight. I received some pictures from Currier & Ives.

Nov. 21. Quite cold. Very dull. A prisoner escaped from jail last night. The jailor, McDermott, had a run of 1½ miles and caught him while he was taking a drink from the ditch. Very dull all day. The faro game did not open, but monte was going full blast. Foster dealt until after 9. When Foster got up the game was a 60- or 70-dollar winner. Ike Brokaw dealt until 12 o'clock--the game closed a loser. They turned to poker and played all night. Charley Butler was a winner, over $100 on the night.

Nov. 22. Cold this morning. The poker game is still running, Speedy and Gifford both losers. 10 a.m.--sunny and quite warm. The stage arrived. I sent for more pictures to Currier & Ives. Very cold this evening. Went to bed at 9 o'clock.

Nov. 23. Cold. The house was open and running all night. The stage came in at 10 a.m.--no mail for me. The monte game was still running at 3 p.m. There was a good game all day and night. Closed at 2 in the morning.

Nov. 24. They are cleaning the streets and it is very dusty. The stage arrived at 10 o'clock. Duke George, alias Mr. McIntee, got in a fight with someone and got flour all over him. He was very much excited.

Nov. 25 (Sunday). Fine cool morning. John Brown and Parker returned from Florence. Dull all day. Old Dublin came to town. Nothing very new. McIntee has not showed up today.

Nov. 26. Colder today. John Hart and Franklin returned from prospecting. I spent the whole day looking over old files of the *Spirit of the Times*. John Brown and Parker opened a faro game in the house.

Nov. 27. Cold. Dull all day. Smith and Banning returned from Sonora. I went to bed at 10 o'clock.

Nov. 28. Very cold. The monte games ran all day. Nothing new. John Miller is on a bust. John Moore was married this evening. Closed up and went to bed at 11 o'clock.

Nov. 29. Thanksgiving Day. I raised the flag. Had beans for dinner. The stores are all closed today, except for some Mexican ones. Jerry Kenny brought us a mince pie. Cold tonight. Closed early.

Nov. 30. Cold morning. Very dull. 11 a.m.--the stage is not in yet. 12 noon--the sun came out warm and it is quite pleasant. I have been working on my scrapbook since breakfast. Did not take a drink until the whistle blew at noon. Very windy and cold this afternoon. Rheumatism took hold in my right shoulder. Ross was on a drunk this evening. He wanted to fight--could lick anybody. He broke down a door on a house in Maiden Lane.

~ ~ ~ ~ ~

December 1. Cold and windy. Joe Steele came in from Florence by stage. Cold all day. John Brown opened a faro game in Levin's. I went to bed at 10 o'clock.

Dec. 2 (Sunday). Cold. Very windy and dusty. Very dull. Joe Steele and two discharged soldiers left on the stage, headed west. Charley White came to town. Boley and Myers came in with their freight wagons. The house was open till 2 in the morning.

Dec. 3. Cold but pleasant. All sorts of vehicles are in requisition today to go to the Feast of San Xavier. I received a letter and some papers from John Shipler, also some papers from brother Milton.

Dec. 4. Cold and dull. The monte game lost $200 last night.

Dec. 5. Cold and very dull. Foster is sick. We closed at 1 o'clock. I had a pain in my side and put on a mustard plaster. Went to bed.

Dec. 6. The weather is more moderate today. I feel pretty well this morning. 12 noon--windy and very dusty. We bought a new stove. Foster is sick and went home early. Very dull in the house. The monte games closed early. I closed the house at 10 o'clock and went to bed.

Dec. 7. Cold, windy, and dusty. The stage came in early. 10 a.m.--very windy and terrible dusty. It got cloudy after dark. Very dull day. Closed at 10 o'clock.

Dec. 8. there was rain and bully thunder at 3 o'clock this morning. The rain has at last set in for good. An old friend of mine has just returned from the City of Mexico. 11:30--no stage yet. 12 noon--the stage came in. It rained nearly all day--the house leaked some. Went to bed at 10 o'clock.

Dec. 9 (Sunday). Muddy and damp. The sun came out very fine. Captain Rogers left and took Charley White with him. I went to bed early after a warm bath. A drunken American lady called on me.

Dec. 10. Fine day. The Sonora stage left with 9 passengers. It broke down and sent back for another coach. A new monte game opened in our house, run by Parker, John Brown, and Gifford. I was sober all day. Went to bed at 9 o'clock. [In 1886, professional gamblers Ben C. Parker and Eli B. Gifford, along with saloon owner W. S. Read, donated 40 acres of land about a mile east of town for the new University of Arizona campus. Old Main, the first university building, was completed on the site in 1891.]

Dec. 11. Got up at 6:30. Pleasant day, a little windy. Nothing new. Last night John Day arrived in town with his family. E. D. Wood is drunk and cursing the Democrats and all other men. I went to bed at 10 o'clock.

Dec. 12. Nothing new today. Very dull. Closed early.

Dec. 13. Mild weather this morning. A telegram from Florence this morning says that the stage was stopped by road agents. They found nothing in the treasure box and did not trouble the mail. The coach came in this morning at 11:30. No further news about the robbers. A telegram from San Carlos says all the Indians jumped the reservation. They attacked a wagon train near Ash Spring below Camp Bowie. A mail rider was also killed.

Dec. 14. Cloudy all day. Nothing was heard of the stage robbers. The stage came in very late. Col. Boyle and others came in today. It commenced raining just before midnight.

Dec. 15. It is raining hard this morning. The house leaks like a sieve. Foster was up playing cards all last night. Some Mexicans are fixing the roof. The rain quit but it is still cloudy. Bill Morgan came in town. Tom Roddick and John Day are trying to drink up all the whiskey in town.

Dec. 16 (Sunday). Still cloudy. There is a heavy fog all around town--you cannot see the hills. Vic [dog] married Prince this morning. Very dull today. George Fields came in this evening. I wrote to Currier & Ives, 938 Chambers St., New York City. Went to bed at 9 o'clock.

Dec. 17. Foggy this morning and quite warm. Some fellows left for the Aztec Mine [in the Santa Rita Mountains south of town] this morning. They took one half of the only bit [12½¢] saloon in town. Wilson returned from Sonora. I received some pictures from Currier & Ives.

Dec. 18. Cloudy and warm. Had venison for breakfast. 3 p.m.--it commenced raining. John Dobbs got drunk. Gibson came in and also got full. The mail stage came in after dark--no through mail. I went to bed at 9 o'clock. It rained quite hard during the night.

Dec. 19. Cold damp morning. The sun came out at 9 o'clock and it is quite pleasant. 3 p.m.--it is cloudy again. No mail today. It cleared off and was cold at night.

Dec. 20. Fine morning. Cold and cloudy later in the day. Sorghum Smith returned from Sonora late in the evening. The mail stage arrived at 9 at night. I went to bed at 10.

Dec. 21. Cloudy and very foggy. The house was open all night. Doc McClary and Jim Speedy returned from Sonora.

Dec. 22. Cold all day. John Hovey returned from Sonora, arriving at 9 o'clock at night.

Dec. 23 (Sunday). Cold this morning. The sun came out at 9 o'clock and it was warm and pleasant. The stage came in at 12 noon. The stage headed for Sonora was stopped and robbed last night and the mail was looked into.

Dec. 24 (Christmas Eve). Fine morning. There were lots of people in the house all day, but very little money. I invested $5 for Foster's children's Christmas. Bill Elliott came to town. Lots of horse talk all during the evening. I closed at 12 o'clock and went to Mass. Came home at 2 in the morning.

Dec. 25 (Christmas Day). It rained all last night. Sullivan got drunk and lay out in the water all night. Very dull this morning. No eggnog today. Pleasant but cold this afternoon. There was a small monte game in the house. The stage came in at 10 p.m. Closed up at 11:30.

Dec. 26. Cold and very dull day. Many of the boys are sick from eating mince pie. The mail stage came in after dark. Closed early.

Dec. 27. Today is the anniversary of the Battle of Trenton. The stage came in--very little mail. I went to a ball at the house of Doña Flavia--had a fine time.

Dec. 28. Cold morning. John Burt came to town and brought me a hind quarter of venison. He also made me a present of a new hat. The mail stage came in--received an invitation to the wedding of my sister Mira's daughter Mary. I also received a letter from Red Hart.

Dec. 29. Very cold and very dull. Doc Atkinson, Matlock, and another man came in from a prospecting tour. Matlock and the other man were arrested this evening on the word of the stage driver as the men who robbed the Sonora stage. They were put in jail. John Burt is drunk. I went to bed at 10:30 o'clock.

Dec. 30 (Sunday). Cold and windy. Very dull day. Went to bed early.

Dec. 31 (New Year's Eve). Cold. Dull. The stage robbers had a hearing and were turned loose. I went to a kept man's dance at the saloon of Ben

Fairbanks. I stayed up till 12 o'clock and then raised the flag to half-mast for the dead year. Went to bed.

~ ~ ~ ~ ~

Charles Shibell was sheriff of Pima County from 1877 to 1880. It was his job to catch the desperados who menaced travelers in southern Arizona in 1878. Buehman photo, Arizona Historical Society, Tucson, #6972.

166

Chapter Four

OUTLAWS TERRORIZE THE ARIZONA COUNTRYSIDE--1878

"The officers on the track of the single robber found him by the treachery of his partner and were obliged to kill him. An ambulance was sent out to bring him in. They laid him on a table in the courthouse. Hundreds went to see him as he was displayed with his guns and accoutrements on." George Hand, August 19, 1878

Prospectors and speculators flocked to southern Arizona in 1878, drawn by reports of the richness of the new silver mines at Tombstone. The population and wealth of Arizona was growing, but effective law enforcement in the countryside was still a scarce commodity. Along with honest miners, the silver boom attracted an undesirable element, and outlaws and road agents proliferated. Travelers were now more threatened by bandits than Apaches. In response, lawmen and vigilantes took to the hills in search of the villains who were causing the trouble.

~ ~ ~ ~ ~

January 1, 1878 (New Year's Day). The new year opened cold. I stayed home all day and drank all the whiskey I needed. Took some candy and nuts to Foster's children. Sullivan took his family to San Xavier, and on returning he turned the wagon over, breaking it very badly. No one was hurt. Election of city officers today. [James H. Toole was elected mayor, Adolph Buttner marshal.] I went to bed at 12 o'clock. Foster stayed up all night.

Jan. 2. Very cold. Several men are drunk this morning, and many are sick from drinking yesterday. Riley Dunton got robbed last night. Telegrams say that the army paymaster's ambulance was stopped near Maricopa Wells by road agents who took $250 and three mules from him. I got full again today.

Jan. 3. Cold this morning. I raised the flag in honor of the Battle of Princeton. There were several dances in town this evening. I went to bed early. Foster stayed up all night.

Jan. 4. Cold. The house was open all night. Blade and Speedy left for the new army post [Camp Huachuca, 80 miles to the southeast] to play cards. H. B. Smith left for Sonora to bring up his herd of cows and horses. Very dull all day. Went to bed early.

Jan. 5. Cloudy. Cleaned my room, and blacked my boots for the first time in two months. Gibson sold his ranch--he went there to bring his property back to town. It was cloudy this evening, with wind and some rain after dark. I went to bed at 10:30. The monte game ran till 2 in the morning.

Jan. 6 (Sunday). The clouds cleared off--pleasant but cold. Very dull all day. The stage came--no news. Nothing to do today but read. It got cloudy in the evening and looked much like rain. Gibson came in and brought a dog.

Jan. 7. Cold but pleasant this morning. Dill went out with the Aztec miners. John Ming left for Hooker's ranch, got drunk on the way, and came back. I wrote to Red Hart in Texas, and received some papers from brother Milton. Went to bed at 10 o'clock. Faro, monte, and other games kept the house open until 4 in the morning.

Jan. 8. I raised the flag before sunrise in honor of the anniversary of the Battle of New Orleans. Dull all day in the house. A few drunken men were in town. A report says that John Burt was arrested at a camp in the mountains for stage robbery. I went to bed early. Some noisy men were singing in the street during the night--nothing new.

Jan. 9. Fine morning. Nothing new, dull all day. Bill Morgan is in town. Sullivan is drunk. Marsh is drunk. Lots of men drunk. A spitz game started at 3 p.m. and was still going when I went to bed.

Jan. 10. Got up at 6 o'clock--the spitz game is still running. Cloudy and cold all day. Sullivan is drunk again. The spitz game ran nearly all day. There was a dance at the Cosmopolitan Hotel in the evening, but it broke up for a lack of ladies. I stayed up till 12 o'clock--got pretty full of rye.

Jan. 11. Cold and cloudy. It rained for a few minutes at 8 o'clock this morning. 10 a.m.--the sun is out and it is quite pleasant. A telegram came today telling of the death of John W. Sweeney in Florence.

Jan. 12. Fine morning. Stage came in--received a new binder for the *Spirit of the Times*. Dr. Handy returned from a visit to Sweeney. A fire broke out in Fairbanks' saloon caused by a falling lamp. It burned everything inside and the roof and floor. A dance was given by T. G. Rusk tonight at Sullivan Hall. I went up and looked on for a few moments. Came home and went to bed.

Jan. 13 (Sunday). Fine morning. Taken with a pain in my side and was sick all day. Quite lively in the house today. Brown opened a faro game this evening. Foster's Indian helper [Charley] won $10 at monte. I went to bed with a mustard plaster.

Jan. 14. Fine morning. The monte games ran pretty well today. John Brown's game is busy. I was sick all day and went to bed early.

Jan. 15. Cold but a fine day. A report says that the Palace Hotel has changed hands. A telegram says that a Mr. Tozer has relieved Magee as manager of the Aztec Mine. I received a Utica [New York] paper with a notice of the marriage and death of my niece Mary Roberts Harbison. Jerry Kenny moved his saloon into Sullivan's house. Very dull all day and evening. I was sick all day, am some better tonight. Went to bed early.

Jan. 16. Fine morning. Received a letter from Sam Jones at Camp Apache. Very dull today. Went to bed early.

Jan. 17. Warm this morning. There was a short shower of rain at 9 a.m. Dave Wilson left for Camp Grant. 11 a.m.--cloudy again. The *Star* came out this morning but failed to take notice of the death of J. W. Sweeney. I sent some papers to Sam Jones. Tom Roddick and Brown are in town. Tom is drunk. Dobbs is drunk. Sullivan is sober. Captain Jeffords is in town.

Jan. 18. Pleasant morning. Nothing new. Wrote to Currier & Ives. Roddick took Tinker [dog] to the Sahuarita Ranch [20 miles south of town]. Jack Dunn and Captain Jeffords dropped in on us this evening. I did not remember Jack until he told of giving Foster an old dog 9 years ago. There was a pretty good faro game tonight--Brown won $60. Parker and Gifford lost a couple of hundred to Jim Blade.

Tom Jeffords was one of the few of George Hand's customers who lived to a ripe old age. He is shown here at his home in the desert north of Tucson in 1914, shortly before his death at the age of 82. Arizona Historical Society, Tucson, #8170.

Jan. 19. Fine morning. Washed out the house. The stage came in at 10 a.m.--no mail for me. There is street cleaning all over town. A report says that one of the *padres* [priests] who returned from Fort Yuma has the smallpox.

The faro and monte games ran till after 12--monte won, faro lost. I went to bed early.

Jan. 20 (Sunday). Fine day. Dull. Pat O'Meara and Shambeck came to town. There was a dance at Fairbanks' house. Foster kept our house open all night--there was a good faro game. I went to bed at 10 o'clock.

Jan. 21. Cold. The house was open all last night. Drunken men are sleeping on every table. Sullivan is drunk. Jim Blade is drunk. John Ming is drunk. Tom Roddick arrived in town and got drunk in 30 minutes. George Atkinson left for Camp Grant this morning. There were good faro and monte games this evening. I retired at 11 o'clock.

Jan. 22. The house is still open and monte still running--did not close last night. Brown's faro game went broke, monte won. The stage arrived at 10 a.m. Windy and very dusty today. Roddick got very tight and left for the copper mine. Panchita [a little girl] died at 9 o'clock this evening. Faro ran all night.

Jan. 23. Cloudy this morning. Faro is still going--Brown kept playing, even after losing badly yesterday. A poker game started after faro closed--Charley Paige was the loser. The stage came--not much mail. Panchita was buried today. We closed at 12.

Jan. 24. Cloudy and cold. Wrote to Pat Connelly at Florence. A telegram from Marshal Buttner says he caught some stage robbers at Burk's Station [between Maricopa Wells and Yuma]. Elisha House died today. Blade is drunk and playing cards against Comstock. 6 p.m.--Blade an $80 loser. He is still drunk and nearly broke. He played seven-up with Dobbs, got robbed, and went home. I retired at 9 o'clock. The faro game ran till three in the morning.

Jan. 25. The house was open all last night. Several drunken men are still around. There is a high wind and it is very dusty. The stage came in early. There was a good monte game all evening. A poker game ran all night--Parker, McClary, Caldwell, and Vedder. I went to bed at 9:30 o'clock with Jo and the other dogs.

Jan. 26. Marsh woke me at 4 in the morning. I got up and found eight men asleep on tables and in chairs--the poker game had just closed. The stage came in this morning--they say two men in a buggy were stopped and robbed on the road between Picacho and Desert Station. Very dull all day. Closed early.

Jan. 27 (Sunday). Nothing new, very dull. I took some pills and went to bed with a mustard plaster.

Jan. 28. Still sick. McCullough lost a horse on the way out of town and came back to find him. The stage came early--light mail. Fairbanks opened a monte game in the house. I was sick all day and went to bed early.

Jan. 29. Cold. Washed out the house this morning. I feel some better today. Stage came--no mail for me. Dull, nothing new. Went to bed early and sick.

Jan. 30. Cold today. Doña Josepha pupped this morning. I received some back numbers of *Country Gentleman* [magazine]. Dull all day. There was a small faro game in the house in the evening--it ran until 2 in the morning.

Jan. 31. Fine morning. The mail stage came early. Dave Knox came in from Globe. He played faro all evening and lost $300. The faro game closed and Knox opened flare, and quit a $2 winner. Nothing very interesting happened today.

~ ~ ~ ~ ~

February 1. Fine morning. The stage came in early. Nothing new.

Feb. 2. Fine morning. News came of another attempted stage robbery, this time at Filibuster Camp [near Yuma]. The driver was shot in the arm but did not stop. There is some sort of a big thing at the convent of the Sisters today. Foster and I had an invitation to a hop at the army post [Camp Lowell] but did not go. Several of the boys went to it and came home full. We closed at 1 o'clock.

Feb. 3 (Sunday). Windy and dusty. There is some excitement about town-- lots of drunken men are around. The games are going fine in the house. Sullivan had a fight with some Mexicans. Ike Brokaw opened a flare game today and won quite a lot. Dull in the evening. Went to bed at 9 o'clock.

Feb. 4. Moderate weather. 9 a.m.--wind and dust. Some packers came in from a camp in the mountains for grub. The stage came in early--received some papers from Mit. Sullivan is drunk again. No faro game in the house this evening.

Feb. 5. Very dusty. Morrison bought 7 gallons of mescal from Steele and left for the country. Charley Butler left for the Point of Mountain [stage station]. Waltemath is drunk. The Pima Mine men came in today--the mine [about 20 miles south of town] is shut down for the present. They all got tight.

Feb. 6. Fine day. The stage came in--received a paper from J. L. Shipler and a letter from William White, State of New York, an old friend of my father. Saw Charley Cannon, in from Florence--he told me that Pat Connelly was very sick and not expected to live. Dobbs and Goodwin are playing cards, $25 a game. Dobbs won $200 on Goodwin's jawbone [promise to pay]. Fernando Otero was buried today. I went to bed at 9 o'clock.

Feb. 7. The *Star* came out early. Nothing very new. The monte games were running all day. Tom Roddick came to town and got drunk in 30 minutes. Sullivan is full as a tick. Gifford opened a faro game in Brown's saloon. Charley Rice is in town--drunk. Dobbs is on the warpath. John Brown is sober. We had a light sprinkle of rain this evening. Went to bed at 10 o'clock.

Feb. 8. Clear and pleasant. Several people came in from Altar, Sonora. Levin's flag is at half-mast for the death of the Pope of Rome [Pius IX]. C. A. Paige and Knox had a row in Brown's saloon over a faro game. Knox had a pistol but was disarmed. He afterward got a shotgun and hunted for Paige but did not find him.

Feb. 9. Cold morning. Nothing new. People are coming to town to attend court. The house was open all night. The faro game won a little.

Feb. 10 (Sunday). Fine morning. Knox and Dr. Porter left for Florence-- Knox did not settle his little bills with the boys. I received a letter from my sister Mira and one from Aunt Elizabeth. Ate a caviar lunch at Levin's. At a dance this evening, several of the boys were invited to leave for not having an invitation card. That broke up the ball. I went to bed at 10 o'clock.

Feb. 11. Very cold--froze the water in the ollas. We scrubbed out the house this morning--Sullivan and Marsh officiated as scrubs. I had fried cabbage for breakfast. Received a copy of a Department of Agriculture report from Delegate H. S. Stevens. It was windy and dusty all day. The games ran till midnight.

Feb. 12. Cold. 9 a.m.--the wind and dust came up. The stage came in-- little mail. Comstock turned his faro table east-and-west for luck. George Fields came in yesterday. I am sick but getting better. Belknap's horseshoer died very suddenly this evening.

Feb. 13. Cloudy. The grand jury is in session. The stage came--received some pictures from Currier & Ives, no letters. Milt Ward is in town. H. B. Smith and Jim Blade returned from Sonora in a *carreta* [a two-wheeled Mexican cart]. They brought three horses. Very dull all day. Went to bed early.

Feb. 14. Cloudy this morning. Nothing new, very dull. Mr. Cummings, alias Dublin, left town today. Jerry Kenny says he has furnished George Foster with drinks for 12 years and never got anything for it. I say it is a lie.

Feb. 15. Fair weather this morning. I sent to Currier & Ives for three pictures. Received a letter from William F. Bradley. There are a great many strangers in town. Bill Gale and Jonesy returned from a surveying trip. H. B. Smith opened a faro game in Brown's saloon. Ben Fairbanks opened a monte game in our house and it ran all night. Chiquita [dog] took her medicine this evening.

Feb. 16. Moderate weather. Gale and Jonesy rented a room next to mine. Kiota [dog] is missing--someone has carried him off. Sullivan left for the mines. Roddick left also. Dull all day and night.

Feb. 17 (Sunday). Fine morning. There was a big time in the church today. There was an eclipse of the moon this morning. Ike Brokaw and Lyons opened a flare game in the house today and doubled their capital. Ed Hudson is in town. Bill Gale left for White's ranch. I went to a dance at the Ohio Saloon--had a fine time. Went to bed at 10:30 o'clock.

Feb. 18. Fine day. Reed left for Sonora. I received some papers from Milton. Charley Lovejoy returned to Tucson. [Charles Lovejoy had been sent to prison at Yuma the previous year for embezzling from the post office. He was subsequently pardoned by the president at the request of several prominent Arizonans.] The trial of Theodore Brown for the killing of Hiram Kennedy [at Safford in October 1877] started this morning. Vic had three pups. Cloudy this evening. Very dull. Went to bed early.

Feb. 19. Cloudy and a little sprinkle of rain this morning. Very windy and awful dusty. We received some Milwaukee beer today. Stanford [Brown's lawyer] talked to the jury for 4 hours. They retired after dark and at 10 o'clock returned a verdict of guilty of murder in the second degree. It rained quite hard for half an hour after dark and the house leaked badly. Very dull. Went to bed early.

Feb. 20. Fine clear morning. The stage came in early. The court adjourned on account of the death of John Farley, brother of [Deputy] District Attorney Hugh Farley. I went to bed at 9:30 o'clock. The faro game ran till two tomorrow morning.

Feb. 21. Cloudy. 10 a.m.--rain. We fixed the roof just in time to prevent leaking. The funeral of John Farley was held at the Catholic church. It rained hard and was very cold all day.

Feb. 22. I raised the flag before sunrise [for Washington's Birthday]. Tom Roddick arrived in town this morning. Tom Britton came in in the evening. Lyons pasted Noriega in the left eye. Roddick, Britton, and Hudson are all very drunk. I went to bed at 10:30 o'clock. Foster kept the house was open till one.

Feb. 23. Fine morning. The mail stage came in at 10 a.m.--nothing for me. John Day came to town and got drunk in 1 hour. His wife had a kid. Nothing very strange happened today. There was considerable drinking, all on jawbone [credit]. Ross and Ed Hudson came very near having a row. Billy Gale had a "quail" in his room and Jones and Hudson had to sleep in the street.

Feb. 24 (Sunday). Cloudy. The churches are running today. The boys are still broke and still trying to get drunk. Ike Brokaw and Lyons opened a monte game and won over $100. I went to bed early.

Feb. 25. The stage came but again no mail for me. I wrote to William F. Bradley and sent some papers to the States. Tom Roddick left for home. Captain Jeffords came to town. John Brown opened a monte game in the house. Court is still going on. I feel pretty well today. It is cold but pleasant.

Feb. 26. Got up early--feel well. Cold and cloudy this morning. The faro game in Brown's saloon was a loser yesterday. Ed Hudson quit drinking mescal and took to beer. Henry Hooker was acquitted of cattle stealing. Cold this evening. Went to bed at 9:30 o'clock.

Feb. 27. Fine morning. The faro game ran all night at Brown's saloon. Jesús Ghanetto, wife of Christopher Ghanetto, was buried today. The trial of John Moore on an indictment for stealing cattle is going on today. The stage came in--no Cal. mail. No [San Francisco] *Chronicles* have come in 5 days. John Moore was acquitted.

Feb. 28. It rained quite hard last night, and is still raining. The roof leaks badly. Very dull in the house. Captain Devers died today. The case of John Ming [charged with stealing cattle] was tried today. Verdict--acquittal. [John Ming and pioneer Arizona rancher Henry C. Hooker were accused of running a cattle-stealing ring, and John Moore, owner of the Tucson Meat Market, was charged with receiving stolen cattle from them. All were acquitted.]

~ ~ ~ ~ ~

March 1. A bogus revenue officer was arrested and confined today. After a hearing before Justice Meyer he was placed under $1,000 bail. Chapman and Billy Wall came to town from Camp Grant. The stage did not arrive until 8 in the evening--very little mail. Dull in the house today.

Mar. 2. Fine morning. The trial of Mr. Graham, the bogus revenue officer, is going on. Marsh is drunk. Jeff Paige is full as a goose. The stage came in at 8 p.m., 15 hours from Florence--very heavy mail. There was a dance at the flour mill--not a success. The boys all got drunk and no ladies went. Very dull all day. I went to bed at 11 o'clock. The house was open all night.

Mar. 3 (Sunday). The house was open when I got up and monte was still running. Foster went to bed early this morning. I received some pictures from Dr. Lord. 11 a.m.--very windy and dusty. There were several dances today. There was one this afternoon upstairs in the hotel--a high-toned dance. Theatre tonight. I went to bed at 11 o'clock.

Mar. 4. Cold. The stage came in late--brought lots of N.Y. papers, none from Cal. Tom Roddick came in town, got drunk very soon, and kept that way. I kept very sober all day and went to bed so.

Mar. 5. Cool this morning. Roddick came up early and got pretty full. He was going to start for home but got too tight and failed to get off. No mail today. Went to bed early.

Mar. 6. Got up early, cleaned the lamps. Got ready for a ride to the post and the farms on Rillito Creek. We started at 9 a.m., Bill Sniffin, a Mexican, and myself, and rode to the post [Camp Lowell]. We did not stop there, but continued on, past Dunham's ranch, and camped in the creek bottom. Bill and the Mexican commenced digging up small cottonwood trees for transplanting in the dooryard of Wheeler Williams. 12 noon--we pulled out the whiskey bottle and went for the lunch. We fed the horses and the boys went at the trees again. I lay under the shade of a tree till Bill was ready and we then came home. This was my first leave of absence from home in a long time--had a fine day. Gale and Jonesy went to the mines. I went to bed early.

Mar. 7. Got up early. I raised the flag to the masthead in honor of the birthday of a celebrated old pisser named George Hand--48 years old. A few less than three thousand people have asked why the flag was up, but they all went away as wise as when they came--I am celebrating this day by myself. Theodore Brown received a sentence of 20 years in prison today [for killing

174

Hiram Kennedy in October 1877]. We have broken all our ollas and water is in great demand. I went to bed early and full.

Officers' row at Fort Lowell in the 1880s. The post's designation was changed from "camp" to "fort" in 1879. Fort Lowell was abandoned by the military in 1891. Arizona Historical Society, Tucson, #42674.

Mar. 8. Cold and cloudy. The wind started blowing early and it is very dusty. The mail stage came early--nothing for me but a paper. Dublin arrived in town. Shaw also came in. Tom Gardner and Santa Cruz Brown came in town last night. The Adobe Club [a recently-organized social club] had a hop this evening. The lager beer and champagne cider supplies suffered.

Mar. 9. Fine morning. Street cleaning today. 9 a.m.--the stage has not arrived from Florence. I sent a money order for the *Trotting Record.* The Rio Grande mail stage arrived at 11:30, and the stage from the west came this afternoon. There was a show this evening in the house opposite ours. Foster went to bed sick. Marsh and I closed up at 1 o'clock tomorrow.

Mar. 10 (Sunday). Fine morning. The stage came in--received a letter from Dr. Jay Porter, Silver City. Parker, Brown, and Sport left for Camp Grant. Dobbs leaves today for Camp Apache. Marsh got tight. There was little monte played--both games closed winners on the day. Theatre tonight.

Mar. 11. Fine day. The mail from both the east and west came in on time--received some papers from Milton. Tom Britton came to town. Marsh is drunk. Foster is sick with a headache. I went to bed early.

Mar. 12. Fine morning. Several of the boys got drunk early this morning. 12 noon--the sun is very warm. I signed over a deed to a mining claim to Tom

Roddick. McKey got very tight today. Marsh, while serving him, also got pretty full. I got just about full and went to bed at 10 o'clock.

Mar. 13. Fine day. I received $50 from Tom Roddick for the Smuggler Mine. Tom left for his ranch. Nothing new. Jim Caldwell arrived with his wagon train.

Mar. 14. Fine morning. The stage came in--very little mail. Very dull, nothing new. I was sick all day. Went to bed at 10 o'clock.

Mar. 15. Fine day. 11 a.m.--the mail stage is not in yet. Young the tinsmith went to Pueblo Viejo. I wrote to my sister Mrs. Roberts. Several thousand dollars worth of mines have been sold in the past few days. Very dull in the house. Went to bed early.

Mar. 16. Fine warm morning. John Allen received a new supply of goods for his store. The stage arrived at 11:30--no mail for me. The sun is quite hot at noon. Captain Gay was on a drunk and making a great noise in the street. He was arrested and sent home. I had my hair cut. Nothing very new today. Went to bed early.

Mar. 17 (Sunday). Cloudy and cold this morning. The stage came at 9 o'clock--very light mail. Lord & Williams' dog Jack got poisoned today. There was some thunder, wind, and lots of dust--very disagreeable. There was a little sprinkle of rain after sundown. The house was open till 2 o'clock.

Mar. 18. Cloudy and warm. 10 a.m.--it rained hard with very heavy thunder and lightning. The house leaked a little. Lightning struck two telegraph poles one mile from town and tore them in splinters. It rained all day. I received a letter from Tom McClellan. Roddick and Brown came to town. Myers and Boley's wagon train arrived. I went to bed at 10:30 o'clock.

Mar. 19. Cloudy and muddy. 12 noon--the sun came out warm. I wrote to Red Hart. There were several new arrivals from San Francisco today. Fred Myers is on a big spree, and Boley is mad as a wet hen--all his teamsters, cooks, and helpers are drunk. There was a little poker game in the house today. I managed to get full of rye by bedtime--10 o'clock.

Mar. 20. Fine warm morning. 12 noon--the stage is not in yet. I wrote a letter to William White. Myers and Boley's wagon train left for Yuma and left two drunken men behind. Cloudy nearly all day. Went to bed at 10:30 o'clock.

Mar. 21. Cloudy this morning. The stage came in late--received some pictures from Currier & Ives. Lovejoy raffled off his watch--Brokaw won it with no. 40. Nothing new or interesting today. Went to bed early.

Mar. 22. Partly cloudy with some sunshine. Stage came in early--no mail for me. No excitement today. Went to bed at 11:30.

Mar. 23. Fine warm morning. John Brown and B. C. Parker arrived in town from Camp Grant. Sport came also. Comstock opened a faro game in the house and quit a loser. Brown dealt monte and won $100--closed the game at 2 in the morning. The Adobe Club had a dance upstairs in the Palace Hotel. There was a meeting at the courthouse of the *Loco Focos* [Democrats] to organize the party and elect officers for the county committee. Five men were present, three of them elected.

Mar. 24 (Sunday). Fine weather. Had bacon and eggs for breakfast. There was a church service in the courthouse--Reverend Anderson gave advice to the young men. Marsh got drunk and could not go to church. The theatre band is touring the town playing music. Professor Caldwell lectured to the young men at the courthouse this evening. Marsh attended and enjoyed it muchly. Theatre is going full blast tonight.

Mar. 25. Fine morning. John Stroud came to town and got drunk. Nothing new or interesting. Very dull.

Mar. 26. Cloudy, cool morning. 9 a.m.--the sun is out and it is quite hot. The stage came--very little mail. Bill Gale came in from the mines. Stroud started for home, but only got as far as Holt's saloon where he camped on the floor. Mr. and Mrs. Martin came in on the stage. Tom Gardner and Santa Cruz Brown arrived in town.

Mar. 27. Cold and windy. Stroud finally got off. Nothing new, very dull. Closed early.

Mar. 28. Cloudy, cold morning. Ross got drunk last night and played off his expense money for his trip to Sonora--he has not showed up today. It commenced raining at 4 p.m. and rained hard until 9 in the evening. Dull in the house all day. Foster went to bed early. Lovejoy and Jim Caldwell had a great Bible argument which lasted 2 hours. Lovejoy had the best of it.

Mar. 29. Got up at 6 o'clock. It was still raining and quite cold. The faro game ran all night at Brown's saloon. 11 a.m.--the sun came out. There were several showers during the day. It was quite cold--we had a fire nearly all day. The stage came in very late. Captain Moore is in town. Several strangers arrived in town, but they are all broke. I went to bed at 10 o'clock.

Mar. 30. Cloudy and cold. Caldwell's wagon train left this morning. He took Miller's dogs with him. I cleaned all the pictures in the barroom. 12 noon--the stage is not in yet. 2 p.m.--the mail coach came in--very light mail. We had a light rain this evening. Very dull in the house. Faro and monte ran late at Brown's saloon. I went to bed at 10 o'clock.

Mar. 31 (Sunday). Still cloudy--it rained during the night. Tom Roddick arrived in town early this morning and is full as a goose this evening. McClary and Smith had a fight in Brown's saloon. There was a theatre performance at Levin's Park this evening. Our games all closed early. Went to bed at 10:30 o'clock.

~ ~ ~ ~ ~

April 1. Fine morning. John Day died at 6 o'clock this morning and was buried at 3 p.m. in the Catholic cemetery. Nothing new today. The faro game ran all night in the house.

Apr. 2. Fine day. Quite warm. Gambling is light today. Parker and John Brown are getting ready to make a trip. Mr. Henry Holt got slightly intoxicated this evening. The boys beat the faro game at Brown's saloon.

Apr. 3. Fine morning. Very warm. Mr. Franklin is missing--people are looking for him. The mail coach came full of dry goods for Zeckendorf & Co. Gale, Hudson, and Co. started to leave again this morning, but did not get off. I did not feel well this evening and went to bed early.

Apr. 4. Pleasant weather. Hudson and Gale got off early. Parker and Brown were to leave but there was not enough room in the stage. William Zeckendorf left for the East via San Francisco. McKey returned from the mines. There was a theatre performance at the Cosmopolitan Hotel corral this evening. Our faro game ran till 3 o'clock in the morning.

Apr. 5. Warm today. I took breakfast at the Palace Hotel. Parker and Brown leave today. John Warner leaves for the Black Hills country. The stage left and took Brown and Parker. I packed them a lunch. There was little gambling in the house all day. Fairbanks went broke dealing faro in Brown's saloon.

Apr. 6. Fine morning. Gifford and McKey commenced playing monte together. Ike Brokaw opened a monte game. Indian Charley got kicked out of the house this morning. Jacob Mansfeld left for the States. I pulled a back tooth out with a string. Sniffin took Rip [dog] home. Metzger came to town. Theatre this evening. The faro game lost $100 the first few deals. Monte and faro ran all night and both closed winners.

Apr. 7 (Sunday). Very pleasant morning. Church services in two denominations were held today. Foster's girls went to Sunday school. The stage arrived at 11:30. Marsh got a shave. Dr. Handy took a pup home. The house was open all night.

Apr. 8. I washed out the house. Faro opened this morning and the game closed a winner at 3:30 o'clock. A report says that Jack Upton died in Florence at 2 o'clock this morning. [The *Arizona Star* gave Cockney Jack (John) Upton this obituary, one that would be fitting for many of George Hand's friends and customers: "Gone--Another genial, whole-souled Arizonian has passed over the breakers of life; this time it was Jack Upton, well known in southern Arizona.... Jack was unfortunate in being a hard drinker, otherwise he might have lived many years. Last Saturday night he gave up his troubles. His age was about forty years. He was honorable and upright, full of wit and wisdom, and probably had but one enemy and that was himself. May he rest in peace."]

Apr. 9. It was cloudy this morning, and remained so all day. The faro game ran nearly all day--faro closed a 90¢ winner on the day. Mr. Franklin returned to town with a swollen head. I went to bed at 11.

Apr. 10. Fine morning. The stage came in early. I saw a notice of the death of Col. Thomas Devin. Ed Hudson came to town and was arrested for beating Franklin. He was put under $1,000 bond to appear before the grand jury. Metzger got drunk and tried to talk me to death. Noriega struck Jonesy in the head with a six-shooter and landed in jail.

Apr. 11. Fine day. Had baked beans for breakfast. The stage came in early--no mail for me. I feel quite well today. Noriega was fined $20. A faro game opened in the house today, closed, and then opened again late and ran all night. Very warm today.

Apr. 12. Fine morning. Had tripe for breakfast, and some fish. Roddick came to town and got drunk in one hour. Tom Britton is in town. They are taking account of the stock in General Allen's store today. [John B. "Pie" Allen, an old Arizona pioneer, had been given the title "general" out of respect, as he had never served in the U.S. Army.] There were two dances in town this evening--I went to one.

Apr. 13. Fine day. The stage came in--no through mail. Roddick gave Foster a money order for $25. Bedford came in from the mountains--the sawmill has shut down. I wrote to Dr. Jay Porter, Silver City, N.M., and to J. C. Robinson, Florence. Windy and dusty today. I got rather full this evening. Had a Dutch lunch at Levin's and went to bed.

Apr. 14 (Palm Sunday). Fine morning. It is Palm Sunday and men, women, and children are going to the Catholic church with bundles of green grass. The stage arrived at 11:30. Very windy and terrible dusty all the afternoon. There was a small monte game in the house. McClary went broke against the faro game at Brown's. Green closed his game early there, and the boys all came over here and went against Comstock. The game ran till 2 o'clock tomorrow morning.

Apr. 15. Pleasant morning. Cloudy and cold, but no wind. Stage came in at 10 o'clock. Buck got tight, had a row at Levin's, and was arrested. Tom Roddick is in town again and is drunk again. 12 noon--windy and very dusty. Levin beat our faro game. John Metzger talked Ed Hudson to death--the funeral is tomorrow.

Apr. 16. Cold this morning--we had a fire. 10 a.m.--the wind rose high and there is dust in great quantities. The stage came in at 12 noon. 2 p.m.-- rain commenced and it is cold and wet. I want to buy some more firewood but there is none to be found. Very dull all day. It rained all day and night.

Apr. 17. Clear and cold this morning. I sent some papers to Roberts, Milton, Shipler, and Chesebro. Sergeant Boutelle, Ike Norris, and McClary went to San Xavier. I took a short ride around town. A man named Miller went to Brokaw's saloon and tried to take charge. He and Ike had a rough-and-tumble fight in which Mr. Miller got a magnificent sore head put on him. Very dull this evening. Went to bed.

Apr. 18. The *Star* came out early--nothing in it. Very pleasant morning. I cleaned my room and combed the pups. Very dull in the house. I read and slept in a chair nearly all day. Williams and Sniffin returned to town yesterday evening. Mrs. Manuela Sweeney, widow of the late John W. Sweeney, died in Florence.

A woodcutter drives his burro loaded with mesquite down a Tucson street. Roskruge Collection, Arizona Historical Society, Tucson, #4012.

Apr. 19. Good Friday. I raised the flag for the anniversary of the Battle of Lexington. A Mexican woman was found this morning standing in the bottom of an abandoned well east of town. Two other women tied her up and let her down, thinking to drown her, but there was not water enough. They are now in jail. [The *Star* reported that the woman was discovered in the well by George Roskruge, a surveyor, who was taking a morning stroll. He heard her cries and went for help to pull her out. Learning that the woman was injured and indigent, George Foster went about town and raised $21 for her relief.] There are a great many drunken men in town today. It is very windy with *mucho* dust.

Apr. 20. Windy and very dusty. The guards are still watching over the tomb of Christ. 11 a.m.--they fired several rounds of musketry. The church is open and the humbug is going on in grand style. The stage from Cal. came in and brought General Rosecrans, Dahlgreen, Charles D. Poston, and others. It was cold all day. Dull. A faro game opened in the house tonight. I went to bed at 10 o'clock.

Apr. 21 (Easter Sunday). Cloudy and warm. Easter Sunday. The cook at Foster's house got her back up and left. The Honorable James Douglass is in town. 12 noon--the wind is blowing hard and it is cold. There was a foot race today. Three entries--2 Frenchmen and one Mexican. Baker, the French barber, won. Dull in the house all day. We had a little faro game at night--it lost $70.

Apr. 22. Cold damp morning--it is cloudy and threatening rain. The women who put the other one in the well were examined today. They were placed back in jail in lieu of $5,000 bail each. They will appear before the grand jury. It rained some in the afternoon. The Acme Minstrels [a local amateur group] performed at the courthouse. The faro game ran all night, lost $300.

Apr. 23. Cloudy this morning. The Acme Minstrels are said to be good-- they gave general satisfaction. I sold two pups this morning. Tom Roddick, still drunk, left for home today. Comstock had a faro game in the house nearly all the afternoon--he won $213. There was no game in the evening. Paige and Pat O'Meara had a little set-to--no damage. I went to bed at 10 o'clock.

Apr. 24. Warm morning. Stage came--very little mail. Metzger and Sales left for the mines. Chiquita pupped this morning. She had 3 gyps [females] and one dog [male]. They are very pretty pups. Layton came and took his dog, and Jo's and Vic's pups are now off my hands. Faro and poker ran all night. McClary came off the winner in the poker game, Comstock's faro game lost some on the day.

Apr. 25. Fine morning. The *Star* came out early. I received a letter from W. Jay Porter, Silver City, N.M. There was a faro game in the house all day. Lyons had two scrimmages with Mexicans this evening. Ed Hudson and Pat O'Meara are drunk. A report says that the Honorable Coles Bashford died at Prescott.

Apr. 26. Fine morning. The boys are all sleepy from overwork. The games were all open by 11 a.m. Nothing very new except a minstrel show this evening. I went to bed at 11:30 o'clock.

Apr. 27. Fine morning. I got up late. The mail stage came in early. [Marshal] Buttner arrested a man for stealing horses. A faro game opened in the house. Hudson and O'Meara are both drunk. There are to be circus and theatre performances this evening and there are lots of musicians in the streets. I went to bed at 10 o'clock. Faro ran till 2 o'clock, lost $290.

Apr. 28 (Sunday). Quite warm. Nothing new. Very dull. John Brown came in on the stage from Florence. Circus and theatre this evening.

Apr. 29. Very warm day. Brown wrote to Parker in Florence and I put in a P.S. James Fitzgerald arrived in town. He got drunk and Hand did also. There are several drunken men in town. I went to bed at 8 o'clock.

Apr. 30. One of the women who tried to drown the woman in the well died in jail [of typhoid fever]. Quite lively in the house today.

~ ~ ~ ~ ~

May 1. Fine weather. We took down the stove in the faro room. Several drunks around--nothing new.

May 2. Quite lively around town today. The sale of mines and claims makes the boys come out with their money. H. D. Williams is drunk and some Mexicans are following him around town, trying to get a chance to roll him. We received news of the deaths of John Morrissey [a great boxing champion] in New York, and William O'Brien [a Comstock Lode mining tycoon] in San Francisco. I went to bed at 10 o'clock. Very warm night.

May 3. Fine warm morning. John Brown packed up his traps [luggage] on Barnett's wagon train to go to Florence. Drunken Williams left for the mines. McKey received the first installment on the sale of his mines. He went around town paying his debts. Plenty of men are looking after him now that he has money. King William and Charley Paige had a row over a faro game--no blood was shed.

May 4. A fine morning before sunrise, but the sun brought wind which made it very dusty. John Burt and Frank Sullivan came to town this morning. Ryland's circus came in town today. I went to see their trained dogs. The first performance is tomorrow evening. [George Ryland's "American Circus" arrived in Tucson on its way to California after a tour of Mexico. Although small by P. T. Barnum standards, it was the most elaborate circus yet to appear in town. The star performer was Ryland's wife, Ellen, who executed acrobatic feats while riding on horseback.] I went to church to see Mr. Carlos Tully get married. The church was full. Quite warm this evening. The night was made hideous by the firing of guns and fireworks until very late.

May 5 (Sunday). This is the anniversary of some Mexican holiday. [*Cinco de Mayo* commemorates the defeat of French forces by the Mexican army at the town of Puebla in southern Mexico in 1862. It is still an important holiday in Mexico.] The circus is driving around town--a goat is riding on a horse's back. I did not go to the circus, but all agree that it was very good. There was plenty of gambling and lots of drunks in the house today. The Mexicans are shooting off fireworks this evening. I felt sick and went to bed early.

May 6. Fine morning. There is a light breeze but no dust. The transit of Mercury across the sun took place today but could not be seen here. The circus made a trip through the streets--there is a show again tonight. Sullivan left town at noon. Very windy and dusty in the afternoon.

May 7. Warm weather. Nothing new. A pain flared up in my side and I commenced taking medicine. There are lots of drunks in town.

May 8. Fine day. Very warm. The games are running pretty well in the house for the dull times. Received a letter from William Bradley. I took some medicine and went to bed early.

May 9. I was quite sick today, obliged to lie down. Johnny Hart came to town from the mountains with two dogs and two burros. He got very tight very quick. Jim Blade is very tight. He played cards with King William and went broke before night. In the evening, the King, playing against faro, went for the "tiger" and blew everything in. I was sick all day.

May 10. I am still sick but feel some better. Windy and dusty. Quite lively in the house today. Every loafer in town is drunk. Parker returned from Florence. I went to bed at 10:30 feeling sick.

May 11. Cloudy and windy. Several of the boys are drunk. The mail stage came in late. Ryland came around posting bills advertizing the circus performance tomorrow night. Very warm. I was sick all day. The faro game ran late--it lost. The monte games all won.

May 12 (Sunday). Fine morning. The circus is promenading through the streets. I was quite busy all day and had no time to take a bath or change clothes. C. O. Brown closed his saloon [to do some remodeling]. I went to the circus--it was very good, but I got tired sitting. I came home before it was out and went to bed.

May 13. Fine weather. No arrivals, no departures. I was sick all day--ate no dinner. I felt very bad in the evening and went to bed early.

May 14. Fine morning. Feel some better. Nothing new except that Holt, McClary, and some girl struck flats and went on a picnic--nice duty for old stiffs. Marsh tended bar for Holt and got full of rot. Hudson and Burt left today with Frank Francis. Report says that Charles Lovejoy was shot yesterday and died today. I went to bed at 10 o'clock.

May 15. Gale, Elliott, and Jones came in this morning. Roddick also came in, and kept sober. The faro and monte games were quite lively all day. Report says Lovejoy was killed by a Mexican at or near Pueblo Viejo. There was a circus performance this evening to benefit the public school--the house was large and it was a good show. Our faro game won. It was quite lively in the house all evening. I went to bed at 11 o'clock.

May 16. Fine day. Jonesy is full. The monte games are running. I feel pretty well today. The stage came in--light mail. No very important things happened today. One monte game ran all night and finally quit a winner. I went to bed at 10 o'clock. Felt sick and got up twice during the night.

May 17. Cloudy before sunrise. The wind commenced to blow at 8:30. The stage came in at 10 a.m. The boys are all drunk. We had some music and dancing. Gale and the boys had a dance up town. We stayed up all night singing.

May 18. The boys are all asleep in the back room and corral. Arey got off for the mines--the boys were to follow but they did not get off till after dark. I went to bed at 9 o'clock, tired and sick.

May 19 (Sunday). Fine day. Feel much better. A very good day for money--lots of soldiers in town drinking. Foster's baby was taken very sick and it was thought for a while that she would die. Report says that Jacob Mansfeld got married in New York. I went to the circus to watch Mrs. Ellen Ryland and had a good time--they had a big house. I did not stay for the draw of the raffle. Smith opened roulette in our barroom. Drunken soldiers and citizens stayed around dancing and singing till 1 o'clock. The faro game ran all night.

May 20. Cloudy, windy, and dusty. A few drops of rain fell in the evening. Puck Ryan is drunk. Smith had a monte game and quit a loser. Bill Elliott had a row--he shot a Mexican and was fined $35. He left for Florence this evening. I went to bed at 9 o'clock.

May 21. Cool morning. Very dull--all the hoodlums have gone and we are waiting for a new gang. The man who killed Lovejoy was brought to town today. We closed quite early.

May 22. Cooler this morning--makes me think of putting up the stove again. Dull today. Smith lost $100. Levin sold the Gem Saloon. Nothing strange happened today. I am still sick. Went to bed at 10 o'clock.

May 23. Very cold for the season. Henry Williams came to town. There is a circus performance this evening to benefit the Sisters' [of St. Joseph] school. Williams the millionaire is spending his money and gambling like a sport. Bedford came in town and got drunk--Foster put him out of the house. Shorty Holt got stung on the lip by a scorpion while sleeping. His mouth, throat, and jaw were badly swollen, and all one side of his face was paralyzed in a few moments.

May 24. Quite cool again this morning. Billy Wood was the first man to get drunk today. T. G. Rusk is drunk and yelling all over town. Holt is some better--Marsh tended bar for Shorty all day. Report says that Franklin Sanford died at his brother's ranch at Sonoita.

May 25. Fine morning. The stage came in quite early--no mail for me. Dull today. Went to the theatre this evening--Bill Oury, Jim Speedy, H. B. Smith, Sanders, Fred Hughes, and numerous greasers were the *cabrones* [fools]. I went to bed at 10 o'clock.

May 26 (Sunday). Nothing new. Quite lively about town today. The circus is promenading the principal streets. They are to perform this evening. There is to be a foot race after the performance between a clown named Tracy and Baker the barber. I was sick and could not go to the circus.

May 27. Cold morning. Tracy won the foot race last night. Mr. Ryland brought me a photo of his wife. H. D. Williams is still very drunk. I had a fearful attack of colic and was obliged to go to bed twice this forenoon. French Louis came in this evening. There was a dance this evening at Alex Wilkins' house. Our house was open all night.

May 28. Warm and pleasant. Ross and Paige returned from Florence this morning. No new arrivals on the stage. Very dull. Judge French left for the East today.

May 29. Cool--4 degrees cooler than yesterday. The stage came in quite early. Ryland's circus got off for Florence early this morning. Williams lost $300 playing cards today, got very drunk, and went to bed. I went to bed at 10 o'clock. Cattle are said to be dying all over the country. [A mysterious disease was killing cattle in southern Arizona. The symptoms described in the *Star* suggest that anthrax was the problem.]

May 30. Fine morning. I raised the flag for Decoration Day. Very dull in town. I spent the day cleaning and covering the pictures with gauze. Feel better this evening than I have in a long time. Only one monte game is running now, no faro game. We closed early.

May 31. Fine morning. I worked all day cleaning and covering pictures. Received a circular from Doc Porter. Nothing new or interesting today. We had cold mornings and it was very windy and terrible dusty during the whole month of May. Went to bed at 10:30.

~ ~ ~ ~ ~

June 1. Quite cool. Stage came in late. John Dobbs arrived from Camp Grant. The first limes of the season came in from Sonora, $2.50 per hundred. Dull today. Smith left with his roulette wheel. C. O. Brown reopened his house. Billy Wood got drunk, made a bluff at a big-headed Mexican thief, and got a plug in the nose for it. I went to bed at 10 o'clock.

June 2 (Sunday). Fine morning. Had cornbread for breakfast. There was dancing and music at Levin's Park all day. Very dull in the house--no gambling, no drinking. There are plenty of Sonoran oranges for sale in town, 3 for 25¢. Nothing new today. Neither Billy Wood nor the man who hit him last night has made an appearance. I retired at 10:30.

June 3. Fine, cool, and very pleasant morning. I sent some papers to Sullivan. Puck Ryan left for the mines to work for Tom Britton. Cattle are reported to be dying everywhere. There was an auction sale of the mules, horses, wagon, harness, shovels, and other farming implements of the estate of John T. Smith. Ed Hudson arrived in town this evening. We sold the last of the Milwaukee beer. Cool and pleasant this evening. Went to bed at 10 o'clock.

June 4. Fine morning. The stage came in at 10 a.m. Roddick arrived in town sober, but did not remain so for long. Quite warm at 2 p.m.--mercury at 103. Charley Bent came in this evening. Nothing new.

June 5. Fine day--very little wind and no dust. I was taken with colic and obliged to lie down for two hours. Roddick left town well-heeled with bottles of whiskey and very drunk. [Deputy Sheriff] Alex Derrick brought in the Mexican who shot Stockton a year ago. Hudson and Bent are pretty tight this evening. Very dull. Went to bed at 11 o'clock.

June 6. Windy and dusty. The *Star* came out early--very little news in it. Bill Keegan is very drunk this morning, lost his hat and had a row with

Coalyard Bill. Charley Kenyon took a pup down to Captain Moore. The Milwaukee beer did not arrive. Ed Hudson is drunk.

June 7. Fine morning. Ed Hudson is sober. The stage came in early--no mail for me. Keegan is drunk again. Holden came in from the mines. Mercury at 2 p.m.--100 degrees. H. D. Williams, Arey, McKey, and others came in this evening from the mines. Foster gave Williams the $100 he owed him and he went broke against monte. Keegan is very drunk. I went to bed at 10 o'clock.

June 8. Very warm morning. Stage came in early. Roddick sent Tinker [dog] in--he looks well. 11 a.m.--cloudy, not much wind. Mercury at 2 p.m.-- 103. Lots of strangers in town and some drunken men. Smith took Tinker home. Wheeler Williams' dog Dick had 5 pups. I went to bed at 10:30.

June 9 (Sunday). Took a bath and changed clothes for summer--all in linen. Arey, McKey, Poindexter, and Co. came to town. The town was quite lively today. There was a dance at the park. Comstock had a good monte game in our house. I went to bed at 10 o'clock.

June 10. Fine morning. Warm and sultry later. Arey and Ed Hudson left for the mines. The stage came in early. Taylor sent his pup in and I cut her ears. It was quite lively in the house in the after-part of the day. Gifford and McClary opened a monte game. McKey was on a big drunk. Charley Bent went out to overtake Arey and Hudson. I went to bed at 11 o'clock.

June 11. Warm morning. McKey, a little on the drink, lost his pocketbook in the privy. We got our lantern and fished it out--it had $5,000 in greenbacks and drafts on St. Louis banks in it. A Mexican tied his wife to a mesquite tree and whipped her nearly to death, shot at her six times, and left her. The man was afterward arrested and confined in jail. It was lively in the house this evening. Went to bed at 11 o'clock.

June 12. The wife beater, Jose Urias Huerta, had an examination this morning before Justice Neugass. He got a $300 fine, in default of which he was sent to jail for 300 days. There is a nice breeze and it is quite pleasant this morning. 12 noon--very warm. Nothing more very new except Company "K" [at Camp Lowell] was ordered to Angel Island [in San Francisco Bay] immediately.

June 13. Cloudy early in the morning, hot during the day. Stage came in-- very little mail. Hefty bought all the remnant of stock from J. B. Allen's store. He will take the goods to the Santa Rita mines. I went to bed at 10 o'clock.

June 14. Cloudy all day. Very dull, nothing new.

June 15. Pleasant day. We had very light sprinkles of rain several times today, but no heavy rain. John Brown opened a faro game in the house. There were not many players and it was dull all day and evening. General Rosecrans and others came in from Sonora. Brokaw, Jim Speedy, and Williams went to the mines this evening. I took a sponge bath and went to bed at 10 o'clock.

June 16 (Sunday). Fine morning. Jerry Kenny is back in town. I wrote a letter to Billy Bradley. Rip [dog] got in on Jacobs' bitch. There was music at the park today. Two buggies collided this evening and one of them was badly smashed up. No one was hurt. It was quite lively in the house today and this evening. Went to bed at 10 o'clock.

June 17. Fine day. Captain Moore came in on the stage. Quite lively in our place today. Mercury at 1 p.m.--104 degrees. Cool and pleasant after sundown. Went to bed at 10 o'clock.

June 18. Fine morning. Joe Phillips came in on the stage. A sergeant from Apache Pass beat Gifford and McClary's little faro game early this morning. Tom Roddick came to town and got drunk in half an hour. Caldwell bought several teams from Samaniego. Carriages and ambulances are going out to the 9-mile horse race. I went to bed sick.

June 19. Cloudy this morning. I washed out the house. Tom Roddick got drunk very early. It is windy and looks like rain. The boys all came in from the race--the Sonoran horse won it by 20 feet. All the smart Americans lost all their money. [The *Star* reported that $5,000 was transferred from Arizona to Sonora as a result of betting on this race between a local horse and one from Mexico.] It rained hard this evening with very heavy thunder. The house leaked some. It is a cool night to sleep.

June 20. Cool and pleasant morning after the rain yesterday. But the sun came out early, burned up the dampness, and by 2 p.m. the dust was blowing all over everything. McKey got pretty tight today. I got him to bed about 4 p.m. and he slept until nearly 11 at night. George Bowen's faro game lost about $100.

June 21. John B. Hart came in from the mountains. Joe Phillips got drunk in a bad-woman house--was drinking *tizwin* [a homemade corn beer] all day. The big nigger from the Cosmopolitan Hotel beat Comstock's monte game-- $100. Mercury 110 degrees this p.m. I went to bed at 10:30.

June 22. Warm and cloudy. I bought some Sonoran limes. Foster gave Kenyon a pup. Dull all day. Went to bed early.

June 23 (Sunday). Warm. The stage came in at 9:30--Billy Bradley came in on it and we had a great time talking over old times. [William F. Bradley was an old comrade from Company "G" of the California Column.] He brought me several ore specimens. We had a few drinks. Report says that Martin Sweeney was killed today [at the new Tombstone mines] by John Boyer, alias Jack Friday. Hamar died at Austin's store [at Camp Lowell]. Billy Bradley slept in my room and we talked ourselves asleep.

June 24 (San Juan's Day). I got up early to see San Juan come into town, but Billy Gale, Jones, Joe Elliott, and Reed came ahead of him. Joe got fearful drunk.

June 25. Very warm. Nothing new. The beer from the States is going quite fast.

June 26. Very warm--mercury 110 degrees in the p.m. No news and quite dull. I am very unwell and have a pain in my side all the time. Faro ran all night in the house, made a winning.

June 27. Very warm. Mercury 107 degrees at 9 a.m. Dobbs was playing short cards and went broke. Col. [Henry] Mizner left by stage for California.

June 28. I put up the flag for the anniversary of the Battle of Monmouth, N.J. Dull today. Went to bed sick.

June 29. I was very much disappointed at the non-appearance of the *Spirit of the Times*, but as I was too sick to read, it made no difference.

June 30 (Sunday). Fine day. People are riding around enjoying themselves. I am sick. The mail stage came in very late. I went to bed early.

~ ~ ~ ~ ~

July 1. Am sick but I knocked around a little today. Ate nothing. George Bowen went to Silver City. No news today. Went to bed early. I took some blue mass. [Blue mass was a dangerous medicinal preparation containing mercury. It was a powerful purgative and was sometimes prescribed to treat syphilis.]

July 2. The medicine did not operate. I took some more and went to bed-- was in bed most of the day. Took some more medicine this evening that I got from Dr. Handy. Jim Carroll took strychnine poison at Holt's bar and died after a terrific struggle.

July 3. Am quite sick and was confined to bed nearly all day. The medicine worked well. Jim Carroll, a native of Lawrence, Kansas, was buried today. Not much excitement in town about the Fourth. Several drunks were around. I went to bed early and sick.

July 4. The day opened fine. Flags are up around town, but not a gun fired. All patriotism seems to be dead among Americans. There was a reading of the Declaration of Independence and speeches were made at Levin's Park. Some refreshments were served up to the children. Altogether it was a very lame performance. There was some drinking and gambling in the house. Private parties had their dinners. There was a dance in the evening. Mrs. W. W. Williams sent me a plate of very nice turkey and the fixings.

July 5. Fine morning. Very warm, a little cloudy. It is a "blue Monday" for many. There was considerable drinking all day. Mr. Cummings, alias Dublin, gave some entertainments during the day--songs, dances, etc. He fell very gently at 6 in the evening, was carried to the rear by the boys, and put on a little pallet on the cold ground. The faro game was up and down all day. It closed at 12:30 a $400 winner. Very warm tonight.

July 6. Very warm this morning. Not a breath of air except that made by the brooms of the street sweepers. I had cucumbers for breakfast. Shut Jo and Vic up today. The telegraph wires were down all day yesterday and we could not hear of the results of the great Kentucky horse race. There was a horse race here yesterday, a single dash of one mile--the Mexican horse won. Learned the result of the great race--Ten Broeck beat Mollie McCarthy. [This famous race inspired a song, "Molly and Tenbrooks," which became part of Bill Monroe's bluegrass repertoire.]

July 7 (Sunday). Fine day. Jonesy is dressed in a swallowtail coat and a plug hat. The stage came in very late. Delegate Hiram Stevens came in on the stage. Some bets on the big race have been paid over already. Rather dull in the house today.

July 8. Very warm this morning. I went with McKey and Foster and called on the Honorable H. S. Stevens--he looks fine and fat. Considerable beer was drank today--mercury 110 degrees. Gale, Jonesy, Reed, and others left for the mines this evening. Dobbs was drunk all day. Bradley drew out $40 from the faro game. We had a good faro game all day. Cloudy and windy at night, but no rain.

July 9. Fine morning. Whipple came in during the night with the body of Finnegan who died on the road of overheat and exertion yesterday. James Farrell, alias Finnegan, was buried this morning. Tom Britton hit Dan Rooney in the right eye. Elliott left for the mines. The monte game ran all night. Very warm at night.

July 10. Warm morning. The stage came in--received a letter from my sister with a photo of her daughter Mary and Aunt Hannah. Very warm day and rather dull. Cloudy in the evening with some wind and dust. Went to bed at 11 o'clock.

July 11. It rained a little at 3 o'clock this morning. I was sleeping outside and it drove me in the house. Mr. E. C. Ledyard shot himself this morning. He had been sick a long time and was tired of living. Still cloudy but no rain yet today. 5 p.m.--cloudy and dark, commenced raining very hard. More water fell and ran in the streets than in a number of years. Many houses were washed away and a great amount of damage was done. A telegram says that lieutenants Henely and Rucker were drowned today [near Camp Bowie]. I slept well.

July 12. Still a little cloudy. Many people were without a place to sleep last night. Sultry and hot all day, cloudy, windy, and thunder and lightning late in the afternoon--not much rain. The stage finally came in.

July 13. Warm, not a breath of air. The mail stage came in at 3 p.m. Dull today. Went to bed at 10:30. The house was open all night and the monte game closed Sunday morning.

July 14 (Sunday). I slept out of doors last night very nicely. Fine morning. Hot all day. Nothing new. I made a bed in the corral but rain drove me in the house.

July 15. Very warm day. There was a big monte game in the house nearly all day. The mail stage came in after 5 p.m. [Deputy Sheriff] Alex Derrick brought in two soldiers who were parties to the killing of Montgomery near Camp Grant. I slept in the house--was too tired to take my bed out. It did not rain.

July 16. Had melons, cucumbers, and tomatoes for breakfast. The Cal. mail stage came after dark--no newspapers or through mail--the storm tore up the railroad west of Yuma. George Foster wrote to H. D. Williams. Indian Charley, our head clerk, got put in jail last night. We had a light sprinkle of rain. I went to bed at 10:30.

July 17. Fine morning but cloudy. Very warm. Still very dull about town-- not much drunkenness today. We were warned to tie up our dogs--Marshal Buttner is out killing stray dogs with poison. The mail stage came in after dinner. Dr. John Handy was married to Miss Mary Page today. [In 1891, Dr. Handy was shot and killed in a fight with his wife's divorce lawyer on a Tucson street.] Foster is sick--he took some medicine and went to bed. I closed up at 12 o'clock.

July 18. Warm and cloudy. Foster is still sick. 107 dead dogs were carted off this morning. Mine are safe yet. There are several drunks in town. The old tinker was put in jail for disturbing the peace. Joaquin had a fight with another Mexican and whipped him. Ike Brokaw came in from the mines. Quite dull this evening. After a codfish and cracker lunch, I went to bed. The house closed up at 12 o'clock.

July 19. Cloudy this morning. Had a good breakfast of fine potatoes brought in by Bill Kirkland--10¢ per lb. Warm and cloudy all day. Foster is still sick. I closed up at 12 o'clock.

July 20. Warm, cloudy, and sultry. Skinner and Lew Burton are on a Milwaukee beer spree. Bob Morrow and Jack McNulty are in town. Murphy also put in an appearance. They are all going out prospecting. The mail stage came in after dark. We had a light rain. Closed after 12 o'clock.

July 21 (Sunday). Slept until 8 o'clock. I washed out the house and cleaned up this morning. Murphy, McNulty, and Bob Morrow played faro all day. Murphy won $140. They all got drunk. I received a letter from Bill Bradley's wife inquiring of Billy. Cloudy and cool this evening. Went to dinner with Foster--we had canned clam chowder from the States. Went to bed at 10 o'clock.

July 22. Fine morning. Murphy is sober. Bob Morrow is trying to get drunk. Soldiers from Camp Lowell are moving through town, bound for Oregon. [The soldiers were being sent from Arizona to the Northwest to take part in the so-called Bannock War. The conflict with the Bannock Indians was soon brought to an end.] No one killed today. Tom Roddick and Stroud came to town. Roddick got drunk in a very short time. The faro game lost. Went to bed at 10:30. The house was open all night.

July 23. Warm and cloudy. It is raining all around us but not here. Frank Sullivan came in. Roddick, drunk all day, went home after dark. Murphy went through his money against faro and then played off his horse. Fred Myers is drunk. Britton and McClary had a growl. Puck Ryan is in town--he is sick with a fever. I went to bed at 11 o'clock.

July 24. Fine day. Billy Gale brought Mr. Reynolds in--he is suffering from the bite of a tarantula. Arey also arrived in town. Fred Myers is still drunk. A report said that thieves were at work at Oury's ranch. The sheriff and others went out there but found no one. Report also says that Jack Friday [John Boyer] has been captured. Dull this evening. Went to bed at 10:30.

July 25. Very warm. Went to the home of W. W. Williams and got a pup-- gave it to Myers. Very hot today. Closed early.

July 26. Hot today. Gale is still in town. Fred Myers and Sullivan are still on the spree. The mail stage came in quite late. I went to bed early.

July 27. Warm. Gale left for the mines. Bedford is drunk and noisy, playing cards for $5 a game and throwing dice for a dollar. The bar wound up with all his money.

July 28 (Sunday). Nothing new this morning. Buttner found the haunt of some horse thieves. [The thieves' camp was in the mountains west of town. Sheriff Charles Shibell, Marshal Adolph Buttner, and gambler and sometime-lawman Ike Brokaw had a shootout with them, but the outlaws escaped.] Thomas Banning died at 10 a.m. from fits. The funeral is at 3 p.m. today. The mail stage came in early. Sullivan and Myers got drunk and went to bed at 7 o'clock this evening. Foster went to bed sick. Report says that C. P. Mason died in San Francisco today. [Mason was one of the four men who discovered the Silver King Mine in Arizona in 1875.] I kept open until 12 o'clock.

July 29. Fine clear day. There is to be an eclipse of the sun today. Smoked glass is in all hands as they look for the eclipse. Sullivan and Fred Myers are sober and ready for business. Fred could not get on the stage. The eclipse commenced on the right side of the sun at 20 minutes after 2 p.m. The smoked glass corps is actively at work. Ross and Shaw had a growl and came near fighting. There was a cool breeze after 10 at night. We closed at 12:50.

July 30. Warm. Very dull all day. Nothing new. Mercury at 110 degrees at 2 p.m. Joe Elliott came in late this evening. Myers left by stage for Florence. Sullivan was sober all day, got drunk at night. I was very tired and went to bed early.

July 31. Very warm. The stage was robbed yesterday evening near Point of Mountain [20 miles northwest of town]. Buttner and Brokaw went out and followed the outlaw's trail. They brought in the mail sacks and torn letters. The robber is supposed to have got about $60. Sullivan and Golden are drunk and fighting in the Gem Saloon. Bedford and several others are drunk. Ross is drunk again. Rather dull today. Foster is still sick. I closed at 12:30.

~ ~ ~ ~ ~

August 1. Warm morning. I got up late. Marsh was very hilarious at breakfast. The *Star* came out early--the best and most newsy one since the first issue. Dull is no name for this--no one has a bit. Closed early.

Aug. 2. Warm. Very dull, no excitement. Cloudy after sundown, some wind, no rain. Warm all night.

Aug. 3. Warm day. Ike Brokaw was made a special policeman by order of Mayor Toole. Knox came to town. Hot all day. Elliott had a dance this evening. The 6th Cavalry band gave a concert at Levin's Park--not a success. George Treanor's son is very sick. I closed at 12:30 and went to bed.

Aug. 4 (Sunday). Fine warm morning. Treanor's boy, George Jr., died this morning at 5 o'clock. I went to the funeral this evening at 5 o'clock. Reverend Anderson performed the ceremony at the grave. There was quite a turnout. We had rain, wind, thunder, and lightning this evening. Not much rain but enough to cool the air and make it very pleasant. Closed early.

Aug. 5. Fine morning--cool after yesterday's rain. Ben Wood opened the Gem Restaurant. Bradley and I went there for breakfast and dinner. We took the big stove out of the barroom this morning. John Miller arrived from Florence. Very sultry at 4 p.m. Cloudy, windy, and plenty of dust at 7 p.m. The [military] plaza was leased to Ghanetto [by the Common Council for the San Agustín feast]--$551. It rained a little and is cool this evening. I closed at 11:30 and went to bed.

Aug. 6. Fine morning. Dobbs and Knox played cards all night in another saloon. They came in here this morning for a drink and played a game of first-seven-over-the-counter for $40. Dobbs won. Rather dull all day. I wrote to the *Spirit of the Times* for some binders. It rained a little in the evening. Very warm night.

Aug. 7. Cloudy and very warm. Dobbs, gambling and drunk, had a row in a house down the street, another one with Parker, beat up his girl, and finally was arrested. He was bailed out by C. O. Brown. I received a telegram from Horton. It rained a heavy shower after dark. Cool night. Rip [dog] is missing.

Aug. 8. Damp and warm. Yesterday's mail stage arrived this morning. Thomas McClellan came in on it. Dobbs landed in jail again. The stage left at 2 p.m., John Miller and a young man from Los Angeles the passengers. As they were riding along, the driver showed Miller where he was stopped by the robber the week before. Just then the same man appeared and said, "I am here again! Throw out the strong box and give up your money!" He got about $500. We had a heavy rain.

Aug. 9. Warm and very damp. There is great excitement in town about the stage robbery last night. Several persons are on the robber's trail. Esslinger and Kelly the barber got put in jail. Count Flannery is drunk. Cloudy and windy in the evening, but no rain. I was very sleepy and went to bed at 9 o'clock. The house was open all night.

Aug. 10. Cloudy and warm. Marshal Buttner came in town at noon. He says the trail is hot and they are sure to get the man before night. Several new deputies are running around hunting six-shooters so they can go out and find the robber, but all to no purpose yet--he is still at large. The stage came in very late, 12 o'clock at night. *Cochi* [Hog] Davis and Wash Evans arrived on it. Warm tonight, a bad time for sleep.

Aug. 11 (Sunday). Cloudy. No news of the stage robber. Saw Cochi Davis--he looks well but is dead broke. 10 a.m.--it rained hard. 1 p.m.--the sky cleared up. Warm in the evening. Cloudy and windy after dark, but no rain. No stage today. Still nothing heard of the stage robber. Closed at 12 o'clock and went to bed.

Aug. 12. Fine morning. Cloudy. Rip came home and was very glad to see us. He is very hungry and tired. By Jesus, Wash Evans bought a clean shirt--blue. Lew Davis and his family arrived from Florence. It threatened rain all day and a few drops fell at night. There was a dance at Levin's. I stayed up late and went to sleep at 3 in the morning.

Aug. 13. I awoke tired and sleepy. Very warm. Count Flannery left for the mines this morning. Nothing new today.

Aug. 14. Fine day. Several new police were put on duty for the public safety. They are still looking for the stage robber. Dave Nemitz was arrested and put in jail for being in possession of the horse ridden by the sandy-haired robber. [A horse matching the description of the one used by the stage robber was recognized at Nemitz' place south of town by a deputy looking for the outlaw. It was assumed, correctly, that Nemitz was in cahoots with him.] Joe Phillips and Tom Britton got notice to leave town from the Committee of Safety. [The Committee of Safety was a vigilante group formed in response to the rash of robberies and hold-ups. The committee began ordering various ne'er-do-wells and rough characters to leave town, some of whom were George Hand's customers.]

Aug. 15. Labaree came in bringing the mail and some passengers. The stage had been robbed in the most approved style [by a new gang of thieves]. They got about $600 besides the express box. Joe Phillips left town, Tom Britton got off by talking to the committee. He went out with a party to catch the robbers.

Aug. 16. Fine cloudy morning. Yesterday's mail stage arrived this morning. Report says that yet another stage was robbed near Burk's Station [on the Yuma road]. I got full of whiskey and stayed up till I know not how late. Very drunk.

Aug. 17. Fine day. I did not get up till 11 a.m. Had dinner and went back to bed again. Stayed in bed till 4 in the afternoon. Feel quite sick. Slept very sound all night.

Aug. 18 (Sunday). Fine morning. Got up early. I am very lame and sore and can hardly walk. Took a few drinks and felt better. Nothing new. Davis is quite sick. He had a fit a few days ago and he looks quite bad. No news of the stage robbers yet. There is a circus performance tonight.

Aug. 19. Fine morning. 8 a.m.--no mail stage yet. The Papago trackers came back to town--they would not follow the trail of the robbers into Sonora. The Americans continued south. The officers on the track of the single robber found him by the treachery of his partner [David Nemitz] and were obliged to kill him. An ambulance was sent out to bring him in. They laid him on a table in the courthouse. Hundreds went to see him as he was displayed with his guns and accoutrements on. [For a share of the loot, David Nemitz, who had a ranch a few miles south of Tucson, helped hide and supply the robber, William Brazelton. In response to a promise of lenience by his jailers, Nemitz confessed and agreed to lead a posse to Brazelton's hideout in a river-bottom thicket. The outlaw was then ambushed and killed in a hail of gunfire. The *Star* reported that the dying man's last words were, as he saw his former partner among the deputies, "You son-of-a-bitch!"]

Aug. 20. Cloudy. A coroner's inquest was held on the dead robber. His photo was taken by Buehman. The robber was named William W. Brazelton and was well known as an outlaw. H. D. Williams came in from the mines and got drunk in a short time. Cloudy and some rain this evening. It rained after dark and during the night--a very good night to sleep. [Henry Buehman came to Tucson in 1873 and went to work for photographer Adolpho Rodrigo the next year. In February 1875 he bought the Rodrigo Photographic Parlor and changed its name to Buehman Studio. Henry Buehman lived in Tucson for the rest of his life, and during his long career he made thousands of images which form the most important collection of early photos of Tucson and its residents.]

Aug. 21. Cloudy. It rained all last night. Very warm today. The stage arrived at 10 a.m., John Miller among the passengers. No mail--another washout on the railroad in Cal. 12 noon--cloudy and quite dark. Commenced raining hard at 3 p.m. and continued until bedtime. There are a great many strangers in town, nearly all of them broke. The new street lamps burned well. Lots of drunk men around. I went to bed early, troubled with piles.

Aug. 22. It rained all last night and it is still coming down. Lots of old drunks around this morning. The *Star* came out early and was full of news, all old. It rained nearly all day. Leaky roofs are the order of the day. Williams is very drunk. No mail today.

Aug. 23. Still cloudy. No mail--the country is all overflowed. The Salt river and the Gila are flooding. No new arrivals today. Hudson and Bent came in from Arivaca. It rained all day. I went to bed at 10. The house was open all night--several men were playing 7½.

Aug. 24. Clear and pleasant. The sun is shining at last. No mail yet. 12 noon--showers. The stage arrived--no through mail. Some of the marshal's party returned from Sonora. J. W. Evans remained there. [U.S. Marshal Joseph Evans had joined the search for the stage robbers--robbing the mails was a federal offense.] The prefect of Sonora says he shall have the robbers arrested if they come there. Dull today. Fairbanks had a flare game in the Alhambra Saloon. I went to bed at 10 o'clock.

Aug. 25 (Sunday). Quite pleasant. The rain has stopped for a while. Very dull today. The stage came in but no mail. Very warm. Esslinger is still on a

spree--he is dirty and stinks badly. Nothing new. I went to bed early. Joe
Ferrin and his wife arrived late in the night.

*The dead outlaw William Brazelton on display in Tucson. Photo by Henry
Buehman. Arizona Historical Society, Tucson, #78140.*

Aug. 26. Very dull. Cloudy but no rain. The stage arrived with the first through mail for 5 days. Many strangers in town.

Aug. 27. Fine morning. All are busy at the feast ground. Gamblers are moving tables in. There was an auction of the household goods of Lt. [Charles] Gordon [the 6th Cavalry quartermaster who was being transferred]. My bill-- $24. I closed at 8 in the evening and went to the feast ground. Had a good time. I won $9, spent it all, and went to bed.

Aug. 28 (San Agustín's Day). Busy all morning taking down and cleaning pictures. I put Mason to work. Went to bed early--drunk.

Aug. 29. We had monte and poker games all day. Nothing new.

Aug. 30. Got drunk. Went to the feast drunk. Went broke. Went home and walked through every mud hole on the way. Was drunk all night.

Aug. 31. Sick this morning. Levin and Comstock had a set-to--nothing serious. I was sober all day. Deputy U.S. Marshal Joe Evans and Tom Britton came in from Sonora. Charley Kenyon got drunk and disorderly and we had a row. He struck Hog Davis, hit me in the eye, and struck the sheriff. He got arrested and put in jail. I went to bed at 7 o'clock.

~ ~ ~ ~ ~

September 1 (Sunday). Still cloudy. Kenyon is very much ashamed about his conduct yesterday. Davis is drunk again. I received some binders for the *Spirit* and a book from N.Y. 2 p.m.--cloudy, looks like rain. Joe Phillips was brought in by [Deputy Sheriff] Tom Kerr and put in jail. I went to the feast, but came home early. Very hot, but I slept well.

Sept. 2. Cloudy. Very warm all day. Joe Phillips was taken before the justice of the peace and was ordered to Pinal County for trial. Charley Conwell is drunk. [Deputy] Alex Derrick came in looking for a horse thief and found him very soon after his arrival. The man was put in jail. I went to the feast ground, had two glasses of beer, and lost $2. Bradley and I came home and ate a big watermelon. I went to bed.

Sept. 3. Quite cool this morning. Dan (a colored man) brought news of two men being killed near Davidson's Cañon [about 25 miles southeast of town]. I worked hard all day cleaning up the house. Parker and Haines are tight. I closed at 7:30 and went to the feast. Stayed 1½ hours and came back. Had two glasses of beer in Brown's saloon and went to bed.

Sept. 4. Cool and pleasant. Prince [dog] fastened himself to the hind end of Chiquita. The Gem Saloon was shut up by the sheriff. Cloudy and very warm. No mail yet--the stage must have been robbed or lost below Florence. A Mexican shot at Marshal Buttner [through the window of his house] and tried to kill two other officers who went after him. I went to the feast ground--the feast was dull. Came home at 12 o'clock.

Sept. 5. Fine sunny morning. No mail stage yet. James Fitzgerald is in town again. I am very busy fixing up the house. Feel well today. Went to the feast ground, stayed a few moments, came home and went to bed. Slept well all night.

Sept. 6. Fine morning. I worked hard cleaning up. Sullivan fixed the counter and got it ready for painting. McKey is tight. Everyone went to the funeral of J. H. Adams and [Cornelius] Finley [the men who were killed by bandits at Davidson's Canyon.] Reverend Anderson gave the sermon. A Mexican shot his wife in the head and killed her, then ran off. John Burt was arrested for the crime. Buttner telegraphed from Florence that he had caught the man who shot at him. I went to the feast ground early, came home and went to bed at 10 o'clock.

Sept. 7. Burt was examined and acquitted. The murdered woman was buried today. There was great excitement on the appearance of the murderer at the grave. Some officers and others turned out armed to arrest him, but it proved a false report. Tonight was the last act in the drama of San Agustín. The 6th Cavalry band gave good music, and with other excitement the feast wound up to the satisfaction of all. I went to bed at 1:30 tomorrow morning.

Sept. 8 (Sunday). Got up early. Feel tip-top. I raised the flag in honor of the anniversary of the Battle of Eutaw Springs, South Carolina, 1781. Already the moving from the feast ground is nearly completed. Three stage coaches came in yesterday. Very dull today. There is a horse race this afternoon. 4 p.m.--people are returning from the race--it was a draw.

Sept. 9. Fine morning. Jerry Kenny commenced papering the house. Bradley got put in jail. There is a lawsuit before Judge Wood--Welisch against Zeckendorf. There are many strangers in town and the hotel is full. The stage came in--no through mail. I closed and went to bed at 11 o'clock.

Sept. 10. Fine morning. Quite warm. We are still fixing up the house. Bill Gale is drunk. Jack the Nailer is drunk. Nothing new. Frank Staples is in town. No other new arrivals.

Sept. 11. Fine day. Very quiet about town this morning. Called on Sam Hughes. I called on the big blonde and then had a 25¢ cigar. Jerry finished papering the house. Shorty Holt is very drunk. Bradley was let out of jail. Miss Mary Byers the dressmaker died today. I closed and went to bed at 9 o'clock.

Sept 12. Fine day, quite warm. Report says that the murderers of Adams and Finley are in Saric, Sonora. The funeral for Miss Byers was held today. Nothing else new. Went to bed early.

Sept. 13. Got up early. Worked on the house all day. There are many drunks in town. Tom Britton got into a row over a poker game and got put in jail. McKey came very near getting me drunk. I stayed with him, brought him home, and put him to bed. I went to bed at 10 o'clock.

Sept. 14. Fine day. We are nearly through fixing up the house. Jim Caldwell is drunk. Hog Davis is drunk. The mail stage came in early. I worked on the front room, put up pictures, etc., and worked quite hard on very little whiskey. Elizabeth Hughes died today.

Sept. 15 (Sunday). Took a bath and changed clothes. Shut the doors, took a walk around town, came home and took a sleep. I passed the day very quietly. Went to Levin's Park in the evening. There were great illuminations, speeches, and the firing of guns and firecrackers. Came home and went to bed at 10:30.

Sept. 16. Today is the 68th anniversary of Mexican Independence. There was a big time at the park. I got drunk early and kept drunk all day--tried to get sober but failed. Duke Flannery arrived today. I found my bed quite early in the night--very drunk.

Sept. 17. Sober and sleepy all day. Flannery and Davis are drunk. There were four monte games in the back room today. Big Ryan and Tom Gates arrived from Phoenix. Quite dull today. Went to bed early.

Sept. 18. Drank buttermilk all day--kept sober. Very dull in the house. Went to bed at 11:30.

Sept. 19. Fine day. A light wind and some dust. Kept sober today. Very dull. The games are running light. Went to bed at 11:30.

Sept. 20. Fine cool morning. The mail stage came in--received a print (barns) from Currier & Ives. Comstock took his monte game away. Lt. Kerr gave a party at Levin's Park. The music was by the Camp Lowell band. Levin bought Joe Goldtree's saloon. Very dull this evening. Went to bed at 10:30.

Sept. 21. The first issue of the *Citizen* in Tucson came out this morning. [John Clum had brought the *Arizona Citizen* newspaper back to Tucson from Florence. Tucson now had two weekly newspapers, both of which would become dailies in 1879. Both the *Star* and the *Citizen* are still published in Tucson.] George Bowen's monte game left the house. In changing pictures, I broke a large piece of glass very carelessly. Was forced to buy another one. The picture looks fine hanging on the wall. I went to bed at 11 o'clock. The house was open all night.

Sept. 22 (Sunday). Fine morning. Several drunks came around before breakfast. Mr. Mansfeld and Dr. Lord arrived back in town. The tinker came in from California and is as drunk as anybody. Dull all day. There was a small monte game in the evening--it lasted all night. I went to bed at 10:30.

Sept. 23. Cool and pleasant. Dull in the house this morning. I drank buttermilk all the time until after the lamp cleaning was finished, then commenced on whiskey. Managed to get pretty tight by evening. Dave Davis left for Florence. McKey is sick--I went home with him. Had a late lunch at George Hucke's and went to bed at 11:40.

Sept. 24. Cool morning. Had a late breakfast. The stage came in at 10:30. Kenyon brought in some buttermilk from Whipple's ranch [about nine miles northwest of town]. Foster and Billy Bradley are both in bed sick. Esslinger is also very bad. He was taken to the hospital this evening. I went to bed at 10:30.

Arizona Citizen *office in Tucson in the 1890s. Arizona Historical Society, Tucson, #2867.*

Sept. 25. Nice cool morning. Had new potatoes and butter for breakfast. George Esslinger died this morning in the hospital. Jim Speedy and Johnny Hart left for Sonora. Roddick, Ed Hudson, and Bent are in town. We bought a faro layout from Fairbanks. I went to bed early.

Sept. 26. Fine day. We received 10 cases of Milwaukee beer from Yuma. Fred Jones, McDaniels, Reed, and others came in from the mines. Quite dull in the house. I called on the big blonde this evening.

Sept. 27. Cool morning. Jones and Reed had a row. There are several drunks in town. Comstock left for the States via California. Foster is sick and went to bed early. The house kept me up till 3 tomorrow morning.

Sept. 28. Got up early but felt sleepy all day. The stage came in. Nothing new. Lots of drunken men around. The monte games ran all day. Foster is sick. Hucke opened a new lunch house. Bob Morrow came to town. I went to bed early.

Sept. 29 (Sunday). Fine morning. Several men were drunk before breakfast, and they kept drunk all day. Nothing new. No one killed. No one robbed. Very quiet all day. I ate dinner at George Hucke's restaurant. Went to bed at 10 o'clock.

Sept. 30. Fine cool morning. Fred Jones left early for the mines. Ed Hudson is drunk again. Whipple brought in some butter and buttermilk. Bradley wrote to his wife. Bob Morrow had a ten-dollar bill--the bar got it. Hand was tight all night.

~ ~ ~ ~ ~

October 1. Fine morning. Got up at 9 o'clock. Went back to bed again and slept till 1 p.m. Candidates for office began to put up their notices. I felt bad all evening. Quite lively in the house at night. Went to bed at 11:30.

Oct. 2. Nice weather. Fred Jones came in from the Cerro Colorado mines [located about 40 miles south of town]. Boley's wagons came in from Yuma. Bradley is getting ready for a trip. Candidates are stirring around quite lively. Nothing very new. Closed early.

Oct. 3. Fine morning. The *Star* came out early. All are anxious to see the statement in it by S. W. Carpenter--he gave William S. Oury a rough handling. Doc Rogers and Bradley got off at 4 p.m., well-heeled for a prospecting trip. The stage came in--A. C. Davis, candidate for delegate to Congress, arrived on it. I stayed up quite late--lively in the house. Got to bed about 12 o'clock.

Oct. 4. Wheeler W. Williams and his wife leave this morning for New York via San Francisco. I called on them and bid them good-bye. They went on their way rejoicing. Knox, Dobbs, and Bedford, all drunk, were playing cards. The game ended in a fight--no one hurt. I saw Mr. Davis. He is a Republican, but cannot get my vote. Went to bed at 11:30.

Oct. 5. Cloudy. Candidates are very thick this morning. Hand commenced getting drunk early, kept so all day until after supper. George Warren came to town and got a little exhilarated. [George Warren was an old prospector who is credited by some with discovering the copper deposits at Bisbee, Arizona. The town of Warren near Bisbee was named for him.] Verde Green is drunk. Lots of fellows are drunk. I went to bed quite sober.

Oct. 6 (Sunday). Pleasant morning. Took a bath and put on clean clothes. Kept sober all day. Hot--mercury today 105. Went to bed at 11 o'clock.

Oct. 7. Anniversary of the 2nd Battle of Saratoga. Very warm today. Cherokee Bob came to town. The election workers are getting after it hot. I got pretty full. Called on the girls. Drank some whiskey. Went to bed early. Miss Zella Johnson [the "big blonde"] entertained a lot of drunken fellows in the house and they kept me awake nearly all night.

Oct. 8. Fine morning. Had doughnuts for breakfast. Bob Johnson, alias Cherokee Bob, left today for Yuma. The would-be delegate returned today from a trip south, and left again. [Deputy] Joe Filmer came in from Sonora with Boyer, alias Jack Friday. The murderer was put in jail. Foster is sick. Harvey Hanson is on a spree. He is very drunk--drinks ale by the bottle. I was sober all day. Quite lively in the monte room tonight. Went to bed at 12:20.

Oct. 9. Fine morning. Hanson is going at the ale, is full as a goose. Shorty Holt went to the Tombstone mines. [The Tombstone silver boom was now getting up steam, would peak about 1883, and be all over by 1887.] Nothing very new. Boyer was put in jail heavily ironed to await the action of the grand jury. [John Boyer was tried in February 1879 for the murder of Martin Sweeney in June 1878. He was found guilty of murder in the 1st degree.] Bill Sniffin has a bellyache. Joe Ochoa got married today. There were lively monte games in our place this evening. Went to bed at 1:30, sober.

Oct. 10. Fine weather. People are returning from the Magdalena feast. I had a lady caller today--Mrs. Fish came by to show me her terrier pup. Had lunch with King William to piano accompaniment. [King William was an accomplished pianist.] Hank Williams came in town this evening and was drunk very soon after. The house was very lively with games this evening. Went to bed.

George Hand's love of dogs and skills as a vet brought him into contact with some women who did not frequent saloons. Maria Wakefield Fish (left) and Mrs. Wheeler W. Williams (right) consulted George Hand regarding their pets. Maria Wakefield, a school teacher, arrived in town in 1873 and married merchant E. N. Fish shortly thereafter. She is thought to be the first unmarried Anglo woman to come to Tucson. Wakefield Middle School bears her name. Arizona Historical Society, Tucson, #8 and #1726.

Oct. 11. Fine morning. We sold two cases of Milwaukee beer to Mr. Labara for his new whorehouse. He is excited about his prospects. Troy and McClary returned from Sonora. Speedy and his family also returned. John B. Hart is in town. Nothing very new except a lawsuit before Justice Neugass. Two girls sued some men for using vulgar language in their presence. The judge dismissed the case.

Oct. 12. A new store opened on the corner of Meyer and Mesilla streets, opposite our place. H. D. Williams left for the mines this morning but forgot something and came back. He got drunk again. Charley Kenyon is in town. The monte games were busy all day and night. Went to bed at 10:30.

Oct. 13 (Sunday). Cool pleasant morning. Today is the anniversary of the surrender of Burgoyne at Saratoga. Took a bath and feel tip-top. Nothing much new today.

Oct. 14. Very dull this morning. Kenyon left for the East via Santa Fe. The games were quite lively this evening. The faro game was a loser. The Milwaukee beer is selling fast. I have a sore mouth. Went to bed at 10 o'clock. The house was open all night.

Oct. 15. Got up at 6 o'clock. The faro game was still open and all the players were losers. Haines' monte game made a small winning. Bill Whalen, Sorghum Smith, and others came to town. Quite lively in the house this evening. I retired at 11:50.

Oct. 16. Fine day. A meeting of electors was called for this evening to make the county nominations. The different political rings are very busy buttonholing people on every corner. The meeting came off at 8 in the evening. Everything went satisfactory to some. Fred Jones killed a Negro. A Mexican fell dead late in the evening. Wash Evans, Bill Henry, and others are very drunk.

Oct. 17. Fine morning. The coroner's jury is sitting on the dead nigger. They found him dead, killed by a pistol-shot from the hand of one Fred C. Jones, wagonmaster for Tully & Ochoa. The man was buried today. [After this shooting, Fred Jones quietly slipped out of town. See Chapter 5, Oct. 16, 1878.] Dull in the house all day. I called on Miss Zella Johnson in the evening and found Captain Jeffords and Martin Maloney sleeping on the floor. McClary and others were there, singing and drinking wine, but I did not drink any. I left there and went to bed.

Oct. 18. Fine morning. Very dull, nothing new. Politics is getting warm. I gave Judge McCarthy a plug hat. A political meeting of the Democrats was called by Mr. Oury this evening. The Carpenter party went up, captured the meeting, and it adjourned. Poker games kept me up all night.

Oct. 19. Got up late. Fine weather. Dull in the house. The stage came in at 2 p.m.--no mail for me. Fred Myers is still drunk. George Warren is drunk and stinking very bad--I was obliged to drive him out. Myers' freight wagons left, he remained. James Speedy has a card up for the legislative assembly. Lively this evening. Closed at 2 in the morning.

Oct. 20 (Sunday). Fine day. Dull, nothing new. The town is full of strangers.

Oct. 21. Fine morning. Fred Myers is still drunk. Hand is drunk. All the boys are drunk. I wrote to Bradley. Got drunk again in the evening.

Oct. 22. Fine day. The drinking commenced early. Lots of drunks are around. The monte games are all busy. The barkeeper was very busy all day and night. Everybody got full--there were several fights and a big time generally. Went to bed at 12:30.

Oct. 23. Nice weather. The stage came in early. Fred Myers is still drunk. Pat Cannon is drunk. George Warren is drunk and stinking--Foster sent him out of the house several times. Johnny Louie came in from Tombstone. Gifford arrived also. Dull this evening. Went to bed early.

Oct. 24. Fine cold morning. Had codfish balls for breakfast. Several people returned from Tombstone and other points. Lots of strangers are in town. There was a trial today of Selden for the murder of a soldier. John Metzger is drunk. Frank Francis is drunk. Had lots of fun today. Went to bed at 11 o'clock.

Oct. 25. Cool morning. Nothing new. The Selden trial closed--he was convicted of murder in the 1st degree. I was called for jury duty tomorrow. Nothing happened today that was very extraordinary. Went to bed at 10:30.

Oct. 26. Fine morning. I was summoned for jury duty, but was excused by Judge French for the term. A soldier was tried as an accessory to the murder of Montgomery. The soldier was acquitted. It was lively in the house this evening for about 2 hours, then everything dropped and the games all closed. I went to bed.

Oct. 27 (Sunday). Fine day. Dull this morning. I have no chewing tobacco. Jim Hart arrived from Dos Cabezas [near Camp Bowie]. Quite lively this evening--the games ran all night.

Oct. 28. The weather is still fine. Politics is getting hot. John Metzger and Bedford are both electioneering. There was a big dance at the Cosmopolitan Hotel. Foster had an invitation but did not go. I had no invitation and did not go. Dull in the house this evening. I hurt myself lifting a trunk and feel bad. Went to bed early.

Oct. 29. Fine day. I was sick all day. No new thing of importance happened today. I sent letters and papers to Bradley. Hereford came in and spent $2. There was a little monte game this evening. The town is very dull. The dance last night was a failure. I went to bed early.

Oct. 30. The trial of Spence commenced today. The jury was only out a short time--Spence was acquitted. Dull during the day, quite lively in the house after dark. Went to bed at 10 o'clock.

Oct. 31. Windy, cold, and very dusty. Dull this morning. Wrote to Peter Brady and Tom McClellan in Florence. Everyone was drunk today and worse at night. Went to bed at 12 o'clock.

~ ~ ~ ~ ~

November 1. Cool morning. Bill Gale is in town. Politics is getting warmer. King Woolsey and Major Cox addressed the people of Tucson at the courthouse. John Wood returned from an election trip and is confident of success. Leatherwood returned, says Shibell will beat his opposition.

Nov. 2. Cool morning. Lots of drunks around this morning. McDaniels came in with Sheriff Shibell. H. S. Stevens came in to see us. Jim Hart got drunk and started for home. He got on the wrong road and ended up at Camp Lowell. He came back for a new start. McKey and Leatherwood left for Cerro Colorado. The wife of S. W. Carpenter died at 4 p.m. today. I received a lithograph of New York City from Currier & Ives. Dull this evening. Closed early.

Nov. 3 (Sunday). Very windy and disagreeable. The funeral of Mrs. Carpenter was held today. Every vehicle in town turned out. Quite lively in the house tonight. Murphy's monte game nearly went broke, but he made it up on faro. The monte games ran till 12. One faro game ran all night and lost $700. I went to bed at 12 o'clock.

Nov. 4. Fine morning. I sent a letter to Bradley and Doc Rogers. Nothing much new. A group of fellows without money or principle had a meeting to discuss offering their votes for sale. They had a row, but finally decided to wait till tomorrow evening and sell their votes to the highest bidder. The street was full of Mexicans fighting in the night.

Nov. 5. The morning opened fine. I went to the Cosmopolitan Hotel for breakfast. Voting commenced early. Wagons with flags flying came around to assist voters in getting to the polls. Flannery got drunk early. There were two fights in the house. The polls closed at sundown. Report says that John Buck was killed at Tubac by John Stroud. I went to bed early.

Nov. 6. The Tucson vote count is finished. Stevens beat Campbell, Shibell beat Wood, and Carpenter beat both of his opponents. Carpenter is very much pleased and set up drinks for the boys. Leatherwood ditto. Lots of drunks around today. The election whiskey is about played out, but Lew Elliott is still campaigning for Hog Davis, and Charley Bushnell is still electioneering for Carpenter. I got a girl and went to bed at 11 o'clock.

Nov. 7. Sick this morning. Cloudy and cold. We put up the stoves today. Stevens is still ahead in the vote count. Nothing very new. Went to bed early.

Nov. 8. Cold and cloudy. I received some letters from Mrs. Bradley asking about Billy. Stevens came in and set up drinks for the boys. He feels easy, says he will win by 250 votes majority. There are lots of strangers in town. I got some medicine from Meyer. Stroud was brought in, had an examination, and was held in jail to go before the grand jury. It commenced raining at three o'clock. It rained all evening and cleared off at 9 o'clock. Cold and windy.

Nov. 9. It is muddy and cold, but cleared off fine. John Stroud is out on bail. Roddick, Lew Elliott, and Britton left for the ranch at noon. Stevens is still ahead. William Oury and C. O. Brown are the worst beaten men in town, especially the former. [Oury and Brown were prominent Tucson Democrats, and were unhappy about the success of Republican candidates.] I received a letter from Bradley with the results of the voting at Tombstone.

Nov. 10 (Sunday). Fine morning, but cold and damp. Bradley arrived this morning and looks well. No excitement, nothing new. Sick this evening. Went to bed early.

Nov. 11. Fine cold morning. We turned the little stove around. Duke Flannery left for the mines. I bought a glass for the picture of New York. Metzger had a birthday. I called on Stevens this evening and then made another bet with Gifford on the election of our delegate. Went to bed early.

Nov. 12. Fine morning. Stevens came down and gave me an invitation to a wedding party tomorrow evening. Received a letter from P. R. Brady. Fred Jones came to town and gave himself up. An indictment being against him, he was obliged to go to jail. Nothing further new. Campbell pulled ahead of Stevens in the vote count for a short time.

Nov. 13. Cold dull day. Nothing new except Stevens is a little ahead. Murphy is tight and playing against monte--he won a pocketful of money. Blade opened a monte game with a soldier's money and lost about a hundred. The soldier closed the game--he thought Blade was throwing him off. The games ran all night. Gifford's game lost. King William and his partner won $150 off of a $1 stake.

Nov. 14. Cold. A report from Clifton [near the New Mexico line] puts Stevens over one hundred votes ahead. Fraud is the cry now. The wedding of Placido Ruelas and Miss Victoria Borquez was held at the church. Being one of the invited guests, I went to the church and from there to H. S. Stevens' house. Had a big time, more fun than ever before in Arizona. Leatherwood and I were the last to leave--two o'clock in the morning.

Nov. 15. Got up late. Got breakfast and then went to call on H. S. Stevens. Came back, my head still full of wine drunk the night before. Went to bed and slept till 3 p.m. After dinner I went back to bed and slept first-rate all night.

Nov. 16. Fine cold morning. Went with [Coroner H. B.] Smith and [Sheriff] Shibell out the old road toward Riley's Well [located about 15 miles southeast of town to look for a body reported by a passer-by]. We found the bones of a man apparently dead about two weeks under a paloverde tree. We buried him--all but the head, which we brought to town. Three of the teeth were filled with gold and silver. No one knows who he is. E. D. Wood and Apache Louise were put in jail this evening. Knox and Dobbs are drunk. [Riley's Well was dug in 1872 by Michael O'Reilly who planned to establish a stage station at the site. The well was a dry hole, and on September 14, 1872, the *Citizen* reported that O'Reilly had gone down 330 feet before abandoning the project.]

Nov. 17 (Sunday). Fine day. Church was held in two forms. Had no time to change clothes today. Sick and sober all day. Bradley cleaned the lamps.

There are lots of people in the streets this evening. Murphy is drunk. I went to bed after taking a sponge bath. The house was open all night.

Nov. 18. Fine day. Quite lively in the house. A telegram from Franklin and Beach to H. S. Stevens says that the Little Colorado vote was a grand swindle. 39 men voted for Stevens, but when the box was opened it only returned 1 vote for Stevens. Judge Silent ordered a grand jury to investigate it. I got a frame for the picture of the City of New York. Went to bed at 10:30.

Nov. 19. Fine morning. Quite cold. The telegraph brought the news of the death of Verde Green at Filibuster Camp [near Yuma] from injuries he received on the upsetting of a stage coach. Nothing else very new. Went to bed at 11 o'clock.

Nov. 20. Fine day. Nothing new except the board of supervisors of Yavapai County threw out every precinct in which Stevens was ahead. Very dull in town. Received a letter from Mrs. Bradley. Went to bed early.

Nov. 21. Fine weather. Sick all day. Very dull. Hanson is on a jamboree. Murphy is sick. Chiquita had one puppy. Bradley finally wrote to his wife. I went to bed at 10:30.

Nov. 22. Fine morning. I was sick all last night and got up very early. The stage came in early--Foster got a letter from Billy Bradley's wife inquiring of Billy. A few feeble guns were fired in honor of the reported election of John G. Campbell as delegate. Foster is sick and went to bed early. I stayed up all night. Faro and one monte game ran until daylight.

Nov. 23. I went to bed at 5 o'clock this morning and slept nicely until after 11. Had some soup and feel well. Drank very little liquor today. McKey was quite full all day and evening. An attempt was made late this evening to set fire to the stores of Lord & Williams and Zeckendorf. Went to bed at 11 o'clock. The house closed at 12.

Nov. 24 (Sunday). Got up early. Not so cold this morning. 10 a.m.--a cold wind came up and it is very dusty. I took a bath and put on clean clothes. Very dull in the house so we closed early.

Nov. 25. Raw cold day. Hanson is on a big spree. Marsh and McKey are drunk, Hand also. Bradley and Foster are sober. A Mexican was arrested for setting fire to the door of the Lord & Williams store. I wrote to John Miller and P. R. Brady. Went to bed early.

Nov. 26. Fine cold morning. Sullivan put a new sash in the front door. Windy and very dusty. McKey and myself got full. A man named Gordon died in the Palace Hotel--I went to see him in the evening. Took a walk with McKey to see a young lady--we "saw" her. I ate some tamales and enchiladas with Brokaw. Went to bed full of grub and whiskey.

Nov. 27. Fine morning. Cold. Got up at 9:30. There was a funeral this morning for E. E. Gordon. The stage came in late--received a letter from P. R. Brady. He says my bitch Fly died from the bite of a snake. McKey, myself, and all the boys are sober--except Roddick. Went to bed at 6 p.m. and slept till 9. Stayed up until 11, then went to bed and slept well.

Nov. 28. Fine morning. I raised the flag early in honor of Thanksgiving Day. The *Star, Miner* [Prescott], and the *Enterprise* [also a Prescott newspaper] all say that Stevens is elected delegate. Roddick is drunk. He is going around looking for bail for his partner Stroud who is still in jail. I had dinner at Dill's--turkey and the trimmings. A good dinner but not the right kind. The lemon pie and rich cake made me sick. Took the flag down at sunset. Went to bed early.

Nov. 29. Cloudy and cold. Had breakfast at the new restaurant *de Kaiser Wilhelm*--boiled spuds, beefsteak, and bad coffee (no eggs). [King William had opened a restaurant associated with the Alhambra Saloon]. Went to work getting intoxicated. Accomplished it. Called on the ladies. Had a good supper. Took a dose of copaiba and retired at 10 o'clock. [Copaiba was a medicine often prescribed in Hand's day to treat gonorrhea.]

Nov. 30. Very cold for the season. Had a good breakfast, fried eggs, etc., poor coffee. Dull all day and night. Went to bed early.

~ ~ ~ ~ ~

December 1 (Sunday). December opened cold. Dull all day. I got drunk in the evening. Nothing new.

Dec. 2. Cold. Dull. Marsh is drunk. I ate apples all day and got full of whiskey in the evening. John Davis got on a bust and was locked in a cell. The house was open all night.

Dec. 3. Cold. I got up early. 9 a.m.--Bradley and Foster are both still asleep. Marsh is as full as a goose. He started off too fast and went back to bed. Henry Hooker's stallion, Mambruno Belmont, arrived from Cal. today. I went to see him. He is a fine-looking horse--has the look of Hambletonian. 3 p.m.--Marsh is still asleep. Joe Elliott came in from San Xavier with a horse thief who was put in jail. Miller and Antoine's saloon went broke. I went to bed at 10 o'clock.

Dec. 4. Fine weather. Hooker left for his ranch driving his stallion in the off lead. The horse travels with his head high and is a fine mover. People are coming back from the San Xavier feast. Knox and Bedford came home stinking drunk. Bedford was noisy as usual and Foster put him out of the house. He troubled Spence for 2 hours and finally Spence put a sore head on him. John Toney, drunk and noisy, broke a pane of glass and cut his wrist badly. There are lots of drunks around. We closed early.

Dec. 5. Cold. The *Star* came out early. Last night's drunks are still around, feeling sore and ashamed. I got up a sweat cleaning pictures until noon. Got up another perspiration in the evening by drinking rot. Went to bed early.

Dec. 6. Fine day. Marsh is trying to get sober but is still drinking. I was sober all day. Called on the girls and got my.... [Hand scratched out several words in his diary.]

Dec. 7. Fine weather. Billy Bradley received a letter from his wife. I bought some limes from Sonora. Sent to Currier & Ives for a picture of the Port of New York. Wiley and Crane opened their new gambling house. Everyone got drunk today. We had lots of fun and whiskey aplenty. There was singing and drinking in the house all night. A nigger sang and was very amusing. I went to bed at 11 o'clock, but the house did not close. Big Lola came to see me.

Dec. 8 (Sunday). Windy, dusty, and disagreeable. Charley Bent, Ed Hudson, Jones, and others got drunk very early and stayed drunk all day. Hand got drunk for the last time. There was a bullfight today. Buck left town for Sonora. All the girls were compromised. I did not change my clothes today. Cause--drunkenness. Went to bed early.

Dec. 9. Got up very early. Marsh took 7 drinks in 15 minutes and put his cash in the box. Frank Francis came in town late last night and broke 2 doors down trying to get a drink. Hudson, Bent, and Co. left this morning. I was busy cleaning and whitewashing my room. Toppy Johnson is in town. Buck returned to town--he got on the wrong road. Hand got drunk again today. I paid for a subscription to the paper to September. Went to bed at 10 o'clock.

Dec. 10. Cloudy and very cold. I finished whitewashing. Bradshaw came in town from the north. Johnny Hart and his burro arrived from Desert Station. Hanson is very tight and on the warpath. Tom Smith's baker got drunk and pulled out a gun. McKey and some others took it from him. In the row a Mexican got a rap on the ear which landed his boat. Several drunks are around. I went to bed sober.

Dec. 11. Cloudy and cold. Buck was going to start out again--he saddled his horse and left him standing at a post all day. I moved into my new room today and was very busy fixing, hanging pictures, and cleaning up. Knox is still tight. Captain Jeffords went home. Doc Rogers left town. The town is very quite this evening. Went to bed and slept in my new room.

Dec. 12. Fine morning but quite cold. Lots of old bums stand with bellies to the bar, telling of the money they spent last night--no go. Nothing new. John Murphy arrived in town today. I worked on my room. Drank some whiskey. Foster bought a new crib board and sent to San Francisco for a faro layout. Dr. Lord came in and had three glasses of beer.

Dec. 13. Cold, dull, and dreary. No games, no drinking, no nothing. I was sober all day. Nothing new today. Wiley opened a bar in the house opposite us. 8 p.m.--it is very cold and we have fires in stoves all over the house. There is a small monte game, no whiskey being sold. Closed up at 11 o'clock and went to bed.

Dec. 14. Very cold morning. Put on a clean shirt today. We bought a load of firewood for $3. Bought a barrel of beer from Major Lawler. Jim McQueen is drunk. Nothing new. Very dull. Strangers are coming to town every day. Oregon Ferguson came up from the Gila. I went to bed early.

Dec. 15 (Sunday). Cold. I got up early. Jo went off on a spree. She came home after breakfast, all muddy. John Justice opened a faro game in the house. Hogan is drunk. There is a baseball game and a horse race today. I rode out to the racetrack. Tom Gardner's Orphan Boy beat Buttner's horse. A very pretty race of 600 yards. Had a lunch at Levin's in the evening. Went to bed at 10:30.

Dec. 16. Fine cold morning. Went to the hospital and took some drawers to Puck Ryan. John Justice is all dressed up this morning. I received a telegram from Lyons asking for money. Montgomery and Wilson also received one. Knox is drunk--very. A wagon load of fish came in town. Went to bed at 10 o'clock. The house closed at 2 tomorrow morning.

Dec. 17. Cold. Had fried fish for breakfast. Hogan is still drunk. Tom Montgomery got drunk early. I tied Jo and Vic [dogs] in my room. Very cold this evening. 8 p.m.--Dick Brown performed on the banjo at the courthouse, assisted by the amateurs of Tucson. A good show, the singing and music was good. They closed by singing "The Sweet Bye and Bye." It is cold tonight. Knox and Montgomery are still drunk. We closed the house early. Hand retired quite sober.

Dec. 18. It is very cold and everything froze. I changed shirts today. Knox got drunk again and had a sleep. He got up and got tight again. John Justice is drunk. Roddick and Brown are in town. They bought a jug of mescal from Steele. Marsh and hand are sober. I sent for the Christmas number of the *Spirit*. Prince married Jo--Rip is very jealous of it. Harper had a piece of his jaw taken out. I went to bed early.

Dec. 19. Cold. The *Star* came out early. The stage came in early--received a letter from my sister, Mira. A man died in the hospital. I saw Harper--he feels good. Roddick was blowing his horn all through the streets. He left this evening for home. Boley returned from Camp Huachuca. Dobbs beat the faro game and then he got drunk. Everybody gets drunk nowadays. I had some enchiladas and went to bed.

Dec. 20. Very cold. Had a good breakfast. Went to Levin's Park and saw his new improvements--the opera house, beer hall, brewery, etc. The streets are full of freight wagons. Bill Wood is drunk. He says he is the best monte dealer in town. Puck Ryan is very sick and is not expected to live. I ate some enchiladas and went to bed.

Dec. 21. Fine morning. Very cold. I gave up the stakes bet on the election to Gifford. [George Hand had bet on Tucson Republican Hiram Stevens, the incumbent, to win the race for delegate to Congress. John G. Campbell, a Democrat from Prescott, finally had been declared the winner in a close and disputed election.] I wrote to Mrs. Bradley and sent $2 to little Charley for

Christmas. Would have sent more but.... Dr. Handy says that Puck Ryan has commenced to mortify and has no chance to live. He eats nothing but a little brandy and sugar. I went to see him twice--he is very low. There were several dances in town this evening. I ate a lunch of broiled quail. Went to bed at 11 o'clock.

Alexander Levin's park and brewery. Arizona Historical Society, Tucson, #14848.

Dec. 22 (Sunday). Very cold. Had breakfast at the Cosmopolitan Hotel. Hogan is drunk. Ryan is some better--he ate two eggs. John Murphy returned to town. The monte games were quite lively today. We had some music in the daytime. I washed up and changed clothes. Ate dinner at Dill's. Went to bed at 11 o'clock. The house was open all night--Knox's monte game ran all night. Bradley did not come home tonight.

Dec. 23. Very cold. Billy Bradley came in and went to bed at 6 o'clock. I got up at 7 o'clock--monte was still open. Jeff Paige and others were full of rot-

-rum and dumb. There was nothing new until 7 in the evening--then I went to the schoolhouse to see the tableaux vivant [a performance in which costumed players strike static poses, accompanied by explanatory singing]. It was very nice. I took Foster's children home while he kicked the stuffing out of a Mexican who kicked Indian Charley a few weeks ago. Closed the house and went to bed.

Dec. 24 (Christmas Eve). Moderate weather. I sent to New York for a [hernia] truss. John Ryan of Whitehall, New York, died in the hospital. The funeral is at 4 p.m. today. Alas, poor Puck--I knew him well. Hand managed to get drunk after attending the performance at the courthouse--Christmas tree, singing, etc. In the evening McKey invited me to go with him to deliver Christmas presents, and afterwards I took him home. I had a lunch at Hucke's. Went to bed.

Dec. 25 (Christmas Day). No eggnog today--no eggs to be had. There were dinners everywhere. I was very busy all day. In the afternoon, McKey and others found some eggs and made them into nog--they all got tight. I had dinner at 5 p.m. at Dill's--very nice turkey, chicken, mock turtle soup, fish, salad, fine coffee and tea, custard pie, cake, and plum pudding. Went to bed early, not well but sober.

Dec. 26. Cloudy. I got up early with a broken back. Suffered some, but mustard leaves helped it. W. W. Williams and his wife returned to town yesterday. No *Star* today. Bedford got a sore head put on him last night--I heard it served him right. Bill Morrison arrived in town. A. E. Fay [editor of the *Star*] left for Prescott. I sat down nearly all day. Felt sick and went to bed early.

Dec. 27. Cloudy and cold. Jerry Kenny came in here very early (before daylight)--he was very tight. Henry Hanson came in town yesterday. Tom Roddick is in town today--sober. A delegation started for Prescott in Mr. Speedy's wagon train this morning. I sent Kendall's things by him. [Prescott was the new territorial capital and the tenth territorial legislature was to convene there in a few days. Delegates from Tucson and other Tucsonans with legislative business now had to travel 250 miles to Prescott and they were not pleased about it.] Jim Taylor left for Tombstone to go into the saloon business there. Leopoldo Carrillo's mother-in-law died today. Shorty Holt got some money for a mine.

Dec. 28. Cloudy and rainy. Big freight wagons are in town. There was a funeral this morning for Leopoldo Carrillo's mother-in-law. The clouds cleared off at noon. Dull in the house all day. Haines is on a spree, taking a drink every 15 minutes. Cherokee Bob Johnson came to town. Nothing new. Andy Cronley and John Warner were fined $25 each for licking a Jew. I went to bed at 11 o'clock.

Dec. 29 (Sunday). It began to rain before daylight. The house roof leaks. Rip was in jail--he got locked in Jacobs' store by accident. Dull today. Cold and rainy. Went to bed early.

Dec. 30. Cold and damp. It is still raining. Very dull in the house. Little Katie Borton died today. The mail stage came in very late--received a copy of the *Spirit*. Nothing new. Went to bed late.

Dec. 31 (New Year's Eve). Cold and damp. The sun came out quite warm at 11 a.m. There are several strangers in town. A race was made between horses owned by Gifford and Kerr--Pumpkins against a three-legged horse. I was sick all evening. Went to bed early and closed the old year sober.

~ ~ ~ ~ ~

John Heath, a member of a gang of six robbers and murderers, was lynched and hung from a telegraph pole in Tombstone on February 22, 1884. His cohorts were legally hanged a month later. Arizona Historical Society, Tucson, #4937.

Chapter Five

MURDER, MAYHEM, AND DEATH IN ARIZONA, 1872-1887

"Mrs. Hunter shot herself this morning. Cause--terrible family." George Hand, April 10, 1881

In the back of his diary for 1885, George Hand compiled a list of deaths and deadly events that occurred in southern Arizona for each year beginning with 1872. It is almost certain that he extracted this information from his diaries, some of which are now missing. The notes in the tabulation for the period 1875-1878 match the diary entries for those years very closely. He continued his morbid log of deaths, separate from his regular diary entries, in the back of his diaries for 1886 and 1887. His tally of mortalities gives insight into the macabre happenings that caught George Hand's attention during his years in Tucson.

~ ~ ~ ~ ~

January 1, 1872. Sam Raglin shot at Roxey, did not hurt him but hit big Price in the hand and a soldier in the hip.

Jan. 16. Maish shot a Mexican at his ranch. Maish and Driscoll were tried for manslaughter on March 9. Verdict--not guilty.

Jan. 24. A. J. Rice and John Petty were found dead 5 miles this side of Apache Pass, killed by Indians. John Bedford and Tom Donovan were attacked by Indians after passing the bodies. Donovan was killed but Bedford escaped, leaving the mules and buckboard.

February 18, 1872. John Ridgeway shot a Mexican who was trying to burglarize his house. The man died on the 19th and Ridgeway got bail. Received a letter on May 20th stating that John Ridgeway was lately killed by Indians near El Paso.

Feb. 20. Lola Moore, under sentence for life for the murder of her husband, was pardoned today with the understanding that she leave the U.S., never to return.

Feb. 26. McFarland (blacksmith) is missing on the Gila. The whole country turned out to hunt for him.

Feb. 29. A man named Keegan killed himself. Indians attacked the herd at Apache Pass. They killed one man and shot John Dobbs through both arms.

March 2, 1872. Pancho Gandara was killed on the Gila.

Mar. 4. The news came of the Gila row. Jack Reynolds (Richards' clerk) and 5 Mexicans were killed at Adamsville [on the Gila River near Florence]. A later report says only 3 Mexicans killed, Gandara, Manuel Rais, and another.

Bedell was killed and another American badly wounded--he was brought to Tucson and died shortly after.

Mar. 6. McFarland's body was found 4 miles down the Gila River. His arms and legs were cut off and there was a bullet hole in his head. Some Mexicans going to Sonora told Pete Kitchen that Pancho Gandara killed McFarland.

Mar. 19. The widow of Bedell, who was killed on the Gila, died this evening.

April 11, 1872. The wife of E. N. Fish died in San Francisco, Cal.

Apr. 28. Received news of the killing of Jack Whitman and a Mexican on Tom Hughes' ranch.

May 3, 1872. Indians killed William Irwin, one of an escort for Appel's wagon train from Camp Apache.

May 10. A mail rider was killed in Stein's Peak Cañon. The buckboard and rider were burned.

May 21. Terrance Cosgrove was killed by Indians on Sonoita Creek.

June 28, 1872. Received a report of the killing of Alonzo Brown by Indians while he was confined to his bed.

July 19, 1872. John P. Perry, who was wounded in the fight with Mexicans on the Gila [on March 2], died in the hospital today. He was a partner with Bedell.

August 6, 1872. Indians went to Roberts' ranch, killed 4 men, and destroyed all their tools and grain--on Sonoita Creek.

Aug. 25. Black Maria died.

Aug. 28. Lt. Stewart was killed by Indians in Davidson's Cañon.

Aug. 31. Corporal Black was found tied to a tree on the Crittenden road. He was full of arrows, his breast cut open, and his heart cut out.

October 3, 1872. Herbert Lord died.

November 28, 1872. Henry Kennedy was killed at Adamsville by John Rogers.

Nov. 29. Robert L. Swope was killed at Adamsville by John Willis.

Nov. 30. Mr. McCartney was murdered in his store at Yuma.

December 6, 1872. John Willis was arrested by Sheriff Ott and confined in jail. He only came out once and that was the day that he was hung. [See August 8, 1873.]

Dec. 24. Johnny Burt (the butcher) shot and killed a Mexican.

~ ~ ~ ~ ~

February 12, 1873. Shoemaker was killed on the Gila by Page.

April 30, 1873. Received the news of the death of Lt. Sherwood from wounds received in the Modoc War [in northern California].

May 30, 1873. Received the news of the killing of Lt. Almy by Indians.

July 21, 1873. George Cox died.

August 7, 1873. Vincente Hernandez and wife were killed by three Mexicans in their own house. They were beaten and their heads mashed in.
Aug. 8. The three Mexicans and Willis were taken from jail by force and hanged on the plaza. They hung from 10:30 a.m. till 3 p.m. [Although vigilantes quite often hung criminals without trial in the countryside, this was the only lynching to occur in Tucson.]
Aug. 22. Received the news of the murder of Ed Lumley at Kenyon's Station.
Aug. 24. Tom Bray died today.
Aug. 29. A Mexican woman died of heart disease on the feast ground. She was frightened by the fireworks.

September 5, 1873. The man who killed Lumley was caught and hanged to a limb of a tree.
Sept. 11. Dave Morgan died this morning.
Sept. 12. Rafael Ron died this evening.
Sept. 15. Joe Dawson shot and killed George Douglas after the hanging of the murderer of Ed Lumley.
Sept. 19. The baby of C. O. Brown died.
Sept. 21. Mark Aldrich died this evening.
Sept. 28. Refugio Pacheco died this evening.

November 4, 1873. Oscar Hutton died this morning. LaFitte and Sam Brown died this summer but I forgot the dates.
Nov. 27. Paymaster Robert Morrow committed suicide by shooting himself at the Occidental Hotel in San Francisco.

~ ~ ~ ~ ~

February 4, 1874. News received of the murder of two men and one woman at Smeardon's ranch near old Camp Grant.
Feb. 21. George Newsom died this evening.

March 10, 1874. Simon Sanchez was killed by Indians.

April 16, 1874. H. D. Smith was killed near O'Reilly's Well.
Apr. 21. Hermann, a German and a cook, died today.

June 5, 1874. Mr. B. Duffield was shot at the Bronco Mine by Holmes. He died immediately.

July 9, 1874. Refugio Rivera cut the jugular vein of Refugia Martez. This was a cold blooded murder. He was arrested, tried, convicted, and sentenced to death, but he escaped before the day was set. He is living in Magdalena, Mex.
July 24. Moore and Hall were arrested for murdering two innocent Mexicans on account of seeing them with plenty of money after making a sale of stock. This was a deliberate murder.

August 21, 1874. Michael Leydon and George Hughes were both murdered and thrown into a mine shaft. They were found a few days ago by Mr. Poindexter. A. J. Long died at San Carlos.

September 26, 1874. James Lamoree died in the hospital.

November 21, 1874. Merced, wife of John Hastings, died of sickness caused by liquor. Her death was hastened by improper care while sick.

~ ~ ~ ~ ~

January 2, 1875. Moore, Hall, Holmes, and Rivera beat Sawyer (jailor) and all escaped.
Jan. 6. Jacob Burch was shot in the French Brewery. He died.

March 8, 1875. Joseph Provencie, "French Joe," was shot in the belly by William Wall. Joe died March 11.
Mar. 9. Fred Eland died this morning.

May 28, 1875. Bob Morrow informed me of the death of Victor Boley in Sherman, Texas. He did not remember the date.

June 1, 1875. Mr. Reise took laudanum and died.
June 14. Pedro Burruel shot and killed a Mexican tramp.

September 1, 1875. Frank Esparza shot Procopio Leivaz in the groin. There was considerable excitement about it and talk of lynching him, but no one took the lead and he was put in jail. The man recovered.
Sept. 9. A Mexican was hung to a mesquite tree for stealing horses. He had no name.

October 10, 1875. Old Martin, the candy man, died.

Oct. 14. Frank Cosgrove died.

Oct. 23. John Farquason died at 4 p.m. today. He was a member of Co. "C," 1st Infantry, Cal. Vols. He always went by the name of Fergy.

Oct. 28. Tom McWilliams died at Ft. Goodwin.

November 21, 1875. Wife and child of W. C. Dunn died.

Nov. 27. Jerome Sawyer, found in arms against Mexico, was shot by the party opposed to Serna. He was very brave in the matter.

December 24, 1875. The wife of Charles Shibell died this morning.

~ ~ ~ ~ ~

January 4, 1876. J. E. McCaffry died today.

Jan. 5. J. G. Phillips shot himself through the head and instantly died. He was agent for the new stage line, the Arizona Express Co.

Jan. 10. Redwood Brown died.

Jan. 12. J. L. Stephenson fell dead in his house.

Jan. 31. Epifania Rivera died today.

February 9, 1876. LaFontaine, the French carpenter, died today.

Feb. 13. Samuel McClatchy died today.

Feb. 15. Mrs. W. C. Davis died.

March 2, 1876. Capt. R. M. Crandall died. He started out as a 2nd lieutenant in Co. "C," 1st Infantry, Cal. Vols. He was promoted soon after to be 1st Lt. of Co. "G," and soon after captain of his old Co. He was mustered out as such in 1864. Bob was a no. 1 man and was loved and respected by the majority of the people wherever he lived. He leaves 2 children, a girl and a boy.

Mar. 7. A soldier named Michael Ryan died from exposure and disease produced by too much whiskey.

Mar. 9. Hattie Davis, infant daughter of Mr. and Mrs. W. C. Davis, died today.

Mar. 11. Rufas Eldred died this evening.

Mar. 19. Martin Gilmartin died.

Mar. 21. Schemerhorn died this evening.

April 10, 1876. Nick Rogers and others were killed by Indians in Sulphur Springs Valley.

Apr. 20. Hank Stafford fell dead in the Gem Saloon.

May 15, 1876. George F. Foster, Jr., aged 18 months, died.

June 2, 1876. A child of Pancho Gomez died.

June 27. Mr. Schwenker accidently shot and killed himself in Tully & Ochoa's store.

July 9, 1876. W. W. Price died at Silver City, N. Mex.

July 18. Received an account of the death of George Toddenworth, killed by Indians. Joseph L. Cadotte was killed at the same time.

July 22. Jack Davis died at Mesilla, New Mex. He and Price belonged to the Cal. Column.

August 4, 1876. A young woman from Sonora named Lula died.

Aug. 15. Received news of the death of my sister Emma.

Aug. 26. Jesús Maria Flores killed himself in the store opposite my house.

September 9, 1876. S. H. Ramsey was shot and killed by a man named Brady at San Carlos.

Sept. 18. One of the men who shot Sawyer was killed in the street after dark this evening.

October 16, 1876. Hon. Judge John Titus died at 10 a.m. today.

~ ~ ~ ~ ~

January 9, 1877. Matt Bledsoe was killed in Hovey & Brown's saloon by Tom Kerr. He was shot in the temple and in the body. Kerr was put in jail by Sheriff Shibell.

Jan. 30. William Teague died today of black measles [smallpox].

February 5, 1877. Bill Morgan came to town and reported the massacre of a number of people by Indians on Sonoita Creek. Names not known.

April 6, 1877. William Tully Osborn [a child] died.

Apr. 22. Manuel Vasquez fell dead in the street today. Another man was brought in town shot through the head. Coroner's jury says he killed himself.

May 9, 1877. John T. Smith died at his home.

May 10. Clara Brown, daughter of C. O. Brown, died. There were a number of deaths today but I did not get the names.

May 11. Eleven deaths today of smallpox. I did not get names.

May 18. Young child of C. O. Brown named Eloise died today.

May 19. Received notice of the death of John Hopkins in Sonora.

May. 30. Adopted child of Adam Linn died.

June 6, 1877. A young child of James Lee died.

June 19. Dr. Goodwin's boy died.

June 25. A Mexican was killed below town. Did not learn his name.

June 26. Learned that his name was Geronimo Morales.

June 27. Morell (stage driver) died of black smallpox.

July 4, 1877. Alfonso Rickman died.

July 24. Received a letter from brother Milton informing me of the death of my brother Lewis in Chicago. Carmen Lopez died today.

August 17, 1877. A man was hung to a tree at Point of Water for stealing a mule.

October 12, 1877. Jim Blade's little boy died of smallpox.

Oct. 16. John Clark died in the pest house of smallpox.

November 11, 1877. Son of Buckalew's brother-in-law H. B. Jones died.

~ ~ ~ ~ ~

January 11, 1878. John W. Sweeney died at his home in Florence.

Jan. 15. Received a paper with a notice of the death of my niece Mary Roberts Harbison of Utica, N.Y.

Jan. 22. Panchita, McClatchy's woman's girl, died.

February 5, 1878. Fernando Otero died.

Feb. 12. Belknap's horse-shoer died. I forget his name.

Feb. 20. John Farley died.

Feb. 27. Jesús Ghanetto died today.

April 1, 1878. John Day died this morning at 6 o'clock. He was buried in the Catholic cemetery.

Apr. 8. John Upton died this morning in Florence.

Apr. 11. Mrs. Manuela Sweeney, widow of the late John W. Sweeney, died.

Apr. 25. Hon. Coles Bashford died at Prescott.

Apr. 30. A woman died in jail.

May 14, 1878. C. V. D. Lovejoy died today from a gunshot wound inflicted by Francisco Grijalva near Pueblo Viejo.

May 24. Franklin Sanford died on Sonoita Creek.

July 2, 1878. A man named James Carroll called for a drink at H. H. Holt's bar. He put poison in it and drank it. He died in a short time in terrible agony.

July 9. J. Farrell (alias Finnegan) died on the road today from heat and over exertion. He was brought to town by Whipple and buried here.

July 11. Mr. Ledyard killed himself.

219

July 28. Thomas Bannon died today in a fit.

August 4, 1878. George Treanor, Jr., (a boy) died this morning.

Aug. 19. William Brazelton, who had been engaged for some time in stopping and robbing stages, was caught and killed today through the treachery of his partner in crime [Dave Nemitz]. Dave was turned loose, but should have been introduced to the penitentiary for a long no. of years.

September 6, 1878. Funeral of Adams and Finley today. They were killed by Indians in Davidson's Cañon. A Mexican shot and killed his wife. Johnny Burt was arrested for the crime but was acquitted. It was the Mexican but he was not found.

Sept. 11. Miss Byers died today.

Sept. 25. George Esslinger died in the hospital this morning.

October 16, 1878. Fred Jones killed a Negro opposite our house. We gave Jones $20 and he left town. He was arrested some time afterwards, tried, and acquitted. He died in Sonora of yellow fever several years after the above circumstance. A Mexican fell dead today.

November 2, 1878. Tomasa, wife of S. W. Carpenter, died at 4 p.m. today. She was the daughter of the wife of C. H. Meyer.

Nov. 5. Buck was killed by John Stroud at Tubac. Stroud was tried, convicted, and sentenced to the penitentiary for 18 years. He was pardoned out in 1884.

Nov. 19. Green, a Tucson merchant, died at Filibuster Camp. He was going to Cal.

December 24, 1878. John Ryan, alias Puck, died in the hospital today. He was from Whitehall on the Hudson River, New York.

Dec. 27. Mother-in-law of Leopoldo Carrillo died today.

Dec. 30. Katie Borton died today.

~ ~ ~ ~ ~

January 2, 1879. Mrs. C. H. Meyer died.

Jan. 6. Heard of the murder of Lazy Bob.

Jan. 9. Arthur Henry died.

Jan. 20. Eli McJones died at 1 o'clock this morning. Charles Cooper died. He was an old timer in Arizona and at the time of his death he was in the employ of Bill Smith and Dr. Jones.

Jan. 30. A child in the next room to me died this evening.

February 13, 1879. A young child of Joaquina died today.

March 2, 1879. A young Mexican named Policarpio something died today.
Mar. 24. A sister-in-law of C. V. D. Lovejoy was buried today.
Mar. 28. A child of Mr. and Mrs. Samuel Drachman died today.

April 7, 1879. Infant child of Murdoc buried.
Apr. 16. Little child of Louis Hughes died.

May 14, 1879. Lew Burton died in the Palace Hotel today.

June 7, 1879. Thomas Roddick died this morning.
June 8. E. P. Head (Prentiss) died this morning.

July 11, 1879. William Quinn, a stranger, went into Mr. Etchells' blacksmith shop to get out of the rain and was struck by lightning, killing him instantly.
July 19. Mrs. Jones, a sister of Buckalew, died at 3 p.m.
July 30. Henry and Mat Shoenbeck (brothers) were killed by Indians in the Santa Ritas.

August 19, 1879. Infant child (Mary) of C. O. Brown died and was buried this morning.
Aug. 23. Powell shot at Simpson, missed him but hit Nelson. He fired again and hit a Mexican in the heart, killing him instantly. He was arrested and confined in jail.

September 4, 1879. Warner Buck died in San Francisco.
Sept. 11. Nephew of Dr. Samaniego died today.
Sept. 23. Ursula Solares, aged 78, died this evening.

October 15, 1879. A telegram announces the death of Billy Jones (son of Col. Jones of Mesilla) in an Indian fight in New Mexico.
Oct. 16. Emilia, wife of Thomas Gale, died.
Oct. 26. A woman was accidentally killed in John Brown's dwelling house.

November 3, 1879. A man named Jennings shot himself with a Winchester rifle, pulling the trigger with his toe. He is said to be the man who put the steel bar in the artesian well.
Nov. 29. Kelly the barber died today. He took too much morphine.

December 6, 1879. The wife of Dr. Guerrero was buried.
Dec. 15. Carpenter died at Camp Grant.

~ ~ ~ ~ ~

January 2, 1880. Funeral today for Santiago's child.

Jan. 7. William LaRose died in Monterey, California. He came to Tucson with me in 1862.

Jan. 25. Child of Dr. and Mrs. Girard died today.

February 24, 1880. Celaya died today.

George Hand (standing) and Eugene O. Shaw. Like George Hand, Shaw evidently was a lover of dogs. This photo was taken in 1880 when Hand was fifty years old. Shaw was elected Pima County sheriff in 1886 but died suddenly the next year. Buehman photo, Arizona Historical Society, Tucson, #1483.

March 3, 1880. Frank Massoletti died at Tombstone.

Mar. 15. Professor Thomas Davis, a native of Pennsylvania and a soldier in the Texan war against Mexico, died today.

Mar. 16. Jim Munroe (colored) was shot and killed today by another nigger who immediately got up and left for Sonora.

Mar. 22. A. C. Benedict died this afternoon of pneumonia.

April 5, 1880. James W. McManus died at the Cosmopolitan Hotel of pneumonia.

Apr. 15. McMorris died this evening from the influence of opium.

Apr. 20. James (Bullet Neck) Halstead of Tombstone died of pneumonia.

May 2, 1880. S. C. Whipple was bitten by a rattlesnake last night and died this morning. His remains were brought here and interred today.

May 7. Mrs. W. Race died of starvation at the Cosmopolitan Hotel. She was buried by Miss Fanny Howard and Rose Gibson.

May 20. F. S. Massey died in St. Mary's Hospital this morning. He was a native of England and had been an employee of the government at the Indian reservation.

June 3, 1880. A Mexican fell dead on Main St. today. The coroner's jury found him dead.

June 4. Mrs. Hart died in a house on Convent St.

June 17. A man named Jim Montgomery took strychnine and died. He was brought to town and buried.

June 27. Mrs. Leopoldo Carrillo died.

July 4, 1880. Frank Foster, infant son of George F. Foster, died today.

July 12. Judge Tom J. Bidwell died in San Francisco.

July 13. Rev. W. H. Dean died this morning and was buried this evening.

July 18. Judge McCarthy died.

July 19. Mrs. Ruelas died.

July 24. William Roberts (Scranton Bob) died at St. Mary's Hospital.

July 26. Guadalupe, widow of Jerome Sawyer (who was shot in Sonora) [in November 1875] died today.

August 23, 1880. The son of Paul Maroney was brought in from Harshaw, dead--caused by injuries received from belting on machinery.

September 6, 1880. A man named Davis killed at Pantano by [rail] cars was brought to town, frozen, and sent to Cal.

October 19, 1880. John Burt died today in St. Mary's hospital.

Oct. 26. A man named Williams died and was buried today. He came from Missouri 32 years ago.

Oct. 29. Dan Moran, a colored man, shot Wilson, a white man. Moran was arrested.

Oct. 30. Wilson was taken to the hospital this morning. He died on the way in the wagon. Moran was tried, found guilty of manslaughter, and sent to the penitentiary. I learned that he died before his time was out.

November 7, 1880. A Negro merchant died in the upper part of town this evening. I did not learn his name.

Nov. 13. The infant child Mr. and Mrs. S. W. Carpenter died today.

Nov. 16. The son of Dr. and Mrs. Goodwin died, aged 18 months.

December 10, 1880. John A. Piggott (a native of Dublin, Ireland) died today, aged 45 years.

Dec. 12. Alex McKey died today. He was buried near John Burt and Whipple.

Dec. 18. Mrs. J. P. Clum died this evening, 5 o'clock.

~ ~ ~ ~ ~

January 5, 1881. Received the news of the killing of Stowe at Arivaca by Joe Elliott.

Jan. 15. Johnny-Behind-the-Deuce was put in jail here for killing W. P. Schneider at Charleston. [Johnny escaped from the Tucson jail and never stood trial for this killing.]

Jan. 18. A man named Lewis died and was buried today. He is said to be the man who struck John Bedford on the head and caused his deafness.

Jan. 23. A soldier's funeral today in the Catholic church. I did not learn his name.

Jan. 30. Dr. Keury buried today.

February 20, 1881. Philip Fisch shot and killed himself.

Feb. 25. Charley Storms was shot and killed by Luke Short at Tombstone.

March 11, 1881. Funeral of a man named Wood today.

Mar. 12. A Mexican was crushed between [rail] cars and killed--don't know his name.

Mar. 16. Chico Foster was shot and killed by a woman in Los Angeles. Road agents stopped the stage between Contention and Benson, 200 yards from Drew's Station on the San Pedro River. They killed the driver, Bud Philpot. Bob Paul was on the box with the driver. He fired two shots at them and then the team ran away. After a while Paul got the reins and drove in to Benson. Philpot's remains were buried at Tombstone, then afterwards were taken to

Calistoga, Cal., for final burial. The men who comprised the gang of agents were Bill Leonard, Jim Crane, and Harry Head. They were all killed a short time afterwards.

Pima County officials prepare to execute a murderer. Haynes Collection, Arizona Historical Society, Tucson, #18866.

April 10, 1881. Mrs. Hunter shot herself this morning. Cause--terrible family.

May 6, 1881. Mrs. Huffaker died on the San Pedro River.

May 15. Archie McBride died in Tombstone.

May 18. A man was killed in the fire at Fish's wood yard at the flour mill.

May 29. Old Fisher died in the hospital this morning. He came to the territory with Shinn's Battery of the army during the Civil War.

June 1, 1881. William Murray died and was buried today. Received the news of the killing of Stiles at Florence. Another man was cut off at the pockets last night up town. I knew none of the above.

June 10. Joe Neugass was buried today.

June 11. Total eclipse of the moon.

June 17. William Shaw committed suicide by drowning near Warner's mill.

June 19. A Mexican was shot in the head and killed. I could not learn his name.

June 27. The big powder explosion in Tucson. The report was heard 110 miles away. [Thirty thousand pounds of blasting powder stored in a special magazine near town accidently detonated. Buildings were damaged and windows blown out, but only a few people were injured and there were no deaths. The blast occurred at 10:50 p.m., and was followed by a huge fireball that lit up the countryside, causing some people to fear that the end of the world was at hand.]

July 7, 1881. A 5-year-old boy was bitten by a snake and died at Smith's ranch.

July 8. Harper was hung by the law a few moments before 3 p.m., Sheriff Paul officiating. He died without a struggle.

July 9. John L. Harris died this morning. Cause--stopped drinking liquor.

July 20. A man was found on the railroad track. A coroner's jury was summoned and they found both of his legs cut off and both arms cut off. His back was broken and the bone was sticking out. His liver and heart were torn out and lying beside the body. The jury said he was dead. No one knew him. He is supposed to have been stealing a ride.

July 23. A woman had a leg cut off and died this morning.

August 11, 1881. The remains of Pat O'Meara were found on the road going to his home. He had been dead some time. His gun was there and nothing taken from him. It is the supposition that he died from thirst and sun stroke. He had been drinking heavily before starting out and whiskey was found beside his body.

Aug. 21. The twin babies of Mr. and Mrs. W. O'Sullivan died last night.

Aug. 26. A Mexican boy shot and killed himself. He was buried today. Name not known.

September 3, 1881. Dispatches from Camp Apache report that 1 officer and 7 men were killed by Indians.

Sept. 19. President Garfield died at 10:55 p.m.

Sept. 25. Infant child of Sam Drachman died today.

October 3, 1881. Bartolo Samaniego, 1 sergeant, and 1 private were killed and several men wounded in an Indian fight.

Oct. 24. Col. Paulison died today.

November 5, 1881. George Teague died in the hospital. McCarthy died sometime in November in Hermosillo, Mexico. He went by the name of Deaf Mac.

Nov. 7. Claude Anderson died of consumption.

Nov. 20. George W. Bowker died.

Nov. 23. Guadalupita Aguirre died yesterday, was buried today.

Nov. 27. DeGraw, a soldier, went into the Palace Hotel, lay on a bed, and died.

December 2, 1881. McGorris died in the hospital today.

Dec. 3. Bop and Congress had a big fight today. Bop got away with the baggage. He licks Congress every time, but Congress comes again some other day. Congress believes in the old saying, "He who fights and runs away may live to fight another day."

Dec. 9. Negley Post No. 35, G.A.R., organized today.

Dec. 10. Negley Post elected officers.

Dec. 20. Hyler Ott died this morning, aged 52 years.

Dec. 26. Cyrus White died this morning. The Masons will bury him tomorrow.

~ ~ ~ ~ ~

January 1, 1882. The brother of E. B. Gifford died today. The service was performed by the Odd Fellows.

Jan. 9. Ike Brokaw died today.

Jan. 11. Washington Evans died last year. I did not hear of it till now.

Jan. 18. A telegram from a hospital in San Francisco states that John T. Pautlind died today.

Jan. 24. J. P. Fuller died at Yuma. His remains were brought here and buried by the Masonic fraternity.

Jan. 27. Col. Edwin A. Rigg died today at Contention City of pneumonia. He was a Cal. pioneer and held many offices of trust in California. He was captain of the Marion Rifles for several years, was a veteran of the Mexican War, and started in the War of the Rebellion as a captain. Before we left sight of San Francisco, he was promoted to major of the 1st Infantry Regiment. When we arrived at Yuma he was a Lt. Col., and on arriving on the Rio Grande he was Colonel of the 1st Infantry Regiment, Cal. Volunteers. After peace was declared, he was transferred to the regular army, but soon resigned. He was a justice of the peace and notary public when he died.

February 14, 1882. Dodge died in the hospital.

March 3, 1882. Received a telegram from Camp Grant stating that the Indians Dandy Jim, Dead Shot, and Skipper were hanged today.

Mar. 9. George Carter died in the hospital.

Mar. 11. Capt. Jenks and Mr. Dodson died today.

Mar. 19. Morgan Earp died today from a gunshot wound he received while playing billiards in Tombstone. He was shot through a window from the sidewalk.

Mar. 21. Frank Stillwell was shot all over, the worst shot-up man that I ever saw. He was found a few hundred yards from the hotel on the railroad tracks. It is supposed to be the work of Doc Holliday and the Earps, but they were not found. Holliday and the Earps knew that Stillwell shot Morg Earp and they were bound to get him.

March 23, 1882. I left Tucson to visit awhile in Contention City, and as a consequence my Tucson diary will not be kept until my return. I shall try, however, to learn by the papers what is going on in the pueblo. Arrived at Contention City on the Rio San Pedro.

Mar. 29. A man living on a sheep ranch at the Mormon settlement was found dead. A coroner's jury was summoned. They brought the body to town and we had a funeral. His name was McMurrain. No clue to the manner of his death.

April 19, 1882. Dave Rickey was killed by Indians at his mine at Bacuachi, Sonora.

Apr. 26. A child died and was buried today.

May 5, 1882. Archie McBride died in Tombstone.

May 17. Received the news of the death of David (alias Hog) Davis at Silver City, N.M.

June 6, 1882. News came of the killing of James Levy last night by John Murphy, Bill Moyer, and Dave Gibson [in Tucson]. They were all tried in due time. Moyer was sentenced for life at Yuma. Murphy and Dave were acquitted. [These men were gamblers and had quarreled with Levy over a card game.]

June 30. Received news of the hanging of [Charles] Guiteau [President James Garfield's assassin].

The Contention Mill on the San Pedro River about ten miles west of Tombstone. George Hand visited Contention City for several months in 1882. The town and mill were abandoned when the silver boom played out a few years later. Carleton Watkins photo, Arizona Historical Society, Tucson, #14822.

July 1, 1882. Started for home. Wm. Bradley came with me to Benson. Rip [dog] and I came the balance of the way alone. Arrived home [in Tucson] in due time with Rip and a pup. Found the [Foster] family all well, but my canary bird had died and the girls had him pressed, feathers and all, and placed in a frame with glass.

July 27, 1882. Went on at the [Pima County] courthouse [in Tucson] as night watchman, $100 per month.

August 4, 1882. Dr. Wilbur died at his father's home in Mass. of heart disease on July 17. News came by letter from his father.

Aug. 21. Andy Hall was killed by road agents on the Globe road while carrying money for Wells Fargo. A man named Vail was killed at the same time.

Aug. 24. Two of the murderers of Hall and Vail were hung today. They confessed to the killing.

Aug. 28. Mariana Dias died today. She is said to be 120 years old.

Aug. 29. Two funerals today, don't know the names.

September 8, 1882. Ben Virgin was shot and killed by pulling his gun out of a wagon. He was brought in to town.

Sept. 11. The supervisors received the new courthouse.

Sept. 12. The prisoners were moved to the new jail.

Sept. 15. A friend of mine died today. I forget her name.

Sept. 16. Mrs. Frank Norton died.

Sept. 17. Thomas Fitzhugh died today in Tombstone of heart disease. He was well known here.

October 9, 1882. Two men are dead. One was a natural death, the other, named Hewett, was beaten to death by someone unknown.

Oct. 11. A man committed suicide in Porter's Hotel.

Oct. 23. Murphy, Gibson, Moyer, and 6 others escaped jail at 6 o'clock this evening. One of the jail keepers went to supper. I was busy with my work, nearly completed, when two ladies came in to talk with me. While we were talking, Mr. George Cooler came running out of the jail saying, "Murphy and the boys are all gone. They gaged me, locked me up, and left." A party was fitted out and went in pursuit. [Jail guard George Cooler was a friend of gamblers Murphy, Gibson, and Moyer and there was suspicion that he aided their escape. They were soon captured.]

November 14, 1882. Fred Fraser died today of consumption. He was a good boy, but he was doomed to die.

Nov. 18. Just received news of the death of Colton in San Francisco.

Nov. 28. Bernard's baby was buried today.

December 9, 1882. L. Lier, brother of Max, died at Contention City. The remains were brought to this town for burial.

~ ~ ~ ~ ~

January 1, 1883. Billy White, the jail guard, while alone, opened a cell door and two fellows jumped out, put a sore head on him, and escaped. They were not found. Sheriff Paul is red hot. Al George was killed at his mine near Tombstone a few days ago.

Jan. 10. William Ganz died.

Jan. 14. Col. A. J. Marsh died of liver disease. We sent for the undertaker and laid him out. He is a complete skeleton. It was no trouble to raise $100--the undertaker's bill is $85. 'Tis a pity that good men must die first. It will be a terrible shock to his parents who are still living and are very old. The Col. was a Mason, but on acct. of the non-payment of dues no Mason attended his funeral. I always had a reverence for Masonry, but if the non-payment of dues to a Masonic lodge keeps Masons from attending a funeral of a better Mason than any one in the community where he lives, then Masonry is in my opinion a humbug. No Mason was at his grave and that settles the secret society biz. with me.

Jan. 17. A man named Powers died in the hospital today.

Jan. 20. A. Lazard's little dog Nelly died of poison. Some son-of-a-bitch gave poison to the little black-and-tan. She died and the son-of-a-bitch who gave it to her should have died two days ago. He is a villain and the curse on the villain who murdered Nell.

Jan. 28. Frank Beale died in the hospital.

February 9, 1883. Samuel Detwiler committed suicide. He shot and killed himself and now lies in the morgue. He blew the whole top of his head off.

Feb. 10. C. S. McMillan died of inflammation of the bowels.

Feb. 13. Mary Antoinette, a Sister of St. Joseph, died.

Feb. 18. Miss Lolo Corey, actress and wife of James Holly of the Fashion Theatre, died today.

Feb. 20. Mrs. Maria Wilkins died.

Feb. 22. Capt. M. Gay was found dead in his house of pneumonia. He had been unwell for some time. Gibson, a policeman, died of smallpox. [There were many cases of smallpox in Tucson at this time.]

Feb. 28. Refugio Mariana died this morning for sure. He was reported dead on the 23rd and I put it down so. He objected to it at that time, but he was buried this afternoon.

March 11, 1883. Henry Crowell died.

Mar. 17. The infant son of W. O'Sullivan died.

April 7, 1883. John Mansfeld and F. W. Schneider died.

Apr. 16. Dr. C. E. Holbrook died.

Apr. 18. Mrs. Lizzie Gardner died this morning from chloroform.

Apr. 21. Samuel E. Rose died.

Apr. 29. Andrew W. Holbrook was killed by Casey this morning. Casey and Sinclair broke the cage, got out, and in the jailor's room got guns. They stood up Holbrook. He resisted them and Casey shot him. Several shots were fired by the guards and deputies. Casey finally gave up his gun, but poor Holbrook got a mortal wound. At 11 o'clock the fire bell commenced ringing and a crowd gathered around the courthouse. They came in to get the murderer, Casey. Quite lively skirmishing for about half an hour, but the mob had no head and they were easily dispersed.

May 19, 1883. Mr. Greenwood was killed near Sahuarita.
May 22. Thomas Belknap was shot at Greaterville. He died in Tucson. He was shot through the bowels, bladder, and kidney.
May 23. Lolo Lopez died.
May 27. Col. John R. James died.

June 6, 1883. Mr. Schabin committed suicide. He formerly kept the I.X.L. Lodging House.
June 8. A man named Cook was found dead, shot through the body, in Tom Gardner's corral. He was put on ice by the coroner.
June 11. Manuel Salazar drowned in a slough above Warner's mill.
June 13. John Drummond died in the hospital.
June 30. Amos Hollister drowned in Silver Lake.

July 8, 1883. Mrs. Smith died today of laudanum and exposure.
July 19. Luciano Telaya and 2 sons were suffocated in an old well in the south part of town.
July 20. George Bannock died in the hospital.

August 24, 1883. Mrs. L. C. Nelson died.
Aug. 26. Cornelius Soult died at Pelton.

September 3, 1883. The people of Florence went into the jail, took Lem Redfield and Joe Tuttle out in the corridor, put some ropes over the beams, and hung them this evening. [These men were accused of robbing the Florence-Globe stage in August 1883 and killing the Wells Fargo agent guarding it.]
Sept. 12. Ramon Montoya died suddenly in El Paso, Tex. He formerly worked for Tully and Ochoa.
Sept. 20. A. B. Barnett died in Hermosillo, Sonora.
Sept. 30. James Lynch, formerly of N. Jersey, died this morning of erysipelas [a blood infection]. His remains are on ice. Louis Shoenberg committed suicide. Heard that George Smeardon, William Eustis, and Fred Jones died of yellow fever in Sonora.

Robert H. Paul served as Pima County sheriff from 1881 to 1886. He hired George Hand as custodian of the new courthouse in July 1882. Arizona Historical Society, Tucson, #1596.

November 12, 1883. Mrs. Joseph Holt died.

Nov. 20. W. L. Brooks died.

Nov. 24. T. C. Webster, R.R. engineer, was killed by robbers at the Gage Station near Deming [New Mexico]. The Wells Fargo Express box was taken, one man robbed, no others hurt.

December 7, 1883. Charles H. Lovell was killed by A. J. Spencer with a knife. They quarreled in Hibbard's saloon and Mr. Lovell was cut in the side and in the thigh.

Dec. 8. Philip Hinkle, proprietor of the Buckeye Saloon, was found dead in the back yard of L. C. Hughes. How he came there is a mystery. His clothing was all on even to his hat, his watch was all right and running, but the poor man was blue as a plum and looked as if he choked to death. I drank with him last evening and he appeared in good health.

Dec. 22. Arthur Anderson died.

Dec. 31. John W. Patterson died at the hospital this morning. A. J. Spencer died today.

~ ~ ~ ~ ~

January 3, 1884. The remains of John W. Patterson were sent by Wells Fargo & Co. Express to Oakland, Cal.

Jan. 6. John T. Logan died in a fit at Logan City, Ariz.

Jan. 8. Henry Glassman died at Tubac.

Jan. 10. Bernardo Bravo died this evening.

Jan. 11. Miss Fanny Huffaker died at Tres Alamos [about 50 miles east of Tucson near Benson].

Jan. 17. Asa Porter of Porter's Hotel died. His remains were taken to California and buried. Joseph Burgmander died today. He was a native of Texas and an old timer here.

Jan. 24. Manuel Ignacio Elias died.

Jan. 28. Albert T. Lea died of pneumonia.

Jan. 29. William S. Morgan died.

Jan. 31. Judge A. W. Sheldon died in San Francisco. He died of constriction of the small intestines.

February 7, 1884. John Ludwig of Contention died at Benson while sitting in a chair.

March 1, 1884. Mrs. W. A. Johnson died.

Mar. 5. John Warner Davis died at Yuma. He was one of the first Americans in Tucson. He was at the time of his death a guard at the territorial prison.

Mar. 7. Constable J. L. Roberts was shot and killed by a man named Adams.

Mar. 11. James Lee died at Silver Lake. An old timer here, he with W. F. Scott were engaged in the flour mill and mining businesses for a number of years. He leaves a large family and many friends to mourn his demise.

Mar. 12. Frank Jewell died today in the hospital. A Mexican and a Chinaman also died.

Mar. 16. Edward Hamilton, a R.R. man, died in the hospital by suicide. He cut his throat and died.

Mar. 17. The little daughter of Charalina died this morning.

Mar. 26. William Handy, brother of the Dr., died at Oakland, California. The infant of Mr. and Mrs. W. F. Kitt died.

Mar. 28. The last of the Bisbee murderers, 5 in number, were hung at 1:18 today in the City of Tombstone, Cochise Co., by Sheriff Ward. Three of them were baptized in the Catholic Church and made Christians. The other two must necessarily go to Hell. [This gang robbed a store in Bisbee in December 1883. A mining company's payroll was in the store's safe, and the robbers made off with several thousand dollars. In an ensuing gun battle, four Bisbee citizens were killed. The outlaws, six in number, were captured, tried at Tombstone (the county seat), and five were sentenced to death. One of the criminals, John Heath, was given a life sentence. The citizens of Cochise County objected to this lenient penalty, and Heath was lynched and hung from a telegraph pole in February 1884.]

Mar. 31. Received news of the death of Dr. Charles H. Lord in Mexico. He leaves many friends to mourn his taking off. Take him all in all, he was one of Nature's noblemen. [Dr. Charles Lord, once a successful Tucson businessman, suffered severe financial reversals in the early 1880s. He went to Mexico and tried to fake his death so that his wife could collect on his life insurance policies. Investigators found him practicing medicine in Mexico City and the fraud was exposed. This time, however, the report of Lord's death was true.]

April 1, 1884. Mrs. N. S. Freeman was buried.

Apr. 10. General George W. Dietzler was thrown from a buggy and his neck was broken. His remains were sent to California.

Apr. 11. Price Johnson was shot yesterday at Casa Grande, and he died this morning. He was shot by a man named Robinson.

Apr. 15. James Casey was hung in the jail yard at a few minutes after one. When the black cap was pulled on, he remarked, "Good-bye. Turn her loose." And down he went to instant death.

Apr. 22. Judge F. N. Smith died early this morning.

Apr. 23. Charles King of Harshaw, a miner, died. I knew him in California as a merchant and as sheriff of Placer County. He had two great faults--one was drinking liquor, but the worst one was, HE WAS A

DEMOCRAT! He was a good man and if there is a better place, I hope Charley will get there.

May 10, 1884. Funeral today of a woman who died from the effects of morphine.

May 11. Edward Lenst and Marcus Cruz died.

May 12. William Keegan died at Harshaw.

May 30. Infant of Mr. and Mrs. Joseph Sersovich died.

May 31. Mrs. John Terwilliger and Pedro Ruelas died today.

June 26, 1884. John Sloan died of heart disease in the hospital.

June 28. The infant son of Fred and Mrs. Austin died.

July 1, 1884. Benoni B. Rogers died.

July 4. James Hersey died in the hospital. He had been crazy for several weeks and then became sick. He was removed to the hospital for treatment. AND THEY TREATED HIM!

July 22. George B. Sheppard died at El Paso today.

August 23, 1884. A child of Hartwell died.

Aug. 27. C. Nimmo died.

Aug. 28. Dr. King died.

Aug. 29. Mrs. George C. Hall died.

September 10, 1884. E. B. Searles died this morning.

Sept. 30. David T. Harshaw died.

October 3, 1884. Mrs. F. H. Mason died today.

Oct. 15. James Carroll died after a long siege of sickness. James H. Toole [Hand's old landlord and former mayor of Tucson] killed himself at Trinidad, Colorado. He was on the way to his family in the state of Wisconsin. Many people here knew that he was crazy and that he should not have gone alone.

November 9, 1884. Guadalupe Alcala died today.

Nov. 15. Mrs. Horace Appel died.

December 9, 1884. Nick, 8-year-old son of Joseph and Mrs. Sersovich, died of pneumonia.

Dec. 17. Judge James Buell died.

Dec. [no day]. John S. Crouch died in N.M. He came to this country with Company "F," 1st Infantry, Cal. Vols. George Matlock and Pasqual Maguey died near Nogales.

~ ~ ~ ~ ~

January 1, 1885. An infant of Johnny Moore died.

Jan. 3. L. Miller died of consumption.

Jan. 7. My little dog Josepha Hand died of poison.

Jan. 11. Demitrio Velasco died.

Jan. 20. Frank Gray died in the hospital of wounds received at the Ray Mine.

Jan. 22. Denton G. Sanford died at 4:30 this afternoon, aged 54. He came to Arizona as a wagonmaster with the Column from California, and was a member of the Arizona Pioneers.

Jan. 25. Four children of Floramina Encina died, all of diphtheria.

Jan. 27. Miss Moreno of Convent Street was buried today.

Jan. 29. James Caldwell died in the hospital, an old timer. The mourners were two Mexican grave diggers and E. J. Smith, the undertaker. Shame.

February 9, 1885. Thomas Brown was badly injured near Casa Grande by the [rail] cars. He died on the cars bringing him here to be placed in the hospital. Miss Mary Rainy and Judge Glassman died.

Feb. 10. Mrs. Costello died.

March 9, 1885. Mrs. E. B. Pomeroy died in Oakland, Cal., aged 28 years.

Mar. 15. William Tuttle died today. I did not know him.

Mar. [no day]. Arvy Katz and Pablo Soto were murdered 50 miles south of Tucson.

April 6, 1885. Col. W. H. Birchard was brought to the city jail. The Dr. came to see him. He was afterward taken to the hospital and died before reaching there. He was a government timber inspector for Colorado.

Apr. 8. Jose Salazar, an old timer, died this morning.

Apr. 22. The infant child of Fred Hughes died.

Apr. 23. H. M. Ellsworth of Wells Fargo Co. Express at Tombstone was stricken with paralysis of the side here last night and died at 6 a.m. this morning.

Apr. 28. Edward Woods of Junction Station on the Arivaca road came to town a few days ago and was taken to the hospital sick with pneumonia. His wife came in to attend him but he died during the night.

Apr. 30. Patrick R. Lee died today at the Mammoth Mine from injuries. He was the son of James Lee and 21 years of age. James Claiborne was shot and killed at Harshaw.

May 3, 1885. Antonio Estrella, a Mexican, was cut and beaten to death.

May 7. Joseph Frates of Pinal Co. died in the hospital here of consumption.

May 27. Leonardo Apodaca died this morning.

June 5, 1885. Harry E. Cook died today at the residence of L. C. Hughes.

June 8. Ferdinand Shantel, in the hospital with consumption, shot and killed himself this morning.

June 10. The infant child of George Martin the druggist died.

July 5, 1885. Ephriam Warner, aged 66, brother of Solomon, died today of congestion of the brain.

July 11. Wong Joy Gin, a Chinaman sentenced to 90 days in jail, died in the hospital.

July 13. Lee Platt, an old soldier, died in the hospital.

July 23. Received the news of the death of General Grant. Flags are displayed at half mast.

August 5, 1885. James Vogan died sitting in a chair. James Stockdale died suddenly at 2 p.m. in the Fashion Saloon from debility and opium.

Aug. 17. Mrs. Messersmith died in Paulusky, N.Y.

Aug. 18. Dr. Handy cut off a leg yesterday from a man who fell under the [rail] cars. The man died this morning.

Aug. 20. Mrs. E. J. Watson died at Fuller's ranch.

Aug. 21. Henry L. Parsons died at the residence of Charles Frye.

Aug. 25. Miss Emma Mellus died today.

September 14, 1885. Juliana Gonzales, a servant woman of the Mexican consul, in lighting a fire with coal oil this evening was frightfully burned. The woman died during the night.

Sept. 22. Con Cutler died in Mexico of yellow fever. Ed S. Mullin of Benson died in the hospital.

October 13, 1885. Mick Mahoney died this morning early.

Oct. 15. Mrs. Rosa Martinez died of old age.

Oct. 29. General George B. McClellan died today in New Jersey at his home.

Nov. 5, 1885. A Chinaman who was murdered at Sanford's ranch was brought to town and buried this afternoon.

Nov. 7. A. G. Buttner, chief of police, died today at about noon. Alexander Bergeot, a waiter at the Elite Restaurant, was found dead in his bed. He was about 45 years of age, a native of Canada.

Nov. 23. Teodora, a sister of Leopoldo Carrillo, and a man who lives near us named Miguel Serenate died today.

Nov. 27. B. M. Jacobs' little boy died today. A great many people are sick.

December 7, 1885. Willie Carnahan, aged 9 years, died today. He was the son of Mr. and Mrs. Robert Carnahan. There are a great many children sick with diphtheria and many have died, but I was unable to get their names.

Dec. 9. William H. Vanderbilt died yesterday in New York.

Dec. 20. Anthony Kirby died in the hospital this morning of pneumonia. He was a member of Co. "D," 88th Ohio Regiment, in the late rebellion.

Dec. 29. Manuelito Villascusa, five years old, died today of diphtheria in Convent Street.

~ ~ ~ ~ ~

January 11, 1886. Samuel Latta died at Tombstone. He was a carpenter and was formerly from Prescott and Nevada Co., California.

Jan. 12. John J. Shuday died in the upper valley from consumption.

Jan. 13. John Hall of Alvarado, Alameda Co., Cal., died of consumption., aged 64.

Jan. 17. Richard West from Pennsylvania died of consumption in the hospital. Santiago Urea, a Papago interpreter who was educated in the East, died. Willie Rice died at Huachuca. W. L. Bailey of Florence died of heart disease.

Jan. 18. Captain Emmet Crawford died at Nacori in Mexico. He was killed in the line of duty by Mexicans.

Jan. 29. The death of Captain Crawford in command of Apache scouts after hostiles in Mexico is said to be true. They were fired upon by Mexican soldiers in the dark, thinking them hostiles.

February 9, 1886. Genl. W. S. Hancock died. Comrade Sampson and myself raised our G.A.R. flag (the American flag) at half mast for the dead comrade.

Feb. 12. Horatio Seymour died in Utica, N.Y.

Feb. 17. Mrs. Millie Creighton died.

Feb. 18. Trinidad Garcia died. She was one of a family of four girls, all down sick. Report says she starved to death. Foster heard of it and immediately went around to the sporting men and collected some money for the family. But the church would not even ring the bell. How is that for Christianity? The bell of the Holy Catholic Church did not tap a tap for the want of one dollar. Christians will do when you need nothing, but when you cannot pay, Hell!

Feb. 20. Malcomb Sinclair, a R.R. man, died in the hospital.

March 2, 1886. Died, in Utica, New York, Mrs. Mira Hand Roberts, aged 58, wife of John E. Roberts and sister of George O. Hand.

Mar. 10. Frank Richardson committed suicide in a frame house.

Mar. 14. Sister Gonzaga died in the convent of consumption.

Mar. 20. Ed Shearer of Willcox died on a visit here.

Captain Emmet Crawford was killed in Mexico in January 1886 while chasing Geronimo and his band of Chiricahua Apaches. He wasn't killed by Indians, however, but by Mexican troops who mistook Crawford's company of Apache scouts for hostiles. Charles Gatewood Collection, Arizona Historical Society, Tucson, #19581.

April 2, 1886. A. G. Post of Yuma, who has been treated for liver disease by Dr. Handy, died in the Sisters' hospital this morning.

Apr. 4. Santiago Espinosa died today.

Apr. 16. William Johnson of Little Rock, Ark., died.

Apr. 18. O. B. Clark died late this evening of strangulated hernia, aged 53.

Apr. 19. William Warford, Jr., a 5-year-old boy, fell in a bad air well and was found dead this afternoon.

Apr. 21. William Gale of Tucson died in the insane asylum in Stockton, Cal.

Apr. 23. J. Macovich, a fruit dealer, died of old age.

Apr. 27. The wife and child of A. L. Peck were killed by Indians on the upper Santa Cruz. A young girl is missing, supposed to have been taken away by the Indians. [She was later recovered unharmed.] Charles K. Owen was also killed. The Indians are all about Agua Zarca and Calabasas. They have killed a number of people in Sonora and are moving this way. Several squads of citizens and soldiers are out after them. We are all in hope they may succeed in killing at least some of them. General Miles has left town. [This was the last chapter in the story of deadly encounters between Apache Indians and White settlers in southern Arizona. In August 1886 Geronimo surrendered to U.S troops and he and his band of Chiricahua Apaches were subsequently sent into exile to Florida. The Apache wars in the Southwest had come to an end.]

Apr. 30. Edward O'Leary died of consumption this afternoon in the Sisters' hospital. Mrs. Concepcion C. Islas died. Mr. J. Shanahan was shot near Oro Blanco by Indians.

Geronimo (mounted, left) and followers in Mexico in 1886. Photo by C. S. Fly. Cañon de los Embudos Collection, Arizona Historical Society, Tucson, #78163.

May 10, 1886. Charles Murray and Thomas Shaw were killed by Indians near Nogales. The soldiers are in pursuit.

May 25. Robert Lloyd was killed by Indians near Patagonia.

May 28. F. P. Wemple was killed by Indians in the Santa Ritas.

May 31. M. G. Roca died.

June 1, 1886. Doña Josepha S. de Haro died early this morning.

June 2. Mrs. Carmen Zuniga died last night and was buried today. I went on top of the courthouse after dark to see Indian signal fires, thought I saw two.

June 3. Dr. Clinton H. Davis was killed by Indians on the new Manlove road. A Mexican lady named Ursula Castro Goldstein died today. Edward Van Hagen, who has been sick a long time with consumption, died this evening.

June 4. Julius Goldbaum was killed by Indians in the Whetstone Mts.

June 6. Thomas Hunt was killed by Indians near Harshaw.

June 7. John W. Hookstraw, a R.R. conductor, fell from the cars and broke his neck.

June 9. Henry Baston was killed by Indians near Arivaca.

June 15. Willie Osborn, Judge Osborn's little boy, died of diphtheria.

July 14, 1886. Carmen Escobosa died.

July 19. Edward Marshall died at Florence.

July 20. Martin Medley died during the night.

July 31. Dr. Thomas Thomas (colored) died in the hospital this morning.

August 1, 1886. Jerome B. Collins was killed.

Aug. 2. Quong Hong Ti died.

Aug. 9. Refugio Montijo was shot and killed by a Yaqui named Teodoro Ramos.

Aug. 16. Carmel Gallego, wife of Antoine Gallego, died.

Aug. 19. Charles Phillips and Luis Redondo died today. Albert Sayles died at Florence.

Aug. 24. Mr. Joseph Betz died.

Aug. 26. Mrs. Pedro Aguirre died.

September 10, 1886. Judge A. L. Heap died at Phoenix.

Sept. 30. Arthur L. Rogers from San Pedro fell dead in Fleishman's drug store.

October 11, 1886. Henry B. Holmes died this morning of heart disease.

Oct. 26. Louise Starr and another little girl died from eating candy bought on the street.

November 8, 1886. Perry, a stranger, died in the Sisters of St. Joseph's hospital. He was from Texas and a Mason. He had plenty of money and was buried by the Masons.

Nov. 18. In New York City at 5 o'clock this morning, ex-president of the U.S.A. Chester A. Arthur died. J. B. Miches died from exhaustion from the effect of a surgical operation. His remains were taken to Florence.

Nov. 20. Gustavo Borquez, aged 12 years, died this morning.

Nov. 25. Stephen Swarkout died in the hospital.

December 6, 1886. Arthur Hamlin, a brakeman who was scalded on the train at San Simon, died in the hospital here.

Dec. 7. A Mexican child unknown to me died. The infant son of Mr. and Mrs. C. M. Williams died this evening.

Dec. 10. D. M. Kalhar died from a wound he received at Nogales from a pistol shot by the hand of one Hamilton. Mrs. Ernest Moreal died at Nogales.

Dec. 13. Miss Ardine Miller of Detroit, Mich., died today.

Dec. 14. Mr. Silas Watters died of brain fever at a ranch near San Xavier.

Dec. 19. Mrs. E. Coker died.

Dec. 20. Calvin Mathews died in the hospital. He was a pioneer of Cal.

Dec. 21. Georgia Cady died this evening of consumption. Pedro Burruel died.

Dec. 26. Genl. John A. Logan died today.

Dec. 27. Jose Leon died today of consumption. He had been sick a long time.

~ ~ ~ ~ ~

January 1, 1887. Frank, son of Mr. and Mrs. Frank Saladin, aged 1 month, died. Mrs. Encarnacion Borquez died.

Jan. 8. Teodora Delis died this morning of old age.

Jan. 10. I. R. Tyler died today. P. I. Garcia also died today. He was the husband of a colored woman called Fanny.

Jan. 13. William Rayl from Detroit, Mich., aged 21, died.

Jan. 18. Mrs. Rebecca Neiveling, mother of Mrs. E. B. Gifford, died.

Jan. 22. Mrs. J. L. Sears died today.

Jan. 23. Teodoro Preciado died today, aged 78, an honest and faithful old man.

Jan. 24. John Hassell, a colored barber, died of heart disease.

February 3, 1887. The infant son of Mrs. Sears (who died a short time ago) was adopted by Mr. and Mrs. Hiram S. Stevens--it died today, aged three weeks.

Feb. 4. A Pima Indian was killed by the [rail] cars.

Feb. 5. Felipe Robles was found dead by the new convent. Ed Burton, in taking a walk this morning to exercise his young dog, found the dead Mexican (the dog found him).

Feb. 7. Richard Woffenden died early this morning. The old man was sick but a short time and died very suddenly. He was 68 years of age.

Feb. 11. An infant of Mr. and Mrs. Al Levin, born yesterday, died this morning.

Feb. 23. An infant of Mr. and Mrs. W. C. Dunn died.

Feb. 28. Amalia Pellon, infant daughter of Mr. and Mrs. Pedro Pellon, died this morning.

March 4, 1887. James Simpson died at Florence. He formerly lived here.

Mar. 8. Henry Knudson, late of the 4th Cav., U.S.A., died in the hospital.

Mar. 10. The 14th Arizona Legislature died of dropsy.

Mar. 11. Duncan S. Glasscott died this evening late. Jesús Burruel of Tubac died in Tucson.

Mar. 21. Received by telegram the news of the murder of Con Ryan at a ranch near Nogales. The wife of L. D. Chillson died today.

Mar. 24. Ernest Follensbee died of pneumonia. Benita, daughter of Mr. and Mrs. Juan Elias, died.

Mar. 25. Sipriano, infant son of Mr. and Mrs. Juan Elias, died. A young child of Oliver Swingle of the lower San Pedro died.

Mar. 28. Mrs. Rafaela Romo died today, aged 58 years.

Mar. 30. Jerry Harrington from Quijotoa died in the hospital.

Mar. 31. Hugh I. Brawley died at Prescott. Wm. S. Oury was taken sick yesterday evening and died this morning.

April 3, 1887. John Aldridge died today, aged 10 years. The infant son of Mr. and Mrs. I. M. Trayer died.

Apr. 4. The Mexican, Quiros, who was shot at San Xavier Sunday night by Enrique Papa, died this evening. Papa is in jail.

Apr. 12. Doña Maria Rivera, aged 70 years, died this morning. She was the mother of Jim Speedy's wife.

Apr. 14. Conquean (Coon Can), the old Papago chief, died today.

Apr. 15. Jose Maria Soso, aged 78, died at noon today. Asa C. Brown, aged 10 years, son of Charles O. Brown, died during the early part of the night of diphtheria.

~ ~ ~ ~ ~

George O. Hand died in Tucson on May 4, 1887, of heart disease. He was fifty-seven years old. Owing to the growth of the city and the closure of old cemeteries, his remains have been moved twice. They are now in Evergreen Cemetery on North Oracle Road.

Arizona Historical Society, Tucson, #28618.

An early Southern Pacific engine and crew. The railroads brought rapid change to the Southwest in the 1880s. Arizona Historical Society, Tucson, #73595.

EPILOGUE

Change Came Rapidly to George Hand's Southwest

The arrival of the railroads in the 1880s changed Arizona dramatically and forever. The iron horse brought in thousands of cattle to occupy the rangelands. The railroads gave Arizona farmers access to outside markets. Rail service made large-scale copper mining possible. No longer was trade with northern Sonora more important to Tucsonans than that with the eastern states. But importantly, the railroads ended the cultural isolation of the region by transporting people with heretofore unimaginable ease. A trip from Tucson to San Francisco that used to take weeks by stagecoach and steamship now could be made in two or three days and at much less cost. Although Hispanics would be in the majority in Tucson until well into the twentieth century, the culture of the community moved rapidly toward that of mainstream America and away from its Mexican roots. The town became more Anglo and Protestant and less Hispanic and Catholic in temperament and outlook. As a result, old traditions were shouldered aside in the rush to join the industrial age. Similar changes were experienced in towns throughout the Southwest.

Among the exotic cultural influences that the railroad helped to bring to Tucson and other Southwestern communities were a number of social reforms that were sweeping the country. Somewhat reluctantly, Arizonans joined the rest of the nation in an attempt to legislate morality. The earliest law making a vice a crime in Tucson was an ordinance passed in 1880 banning the smoking of opium and the keeping of opium "dens" within the town limits. Opium smoking was introduced to the Southwest by Chinese workers who helped build the railroads, and was practiced almost exclusively by them. The non-medical use of opium was outlawed throughout the United Sates by federal legislation passed in 1914.

In an attempt to bring Tucson even closer to the Victorian norm, the common council passed Ordinance 44 in 1883. Among other things, this decree prohibited "indecent or lewd dress," "indecent or lewd books," and "indecent, immoral or lewd plays." The ordinance banned public drunkenness and the public use of "obscene or abusive language." It did not ban prostitution outright, but Ordinance 44 enjoined "courtesans or lewd women" from soliciting on the streets, from windows or doorways, or at any public place. The council formally proscribed "houses of prostitution or assignation" in Tucson in 1905.

Chief among the reform crusades of the day was the temperance movement. A uniquely American and Protestant phenomenon strongly supported by women, its goal was not temperance but abstinence and the abolition of the manufacture and sale of all alcoholic beverages. The champions of this ideology found in the consumption of alcohol the root of all of society's ills, from crime to insanity. They sincerely believed that if the breweries and distilleries were shut down and the saloons padlocked, virtually all American families would be happy and prosperous.

PROHIBITION IN ARIZONA

will result in

HUNDREDS OF UNREGULATED DIVES OF THE VILEST NATURE

across the international line at

Nogales, Naco, Douglas

and other border cities.

These Arizona cities will have no control over the liquor business in Mexico, but will suffer the consequences which will be incomparably worse than could arise under present conditions.

IS IT FAIR

for other parts of Arizona to force
such conditions on the border cities?

Vote NO on Prohibition

and let each community decide what is best for itself.

Anti-Prohibition propaganda printed in the Arizona Daily Star *in 1914.*

Shortly after the southern railroads were completed, proponents of Prohibition made their way to the Southwest and began their work with missionary zeal. In 1883, Frances Willard, founder of the Women's Christian Temperance Union, arrived in Tucson and organized a WCTU chapter there. She was hosted by Josephine Hughes, wife of *Arizona Daily Star* owner and governor-to-be Louis C. Hughes. Thirsty Arizonans were slow to "take the pledge," but the "drys" made progress nonetheless. In 1885, the Arizona legislature passed bills prohibiting the sale of liquor on election days and barring boys under sixteen from entering saloons. Two years later, the territorial lawmakers raised the license fees charged saloon keepers. In 1901 they enacted a "local option" law permitting towns and counties to abolish the "liquor traffic" within their jurisdictions. The year 1907 saw the legislature bar women and minors from working in or "loitering" in saloons. The final blow to John Barleycorn came in 1914 when, by a close vote, Arizonans approved an initiative measure banning the sale of liquor in the state--Arizona went dry. The words of the prohibitionists' song of joy and victory, a takeoff on Stephen Foster's "My Old Kentucky Home," were published in the *Arizona Daily Star*:

The sun shines bright in our Arizona home.
There's gladness where once was dispair.
The children sing and the mothers happily smile,
For no longer waits the evil snare.
The fathers save all the daily wages earned.
They too are happy that we're dry.
The time has come when all liquors have to go,
Then to old vile Alcohol, Good-bye.

Weep no more the mothers.
No more the children cry.
Let us sing glad songs and we'll make our dear state ring
As we bid old Alcohol, Good-bye.

The reformers jubilantly proclaimed that now two-thirds of the United States had turned its back on demon rum through local or state laws. The adoption of the 18th amendment to the U.S. Constitution in 1919 brought the total to 100%. It remained so until 1933 when the amendment was repealed.

Gambling, an accepted feature of frontier life, was closely associated with drinking and saloons and suffered a similar fall into disfavor. Gambling houses were prohibited within one mile of the Tucson city limits in 1905, and two years later the legislature passed a law forbidding all forms of gambling throughout Arizona.

Many elements of Hispanic culture were swept away in the campaign to improve the behavior and morals of Tucsonans. Cockfights and bullfights were banned in Tucson in 1893. And, while cockfights remain technically legal in rural Arizona, betting on the contests--an integral part of the sport--is not. A statute prohibiting the killing of animals for the entertainment of spectators was adopted shortly after statehood was achieved in 1912. This decree effectively outlawed bullfights throughout Arizona (cockfights were exempted from the provisions of this law). The sale and use of fireworks within the city limits of Tucson were prohibited in 1910.

A conspicuous victim of these reforms was the Feast of San Agustín. Protestants brought up under the strictures of the Puritan Ethic were not noted for enthusiastic celebrating, and in the late 1800s they tended to equate exuberant revelry with depravity and sin. Many of the activities that the reformers sought to suppress blossomed during the ten-day feast, and even in George Hand's time there were calls from intolerant Anglos to curtail the annual carnival. By the 1890s, some upper-class Hispanics and Catholic clergymen had begun to view the raucous merrymaking associated with the feast as something of an embarrassment. The fiesta was banished to the outskirts of town and deleted from the roster of important local celebrations. A Tucson "booster book" designed to lure visitors and investors to town was published in 1897--it did not mention the Feast of San Agustín as a feature of local culture. Tucson's patron saint was still honored each August 28 by special services held in the cathedral named for him, but few residents celebrated the event as in days of old. After the turn of the century, prohibitions against gambling and drinking put an end to what was left of the feast.

Of course, vice did not disappear from the Southwest after the enactment of restrictive laws, it only went underground. Bootleg whiskey flowed freely in Tucson during Prohibition, and smuggling booze into the United States from Mexico became a flourishing business. The authorities mostly winked at the roadhouses that sprang up a few miles from town, where a shot of tequila, a game of cards, or a tryst with a woman of easy virtue could be had on the sly. Drinking and high-stakes gambling were carried on in the back rooms of many private clubs, and often these clubs counted important civic leaders among their members. George Hand's old neighborhood on Meyer Street and nearby Gay Alley became Tucson's semiofficial tenderloin and remained so until shortly after World War II. In those days, the city fathers usually opted to contain and control vices such as prostitution rather than engage in a never-ending struggle to stamp them out entirely.

~ ~ ~ ~ ~

Thankfully, many of the excesses of the reformers of the past have now been redressed. And, although all is not totally rosey in modern, industrialized Arizona, some refreshing new attitudes have arisen in recent years. Chief among them is our growing appreciation of the cultural diversity found in the Southwest. In recognition of our Hispanic past, the secular, festive half of the Feast of San Agustín was revived in Tucson in 1983 by the Arizona Historical Society. Although the new one-day fiesta does not yet dominate the attention of the whole town each August as the ten-day fling did in George Hand's time, interest in it grows every year. We have come to understand that old traditions can enhance modern lives. Other festivals celebrating ethnic pluralism have sprung up in Tucson and are flourishing.

~ ~ ~ ~ ~

Yes, sin was legal in old Tucson. Personal liberty was unabridged. But George Hand's diaries reveal the brutal harshness of life on the frontier. The physical comforts enjoyed by most modern Southwesterners stand in stark contrast to the daily hardships endured by Hand and his friends and neighbors. One has to admire our forebears who faced the rigors of frontier life with such good humor and optimism. Hopefully, we will meet our trials and tribulations with equal fortitude.

Looking east across the Santa Cruz River floodplain from the base of Sentinel Peak (now "A" Mountain) in 1880. The building on the left houses Solomon Warner's water-powered flour mill. The ruins of an abandoned two-story adobe convent can be seen amid the fields. Beyond the irrigated fields lies the village of Tucson. Arizona Historical Society, Tucson, #6608.

The same view as above as seen in 1994. The flour mill and convent are long gone, the agriculture that nourished George Hand's Tucson has disappeared from the valley, and tall buildings rise where Hand's saloon once stood. Even the natural vegetation in the foreground has changed. Photo by Neil Carmony.

BIBLIOGRAPHY

Books and Articles

Altshuler, Constance Wynn. 1983. *Starting with Defiance: nineteenth century Arizona military posts.* Ariz. Hist. Soc., Tucson. 80 pp.

------. 1991. *Cavalry yellow & infantry blue: army officers in Arizona between 1851 and 1886.* Ariz. Hist. Soc., Tucson. 406 pp.

Ball, Larry D. 1978. *The United States marshals of New Mexico and Arizona territories, 1846-1912.* Univ. of New Mexico Press, Albuquerque. 315 pp.

------. 1992. *Desert lawmen: the high sheriffs of New Mexico and Arizona, 1846-1912.* Univ. of New Mexico Press, Albuquerque. 414 pp.

Barnes, Will C. 1935. *Arizona place names.* Reprint: 1988, Univ. of Arizona Press, Tucson. 503 pp.

Barter, G. W. 1881. *Directory of the City of Tucson for the year 1881.* G. W. Barter, San Francisco. 114 pp.

Beck, Warren A., and Ynez D. Haase. 1969. *Historical atlas of New Mexico.* Univ. of Oklahoma Press, Norman. 62 maps plus index.

Bourke, John G. 1891. *On the border with Crook.* Reprint: 1969, Rio Grande Press, Glorieta, N.M. 506 pp.

Browne, J. Ross. 1869. *Adventures in the Apache country.* Reprint: 1974, Univ. of Arizona Press, Tucson. 297 pp.

Butler, Anne M. 1985. *Daughters of joy, sisters of misery: prostitutes in the American West, 1865-90.* Univ. of Illinois Press, Urbana. 179 pp.

Carmony, Neil B., ed. 1985. "The California Column occupies Tucson: George O. Hand's diary, Aug. 8-Dec. 2, 1862." *J. of Ariz. Hist.*, Vol. 26, No. 1 (spring), pp. 11-40.

Carmony, Neil B., and David E. Brown, eds. 1992. *Tough times in rough places: personal narratives of adventure, death, and survival on the Western frontier.* High-Lonesome Books, Silver City, N.M. 296 pp.

Chambers, George W., and C. L. Sonnichsen. 1974. *San Agustin: first cathedral church in Arizona.* Ariz. Hist. Soc., Tucson. 55 pp.

Clark, Nancy Tisdale. 1977. "The demise of demon rum in Arizona." *J. of Ariz. Hist.*, Vol. 18, No. 1 (spring). pp. 69-92.

Clum, Woodworth. 1936. *Apache agent: the story of John P. Clum.* Reprint: 1978, Univ. of Nebraska Press, Lincoln. 297 pp.

Colley, Charles C. 1972. *Documents of Arizona history: a guide to the manuscript collections of the Arizona Historical Society.* Ariz. Hist. Soc., Tucson. 233 pp.

Colton, Ray C. 1959. *The Civil War in the western territories: Arizona, Colorado, New Mexico, and Utah.* Univ. of Oklahoma Press, Norman. 230 pp.

Cooper, Evelyn S. 1989. "The Buehmans of Tucson: a family tradition in Arizona photography." *J. of Ariz. Hist.*, Vol. 30, No. 3 (autumn). pp. 251-278.

Cosulich, Bernice. 1953. *Tucson.* Arizona Silhouettes, Tucson. 310 pp.

Cramer, Harry G. 1976. "Tom Jeffords--Indian agent." *J. of Ariz. Hist.*, Vol. 17, No. 3 (autumn). pp. 265-300.

DeArment, Robert K. 1982. *Knights of the green cloth: the saga of the frontier gamblers.* Univ. of Oklahoma Press, Norman. 423 pp.

Drachman, Mose. 1973. "The Tucson gamblers." *J. of Ariz. Hist.*, Vol. 14, No. 1 (spring). pp. 1-9.

Earp, Josephine Sarah Marcus. 1976. *I married Wyatt Earp.* Ed. by Glenn G. Boyer. Univ. of Arizona Press, Tucson. 277 pp.

Earp, Wyatt. 1896. "How I routed a gang of Arizona outlaws." In: *Tough times in rough places: personal narratives of adventure, death, and survival on the western frontier.* Ed. by Neil B. Carmony and David E. Brown, 1992. High-Lonesome Books, Silver City, N.M. pp. 207-215.

Erdoes, Richard. 1979. *Saloons of the old west.* Reprint: 1985, Howe Brothers, Salt Lake City. 277 pp.

Fierman, Floyd S. 1981. "The spectacular Zeckendorfs." *J. of Ariz. Hist.*, Vol. 22, No. 4 (winter). pp. 387-414.

Fontana, Bernard. 1961. "Biography of a desert church: the story of Mission San Xavier del Bac." *Smoke Signal* No. 3, Tucson Corral of the Westerners. 24 pp.

Fulton, Richard W. 1966. "Millville-Charleston, Cochise County, 1878-1889." *J. of Ariz. Hist.*, Vol. 7, No. 1 (spring). pp. 9-22.

Gipson, Rosemary. 1972. "The Mexican performers: pioneer theatre artists of Tucson." *J. of Ariz. Hist.*, Vol. 13, No. 4 (winter). pp. 235-252.

Goff, John S. 1975. *Arizona territorial officials, Vol. I: the supreme court justices, 1863-1912.* Black Mountain Press, Cave Creek, Ariz. 200 pp.

------. 1978. *Arizona territorial officials, Vol. II: the governors, 1863-1912.* Black Mountain Press, Cave Creek, Ariz. 212 pp.

------. 1983. *Arizona historical dictionary.* Black Mountain Press, Cave Creek, Ariz. 107 pp.

------. 1985. *Arizona territorial officials, Vol. III: the delegates to Congress, 1863-1912.* Black Mountain Press, Cave Creek, Ariz. 193 pp.

Goff, John S. and Mary E. Gill. 1984. "Edmund Francis Dunne and the public school controversy, 1875." *J. of Ariz. Hist.*, Vol. 25, No. 4 (winter). pp. 369-384.

Griffith, James S. 1992. *Beliefs and holy places: a spiritual geography of the Pimería Alta.* Univ. of Arizona Press, Tucson. 218 pp.

Gustafson, A. M. ed. 1966. *John Spring's Arizona.* Univ of Arizona Press, Tucson. 326 pp.

Hall, Dick. 1979. "Jesús Camacho: the mayor of Meyer Street." *J. of Ariz. Hist.*, Vol. 20, No. 4 (winter). pp. 445-466.

Hill, Ben C. 1926. *Charter and ordinances of the City of Tucson.* City of Tucson. 527 pp.

Hilzinger, George J. 1897. *Treasure land: a story.* Reprint: 1969, Rio Grande Press, Glorieta, New Mex. 160 pp. plus index.

Hinton, Richard J. 1878. *The hand-book to Arizona: its resources, history, towns, mines, ruins, and scenery.* Reprint: 1970, Rio Grande Press, Glorieta, New Mex. 431 pp. plus app.

Hodge, Hiram C. 1877. *Arizona as it is.* Reprint: 1965, Rio Grande Press, Chicago. 273 pp.

Kelly, George H. 1926. *Legislative history of Arizona, 1864-1912.* Office of the State Historian, Phoenix. 399 pp.

Lockwood, Frank C. 1928. *Arizona characters.* Times-Mirror Press, Los Angeles. 230 pp.

------. 1943. *Life in old Tucson.* Tucson Civic Committee. 255 pp.

Lutrell, Estelle. 1949. *Newspapers and periodicals of Arizona, 1859-1911.* Univ. of Ariz. Bull. No. 15. 123 pp.

Martin, Cy. 1974. *Whiskey and wild women.* Hart Publishing, N.Y. 304 pp.

Martin, Douglas D. 1951. *Tombstone's Epitaph.* Univ. of New Mexico Press, Albuquerque. 287 pp.

------. 1963. *An Arizona chronology: the territorial years, 1846-1912.* Univ. of Arizona Press, Tucson. Unpaged.

Meyer, Shelby. 1983. "There is beer in this town!" *J. of Ariz. Hist.*, Vol. 24, No. 1 (spring). pp. 29-54.

Miller, Darlis A. 1982. *The California Column in New Mexico.* Univ. of New Mexico Press, Albuquerque. 318 pp.

Myrick, David F. 1975. *Railroads of Arizona, Vol. I: the southern roads.* Howell-North Books, Berkeley. 477 pp.

Officer, James E. 1987. *Hispanic Arizona, 1536-1856.* Univ. of Arizona press, Tucson. 462 pp.

Ortiz, Alfonso, ed. 1983. *Handbook of North American Indians, Vol. 10: Southwest.* Smithsonian Institution, Wash. D.C. (Apaches, pp. 368-488.)

Orton, Richard H. 1890. *Records of California men in the War of the Rebellion, 1861-1867.* Adjutant General's Office, Sacramento. (Company "G," 1st Reg. of Infantry, pp. 363-367).

Oury, William S. 1885. "The Camp Grant massacre." In: *Tough times in rough places: personal narratives of adventure, death, and survival on the western frontier.* Ed. by Neil B. Carmony and David E. Brown, 1992. High-Lonesome Books, Silver City, N.M. pp. 163-172.

Pearce, T. M. 1965. *New Mexico place names: a geographical dictionary.* Univ. of New Mexico Press, Albuquerque. 187 pp.

Peters, Harry T. 1942. *Currier & Ives: printmakers to the American people.* Doubleday, Doran, Garden City, N.Y. 41 pp., 192 plates.

Peterson, Thomas H. 1970. "A tour of Tucson--1874." *J. of Ariz. Hist.*, Vol. 11, No. 3 (autumn). pp. 180-201.

Pettis, George H. 1908. *The California Column.* Hist. Soc. of New Mex. Pub. No. 11. 20 pp.

Quebbeman, Frances E. 1966. *Medicine in territorial Arizona.* Ariz. Hist. Found., Phoenix. 424 pp.

Ronstadt, Edward F., ed. 1993. *Borderman: memoirs of Frederico José María Ronstadt.* Univ. of New Mexico Press, Albuquerque. 154 pp.

Rorabaugh, W. J. 1979. *The alcoholic republic: an American tradition.* Oxford Univ. Press, New York and Oxford. 302 pp.

Salpointe, J. B. 1898. *Soldiers of the Cross: notes on the ecclesiastical history of New Mexico, Arizona, and Colorado.* St. Boniface's Industrial School, Banning, Calif. 296 pp.

Schellie, Don. 1970. *The Tucson* Citizen: *a century of Arizona journalism.* Tucson Citizen [newspaper]. 96 pp.

Sharlot Hall Museum. 1982. "Times and trials of Mollie Monroe." *Sharlot Hall Gazette*, Vol. 9, No. 4 (December). pp. 1-3.

Sheridan, Thomas E. 1986. *Los Tucsonenses: the Mexican community in Tucson, 1854-1941.* Univ. of Arizona Press, Tucson. 327 pp.

Simmons, Alexy. 1989. *Red light ladies.* Anthropology Northwest No. 4. Dept. of Anthropology, Oregon State Univ., Corvallis. 150 pp.

Sonnichsen, C. L. 1982. *Tucson: the life and times of an American city.* Univ. of Oklahoma Press, Norman. 369 pp.

------. 1982. "Who was Tom Jeffords?" *J. of Ariz. Hist.*, Vol. 23, No. 4 (winter). pp. 381-406.

------. 1984. *Pioneer heritage: the first century of the Arizona Historical Society.* Ariz. Hist. Soc., Tucson. 230 pp.

Theobald, John, and Lillian Theobald. 1961. *Arizona Territory post offices and postmasters.* Ariz. Hist. Found., Phoenix. 178 pp.

------. 1978. *Wells Fargo in Arizona Territory.* Ariz. Hist. Found., Phoenix. 210 pp.

Thrapp, Dan L. 1967. *The conquest of Apacheria.* Univ. of Oklahoma Press, Norman. 405 pp.

Tucson Corral of the Westerners. 1992. *Tucson: a legacy--a collection of Smoke Signals.* Tucson Corral of the Westerners. (Includes several individually paginated monographs.)

Wagoner, Jay J. 1970. *Arizona Territory, 1863-1912: a political history.* Univ. of Arizona Press, Tucson. 587 pp.

------. 1975. *Early Arizona: prehistory to Civil War.* Univ. of Arizona Press, Tucson. 547 pp.

Walker, Henry P. 1973. "Wagon freighting in Arizona." *Smoke Signal* No. 28, Tucson Corral of the Westerners. 23 pp.

Walker, Henry P., and Don Bufkin. 1979. *Historical atlas of Arizona.* Univ. of Oklahoma Press, Norman. 65 maps plus index.

Newspapers

Arizona Citizen (Tucson), October 1870-October 1877 (weekly).

Arizona Citizen (Florence), November, 1877-September 1878 (weekly).

Arizona Citizen (Tucson), September 1878-February 1979 (weekly); *Arizona Daily Citizen*, February 1879 to date. Name changed to *Tucson Citizen* in 1903.

Arizona Weekly Star (Tucson), March 1877-June 1879; *Arizona Daily Star*, June 1879 to date.

Weekly Arizonian (Tucson), January 1869-April 1871.

INDEX

258

~ ~ ~ ~ ~

Editor Neil Carmony is a native Tusconan. He grew up reading excerpts from George Hand's diaries as they appeared in the *Arizona Daily Star* newspaper. The *Star* featured entries from Hand's diaries on their editorial page from 1927 to 1972 with, however, the more ribald and controversial commentaries censored out. Encouraged by the late C. L. Sonnichsen, Mr. Carmony, magnifying glass in hand, began in 1984 the tedious task of a new transcription of the original diaries, housed in the archives of the Arizona Historical Society. The result of his work is a complete, accurate and unexpurgated transcription of the diaries of George O. Hand. The diaries covering the "saloon years," with Mr. Carmony's introduction and notes, is presented in *Whiskey, Six-guns, and Red-light Ladies.*

Author George O. Hand was born in Oneida County, New York, in 1830. He went west with the California gold rush in 1849 and served with the California Column for the Union cause in the Civil War. After the war he settled in Tucson, Arizona, where he worked alternately as a butcher, saloon keeper, and night watchman and custodian at the Pima County courthouse. He kept a personal diary during much of the adult portion of his life, up until two weeks before his death on May 4, 1887.